Who Should This Book?

"Read" may be the wrong word. "Engage" would be better, because this is not so much a book as it is a classic text, and Jewish classics are not read so much as they are engaged. Included here are a classic text of Jewish prayer, spanning 2,000 years of Jewish experience with the world and with God; and nine thoughtful commentaries on that text, each one reaching back in a different way, again through 2,000 years of time. The question ought to be "Who should engage this book in personal dialogue?"

If you like to pray, or find prayer services baffling: Whether you are Orthodox, Conservative, Reconstructionist, or Reform, you will find that *My People's Prayer Book* tells you what you need to know to pray.

- The Hebrew text here is the most authentic one we have, and the variations among the Jewish movements are described and explained. They are all treated as equally authentic.

- The translation is honest, altogether unique, and outfitted with notes comparing it to others' translations.

- Of special interest is a full description of the Halakhah (the "how-to") of prayer and the philosophy behind it.

If you are a spiritual seeker or Jewishly curious: If you have wondered what Judaism is all about, the prayer book is the place to begin. It is the one and only book that Jews read each and every day. The commentaries explain how the prayers were born and synopsize insights of founding Rabbis, medieval authorities, Chasidic masters, and modern theologians. The layout replicates the look of Jewish classics: a text surrounded by many marginal commentaries, allowing you to skip back and forth across centuries of insight.

If you are a teacher or a student: This is a perfect book for adult studies, as well as for youth groups, teenagers, and camps. Any single page provides comparative insight from the length and breadth of Jewish tradition about the texts that have mattered most in the daily life of the Jewish people.

If you are a scholar: Although written in friendly prose, this book is composed by scholars: professors of Bible, Rabbinics, Medieval Studies, Liturgy, Theology, Linguistics, Jewish Law, Mysticism, and Modern Jewish Thought. No other work summarizes current wisdom on Jewish prayer drawn from so many disciplines.

If you are not Jewish: You need not be Jewish to understand this book. It provides access to the Jewish wisdom tradition for everyone. It chronicles the ongoing Jewish-Christian dialogue and the roots of Christian prayer in Christianity's Jewish origins.

The *My People's Prayer Book:*
Traditional Prayers, Modern Commentaries series

Volume 1—The *Sh'ma* and Its Blessings
     168 pp, ISBN 1-879045-79-6

Volume 2—The *Amidah*
     240 pp, ISBN 1-879045-80-X

Volume 3—*P'sukei D'zimrah* (Morning Psalms)
     240 pp, ISBN 1-879045-81-8

Volume 4—*Seder K'riat Hatorah* (The Torah Service)
     264 pp, ISBN 1-879045-82-6

Volume 5—*Birkhot Hashachar* (Morning Blessings)
     240 pp, ISBN 1-879045-83-4

Volume 6—*Tachanun* and Concluding Prayers
     240 pp, ISBN 1-879045-84-2

Volume 7—Shabbat at Home
     240 pp, ISBN 1-879045-85-0

Volume 8—Shabbat in the Synagogue
     240 pp (est.), ISBN 1-58023-121-7, Projected Fall 2004

My People's Prayer Book

TRADITIONAL PRAYERS, MODERN COMMENTARIES

Vol. 7—Shabbat at Home

EDITED BY RABBI LAWRENCE A. HOFFMAN

CONTRIBUTORS

MARC BRETTLER

MICHAEL CHERNICK

ELLIOT N. DORFF

DAVID ELLENSON

ELLEN FRANKEL

ALYSSA GRAY

JOEL M. HOFFMAN

LAWRENCE A. HOFFMAN

LAWRENCE KUSHNER

DANIEL LANDES

NEHEMIA POLEN

Jewish Lights Publishing
Woodstock, Vermont

My People's Prayer Book: Traditional Prayers, Modern Commentaries
Vol. 7—*Shabbat at Home*

First Printing 2004
© 2004 by Lawrence A. Hoffman

For information regarding permission to reprint material from this
book, please mail or fax your request in writing to Jewish Lights
Publishing, Permission Department, at the address / fax number listed
below, or e-mail your request to permissions@jewishlights.com.

Library of Congress Cataloging-in-Publication Data
My people's prayer book : traditional prayers, modern commentaries /
edited and with introductions by Lawrence A. Hoffman.
p.   cm.
Includes the traditional text of the siddur, English translation, and
commentaries.
Contents: vol. 7. *Shabbat at Home.*
ISBN 1-879045-85-0 (hc)
1. Siddur. 2. Siddurim—Texts. 3. Judaism—Liturgy—Texts.
I. Hoffman, Lawrence A., 1942– . II. Siddur. English & Hebrew.
BM674.39.M96 1997
296.4'5—dc21   97-26836
                                CIP

First Edition

10 9 8 7 6 5 4 3 2 1

Manufactured in the United States of America

Published by Jewish Lights Publishing
A Division of LongHill Partners, Inc.
Sunset Farm Offices, Route 4, P.O. Box 237
Woodstock, VT 05091
Tel: (802) 457-4000   Fax: (802) 457-4004
www.jewishlights.com

Contents

ABOUT *MY PEOPLE'S PRAYER BOOK* . . . . *vii*

INTRODUCTION TO THE LITURGY OF SHABBAT AT HOME:
   WHY THE HOME? 1
   Lawrence A. Hoffman

INTRODUCTION TO THE LITURGY OF SHABBAT AT HOME:
   WHY SHABBAT? 11
   Lawrence A. Hoffman

SHABBAT *Z'MIROT*: AN EXPANDING FRONTIER OF THE JEWISH SPIRIT 23
   Lawrence A. Hoffman

S'UDAH SH'LISHIT: A RITE OF MODEST MAJESTY 30
   Michael Chernick

INTRODUCTION TO THE COMMENTARIES:
   HOW TO LOOK FOR MEANING IN THE PRAYERS 37
   Lawrence A. Hoffman

THE LITURGY

1. WELCOMING SHABBAT 41
   A. *HADLAKAT NEROT* ("CANDLE LIGHTING") 41
   B. *BIRKAT BANIM* ("BLESSING OF CHILDREN") 57
   C. *SHALOM ALEIKHEM* ("PEACE TO YOU") 65
   D. *ESHET CHAYIL* ("A WORTHY WOMAN") 74
   E. *KIDDUSH* ("SANCTIFICATION") 91
   F. *Z'MIROT* ("TABLE SONGS") 116

      I. *YOM ZEH L'YISRA'EL* ("THIS IS ISRAEL'S DAY")......116

      II. *D'ROR YIKRA* ("LET HIM PROCLAIM FREEDOM")......127

      III. *Y'DID NEFESH* ("SOUL'S COMPANION")......135

      IV. *SHABBAT HAMALKAH* ("THE SHABBAT QUEEN")......147

2. KIDDUSHA RABBAH ("THE GREAT KIDDUSH")......**155**

3. BIDDING SHABBAT FAREWELL......**164**

    A. *HAVDALAH* ("SEPARATION")......164

    B. *SHAVU'A TOV* ("A GOOD WEEK")......181

    C. *ELIYAHU HANAVI* ("ELIJAH THE PROPHET")......185

About the Contributors......**191**

List of Abbreviations......**195**

Glossary......**196**

CONTRIBUTORS

MARC BRETTLER......*Our Biblical Heritage*

MICHAEL CHERNICK......*S'udah Sh'lishit: The Third Shabbat Meal*

ELLIOT N. DORFF......*Theological Reflections*

DAVID ELLENSON......*How the Modern Prayer Book Evolved*

ELLEN FRANKEL......*A Woman's Voice*

ALYSSA GRAY......*Our Talmudic Heritage*

JOEL M. HOFFMAN......*What the Prayers Really Say*

LAWRENCE A. HOFFMAN......*History of the Liturgy*

LAWRENCE KUSHNER AND NEHEMIA POLEN......*Chasidic and Mystical Perspectives*

DANIEL LANDES......*The Halakhah of Prayer*

About My People's Prayer Book

My People's Prayer Book is designed to look like a traditional Jewish book. Ever since the dawn of modern printing, Jews have arranged their books so that instead of reading in a linear fashion from the first line of the first page to the last line of the last one, readers were encouraged to linger on a single page and to consult commentaries across the gamut of Jewish thought, all at one and the same time. Every page thus contained a cross section of the totality of Jewish tradition.

That intellectual leap across many minds and through the centuries was accomplished by printing a text in the middle of the page and surrounding it with commentaries. Readers could scan the first line or two of the various commentaries and then choose to continue the ones that interested them most by turning the page—more or less the way newspaper readers get a sense of everything happening on a single day by glancing at all the headlines on page one, then following select stories as they are continued on separate pages further on.

Each new rubric (or liturgical section) is, therefore, introduced in traditional style: the Hebrew prayer with translation is in the middle of the page, and the beginning lines of all the commentaries are in the margins. Commentaries are continued on the next page or a few pages later (the page number is provided). Readers may dwell for a while on all the comments, deciding which ones to pursue at any given sitting. They may want to compare comments, reading first one and then another. Or having decided, after a while, that a particular commentator is of special interest, they may instinctively search out the opening lines of that commentator's work, as they appear in each introductory page, and then read them through to arrive at a summary understanding of what that particular person has to say.

Introduction to the Liturgy of Shabbat at Home

Why the Home?

Lawrence A. Hoffman

PRAYER BOOKS, SYNAGOGUE, AND HOME

Normally, we think of the prayer book (or Siddur [pronounced see-DOOR or, commonly, SIH-d'r] as it is called) as containing the liturgy for the synagogue, and indeed, that is correct. But the original prayer books from the period called the geonic era (c. 750–1034), and their medieval successors, too, contained much more than that. They were compendia of prayer in general and included not only synagogue prayers for the entire year, but also prayers said privately (such as the bedtime *Sh'ma*) or at home with the family (the entire Passover Haggadah, for instance, or the home liturgy for Shabbat, the topic of this volume). Instructions were liberally interspersed alongside the prayers, providing the information people needed for their life of prayer, whether communal or private.

The important point is that the printing press had yet to be invented, so these early prayer books were hard-to-get handwritten documents copied painstakingly by scribes, and not for private use but for the community. Prayer leaders might read from the book as they recited the liturgy aloud at services; individuals who, normally, didn't have their own copies would request instructions on how to pray at home and receive answers based on what the leaders read in the town's official copy. The Siddur became not just a book of prayer, but also a standard reference guide to be consulted for everything from how to say the morning *Sh'ma* to the requisite customs for a funeral. All of that would change with the invention of printing.

Europeans were not the first to develop the modern technology of printing. Koreans were using it as early as 1403. But it was being studied independently by Europeans—including at least one Jew, Davin de Caderousse of Provence—by the 1440s, when Johannes Gutenberg (1400–1468) set up his epochal printing press. Its breakthrough was its use of a technology that made it possible to print from individual letters cast in moveable metallic type, rather than inking a wood or metal block that could print only an entire page (or part, thereof), but could not be disassembled and put back together again, letter by letter, in other combinations. Scribal replication of manuscripts would soon become obsolete, a consequence not lost on scribes who frequently opposed the new technology on theological grounds. But the revolution was not immediate. Printed books were still costly and rare. William Caxton, for instance, the first British printer, set up a press in Westminster in 1476 but managed to produce only about a hundred items in almost twenty years.

About the same time (1475), the first dated Hebrew books were being printed (some, without dates, may have come somewhat earlier); and by the sixteenth century, printing was becoming feasible on a wide-scale basis. Up until then, reading had been a public, not a private, matter—Benedictine monks, for example, spent four hours a day being read to. But by 1597, books were becoming sufficiently standard, at least among the élite, that it was felt necessary to impose imperial censorship over the Frankfurt book fair. Also in the sixteenth century, the great publishing houses for Jewish books made their appearance.

Still, with output necessarily limited, printers had to choose their Jewish titles carefully and design them to the taste of what was still a very tiny moneyed clientele. Liturgical works were obvious candidates for inclusion. A prayer book was the first publication of a Hebrew printing press established in Prague in 1512, and beautifully designed versions of Italian prayer books printed on parchment were issued in Bologna from 1537 to 1540. But new technologies take shape only slowly—think how long people continued to use typewriters after computerized word processing became available. So for some time, "old-fashioned" scribal copies existed side by side with printed versions, and even where there were printed prayer books, communities might use them much as they had their handwritten predecessors—owning a single book for an entire community. Printers could, of course, choose any prayer collection to publish, errors and all, and they frequently did not even replicate the complete set of prayers that the old original prayer books had contained; sometimes they lopped off a poem's final verse so as to fit what was left on a single page. Some books were not even intended for use; they sat as coffee-table volumes for the wealthy.

In every technological innovation, production and the market's readiness to receive the product advance together. In a continuing spiral of mutual influence, then, every increase in publishing output galvanizes an equal increase in literacy, which expands the market of readers, and then further increases the publishing output all over again. For the publication of prayer books to mature, three factors had to coalesce: widespread literacy, a market for new prayer books, and the technological capacity to print multiple copies of these books at an affordable price for the average reader.

All three contributing factors came together in the late eighteenth and, especially, in the nineteenth century. Continuing Jewish emancipation heightened literacy in both Hebrew and the vernacular. The rise of liberal Judaism created the desire for prayer books newly composed according to the dictates of local rabbis, each one convinced that his reform of tradition surpassed those of others. And with the industrial revolution, costs fell dramatically. Most of our early prayer books, therefore, come only from the 1800s.

Until then, home and synagogue had played equally important roles in Jewish life, but as Jews became dependent on printed prayer books, the balance changed. What printers included in their books had an impact on the centrality of the Jewish home.

How Home Prayers Began

Before continuing our story of prayer in Jewish homes, we should look back at how prayer got there in the first place. "Liturgy," the word we use for collections of prayer intended for ritual use, comes from the Greek *leiturgia,* meaning "public works." In pagan cultures, it was the sacrificial system that pleased the gods—perhaps the most important public work imaginable. So liturgy, by definition, is public.

But what constitutes the public? Sacrifice in antiquity was both civic and familial. Shrines to gods responsible for the welfare of large collectivities of people existed side by side with a domestic cult devoted to a single family's divine benefactors. In imperial Rome, for example, large-scale public cults were dedicated not just to the old Roman pantheon, but also to gods such as Cybele, Isis, and Mithra; and these late importations from the East existed side by side with a cult of the emperor, as well as others for gods who were seen as local favorites in one city or another. From the beginning, however, the family worship of household gods was also the norm.

To some extent, Jews in the Roman Empire fell into line with custom elsewhere, but with limitations. Their commitment to monotheism prohibited their establishing cultic centers for more than one God, whose sacrifices, moreover, had long been reserved for the Jerusalem Temple alone. If Jews were to establish ritual centers on street corners and in homes, they would need something other than a proliferation of sacrificial altars. Non-sacrificial liturgies therefore arose, but as with sacrifice in the empire generally, Jewish liturgies were established with more than one public in mind. For Jews, the only large collectivity that was fully Jewish was the Jewish People as a whole, represented ritually wherever representational groups of Jews cared to gather. The liturgy—non-sacrificial, of course—that the Rabbis established for them would eventually become synagogue prayer. The Rabbis also invented prayers to be said around a dinner table: prayers, that is, for a smaller public, a public that would eventually become the family.

Neither synagogue nor family liturgy emerged all at once. Synagogue worship appeared first in rabbinic circles as part of a daily regimen of Torah study. Home worship evolved out of the practices associated with a rabbinic institution called a *chavurah* (pronounced khah-voo-RAH), best identified as a "tableship" group—an ad hoc or regularized gathering for food, conviviality, and conversation. How synagogue prayers reached maturity is the topic of the introductory essay in Volume 1 (*The Sh'ma and Its Blessings,* pp. 1–13). In this volume we explore how home prayer came to occupy such an important place in Jewish life.

Throughout the Roman Empire, not just for Jews, it had long been common for those who could afford it to celebrate holidays and life-cycle events by sharing lavish meals accompanied by conversation of a philosophical or religious sort. The earliest well-known testimonial to such a thing comes from Plato, whose dialogue *Symposium* receives its name from a Greek word meaning "to drink together," an apt description of the institution in question. The Jewish version of this is still alive and well in the form of the Passover Seder, but echoes of these tableship celebrations can also be found in such daily staples as the Grace after Meals (the *Birkat Hamazon,* pronounced beer-KAHT hah-mah-ZOHN), blessings over various kinds of food, and for Shabbat, the prayer with which Shabbat begins—the *Kiddush* (pronounced kee-DOOSH or, commonly, KIH-d'sh)—and the ritual with which Shabbat ends—*Havdalah* (pronounced hahv-dah-LAH or, commonly, hahv-DAH-lah).

By the second century, then, with the Temple destroyed and no sacrificial system possible anywhere, Jews were able to substitute prayer: the synagogue service, which was seen as a substitute for the moribund Temple sacrifices on behalf of the corporate Jewish People; and a set of rituals, mostly for tableship gatherings and particularly at holidays (including Shabbat). These table rituals moved from the specialized format of the *chavurah* to the everyday home of ordinary Jews, who adopted rabbinic Judaism as their own.

As the ritual for both places expanded, and as rules for the expanding prayers multiplied, fixed texts and written instructions came into being, and these eventually became the first prayer books described above. Appropriately, they gave equal weight to synagogue and to home.

If Jews today mistakenly identify "liturgy" as the prayers of only one of these publics, the synagogue, not the family, it is because we have mistakenly accepted the Christian definition of the subject. Jesus, who was Jewish, knew all three places for first-century Jewish worship: the Temple cult, which was still in effect in his lifetime; the synagogue, which he frequented (even though rabbinic prayers that eventually found their way there were just in their infancy and had yet to become part of the synagogue's offerings); and the *chavurah,* or tableship group, the rituals of which he observed with his disciples. By the end of the first century, however, Christianity, which was becoming an independent religious entity, was developing its own sacred scriptures and unique liturgy. The process of separation reached its zenith in the fourth century, in the wake of the Roman Empire's Christianization. At first, Christian celebration had been entirely in homes. But these simple home gatherings now took on the pomp and ceremony of the imperial Roman cult. As state religious practices expanded exponentially, home ritual atrophied. And that is why, in Christian parlance, "liturgy" became primarily associated with church, not home.

For Jews not to call home ritual a "liturgy" as well would be to judge Jewish prayer by Christian standards. For Jews, too, liturgy is public, but it varies with the particular public we have in mind: synagogue or home. Unlike Christianity, Judaism was never imperialized; to this day, all Jewish holidays, including Shabbat, have both a synagogue and a home component. Prayer books throughout the ancient and medieval periods honored these parallel foci of Jewish devotion. But what imperialization was to Christianity, modernization was for Jews. In what follows, we will see that modernity let the synagogue overshadow the home. And we will see also why the balance is now shifting back to what it was when Jewish prayer began.

THE AGENDA OF MODERNITY

We have seen how synagogue and home became parallel centers of Jewish worship. But prayer functions not only spiritually; insofar as it is a *public* ritual, it also provides a public display of personal identity. Examples are universal and legion: the question is never *whether* people keep rituals, but which rituals they keep. Every winter and spring, for instance, Christians gather for Christmas and Easter, while Jews keep Chanukah and Passover. Rosh Hashanah and Yom Kippur are Jewish High Holy Days, but the Jewish socialists who settled the Land of Israel preferred May Day. Christians broke away from Judaism by ending circumcision but demanding baptism. Sixteenth-century Baptists (called then Anabaptists, meaning "rebaptizers") reinstated the original Christian practice of adult baptism in place of infant baptism, which had become standard in the Church of Rome three hundred years earlier. Reform Judaism did away with head covering for men, then made it optional; Orthodox Jews have always worn it, as do Conservative Jews, who, however, prefer tiny knitted versions, while Chasidic Jews are actually sometimes referred to (with negative connotations) as "Black Hats," the head covering that typifies their attire.

As long as worship had to get along without printing, determinative ritual differences often had little to do with the words one said. To be sure, even in the Middle Ages, different groups of Jews memorized versions of prayer that marked them off from what others were saying, but the most obvious ways to stake out a unique religious identity were nonverbal, and to some extent (as the above examples demonstrate) they still are. But even changes in prayer wording has regularly agitated people in the know, who insist that their worship remain uncontaminated by the preferences of the people they are "not," and as printing made its appearance, it was the printed book that best established who one was and who one wasn't. This was all the more so because prayer books, which had always included halakhic instructions, were planned with room to tell people not to behave the way other people did.

Take these obvious examples. The 1866 High Holiday Prayer Book of Isaac Mayer Wise, the founder of Reform Judaism, opens with a page of ritual instructions that informs worshipers, "It is no more necessary to wear a TALITH in the temple than anywhere else outside thereof.... As a memorial, it will suffice that the minister wear it." From the other side of the religious spectrum, a 1985 collection of life-cycle liturgical halakhah (Benjamin Adler, *Sefer Hanissu'in K'halakhah,* vol. 2 [Jerusalem: Hamesorah Press, 1985], p. 224) observes that the traditional Jewish marriage ceremony has the groom say to his bride, "Behold you are sanctified to me"; the author then warns, "If she [the bride] answers [the groom], 'Behold you are sanctified to me'—as is common in Reform congregations—there is reason to question whether the marriage is thereby rendered null and void." Even medieval hand-copied prayer books had polemicized against alternatives, as when Amram Gaon, from Babylonia, tells Palestinian Jews that by following their custom of standing up to say the *Sh'ma* (instead of sitting for it, the Babylonian rule), they are guilty of "piling error upon error, foolishness, ignorance, and nonsense." But the possibility of having such instructions circulate in printed form among masses of people only exaggerated the role prayer books played in differentiating right from wrong in worship. Authors do not condemn their opponents out of simple mean-spirited self-pride, nor from political motives alone, even though issues of power are closely tied to liturgical debates like these. They denounce opponents out of honest religious scruple. But the end result does not change just because the motive is honorable. From time immemorial, the way people ritualize is the most obvious way of declaring their group identity. And with printing, prayer books bore the primary responsibility for helping people announce who and what they were.

That was why the emerging Church of England depended on a *Book of Common Prayer* to demonstrate its break with Rome. The breakaway had coincided with the sixteenth-century printing boom, so prayer books were newly possible. That is why, also, when printing became inexpensive in the nineteenth century, every Reform rabbi of significance insisted on publishing his own prayer book and why, equally, Chasidic rebbes from the same era did likewise. It was because they could. The technological capacity to produce written scripts for ritual identity only exacerbated the splintering of religions into competing factions. The shaping of religious identity became more and more dependent on books.

But displays of identity must be public things if they are to matter. In antiquity, Chanukah candles had emerged as a sign of religious allegiance. Although lit at home, they were to be put in windows for the public to see, *l'parsomei nisa,* as the talmudic rationale went, "to [publicly] proclaim the miracle." We shall see later (see pp. 41–55) that Shabbat candles were also signs of allegiance to a specific Jewish identity. They could be seen from outside the home. In modern times, however, the home was increasingly marked off as private, separate in essence from one's public persona. Victorian mores made the home the bastion of women, who were assigned such chores as inculcating virtue in children, while men went off to work. Early Jewish modernists could make it their motto to be "a man *[sic]* in public, but a Jew at home." What mattered was not what you did around your dining room table, but what you did in the public arenas of ritual, the places where you were deliberately on display for yourself as well as for others.

Originally, the purpose of prayer books had been halakhic—providing instructions about the right way to pray, a matter equally relevant in home and in synagogue. In the nineteenth century, however, prayer books became vehicles for taking a public stance by praying according to one tradition rather than another. With home ritual unobservable, and therefore shrinking in importance, printers filled their prayer-book pages with the liturgy of the synagogue, not the liturgy of the home.

All of this is by way of explaining why we, today, think of public liturgy as synagogue prayer, not home devotion. Liberal prayer books, in particular, tended to eliminate home prayers—not because Jews were not supposed to pray at home, but because Jewish identity did not depend on what outsiders could not see. The dichotomy between synagogue and home was so complete that, to this day, most seminaries that include courses on liturgy overlook home prayer altogether, even as they go painstakingly through the history, theology, rules, and customs associated with the public liturgy of the synagogue.

Especially among twentieth-century liberal Jews in North America, home ritual shrank in significance. Partly, that was because their prayer books (such as the *Union Prayer Book,* which dominated Reform consciousness from 1894 to 1975) omitted much or all of home ritual, giving the impression that it was not altogether that important. Then, as immigrants brought with them memories of home prayer and memorization of what was to be prayed, successive generations of Jews born in the New World lost all such memories and found going through traditional home rituals increasingly difficult. The prayers were no longer memorized or even familiar. And they could not be looked up in prayer books that lacked them. Among Reform Jews, a late Friday night service at synagogue began to take the place of home ritual, as candle lighting (once the sole province of the home), for instance, dominated the public service.

This long-term trend toward public ritual can be linked to wider patterns in North American culture. To begin with, because Christians (as we saw) had relatively little home liturgy, thoroughly acculturated Jews did not need to have much either. Of greater importance, however, was the parallelism between economy and worship. One need not be a philosophical Marxist to see that economic developments intertwine with the means of production and with social trends. Economy and social consciousness do go hand in hand. A rising economy allows for investment, inventiveness, and a rapid spread of new technology, which in turn influences how we approach the world of experience (we think differently with television and computers than we did without them). But it is a two-way street: a feedback loop allows changing consciousness to instruct the economy where to invest as well.

Economically speaking, industrialization dominated the last half of the nineteenth century, reached maturity by 1900, and continued through 1950. Artists such as Fernand Léger (1881–1955) painted cubist scenes of machinery and factories. The Bauhaus school of architecture glorified the factory look with visible pipes, ducts, and beams. The very concept of labor, a working class, and unions dominated consciousness. Steel had become king, along with railroads to move it. The Midwest, with its factories, was America's heartland, enjoying its day in the sun, even as the newly revised Reform *Union Prayer Book* prayed for "those who dig far away from" it [the sun], that we might have coal to fuel our future. World War II, however, produced a shift to jet travel, so airlines and restaurant and hotel chains emerged—Holiday Inn in the 1960s, Hyatt and Marriott soon after. We entered the service economy.

The fate of home liturgy among liberal Jews who were not tied halakhically to its absolute necessity varied with these economic and industrial changes. The industrial economy accustomed people to assembly-line mass production, changing the cultural ideal from individuality to uniformity. The mass production of books only hastened that goal, as everyone could now be expected to look up a single set of instructions and abide by them. It was just this expectation of uniformity that eventually created denominations, each with its own prayer book.

To some extent, that changed with the advent of the service economy in the 1960s and beyond. But the 1950s bequeathed the next decade an equal admiration for uniformity—the company man, and the idealized suburban family of mother, father, two children, and a dog. So the economic emphasis on being served was not immediately devoted to individualization. Madison Avenue still advertised mass identity, not becoming one's own person. The accent on public ritual continued.

All that has begun to change. The economic parallel is the new experience economy. As of the 1990s, Ziggy, the perfect cab driver from TV's *Taxi,* sings Sinatra songs while serving his passengers food. At theme restaurants such as Hard Rock Café and Planet Hollywood, customers go for "eatertainment." Thousands of tourists exit Northwest airplanes in Minneapolis to vacation at the Mall of America, where they go dancing and take in floorshows between purchases. Customers at Sharper Image and Brookstone play with gadgets. We have moved from industrial output, to service, to experience. Whereas industrial goods were standardized and services were customized, experiences are personalized. Worship in the industrial era asked us all to be the same, without regard to whether we liked it or not. Worship in the service economy emphasized *"religious services,"* still an exercise in uniformity, but catering more and more to changing tastes, so that people would feel well served by what their synagogues offered. Worship in an experience economy offers individuals exciting personal experiences: spirituality, warmth, belonging, and appropriate emotionality because people are moved to identify personally with a ritual's meaning. None of this is necessarily bad. Judaism has always valued personal experience—it even provides benedictions that accompany moments of private enjoyment. This is simply a description of the way things are. A raft of studies has demonstrated the extent to which the American glorification of what has been called "expressive individualism" has led to our sense of personal entitlement to lives that are anything but mass-produced. Even the U. S. Army began marketing itself with the motto "Be all that you can be." We have been encouraged to manufacture who we are irrespective of what others think. We expect religion to fall into line and give us the experiences we want. And part of what we want is the experience of family.

Why the family? In part, it is because the generation now reaching adulthood has an extraordinary number of members who grew up in broken families. Part of it, also, is the ubiquitous two-career family, where parents worry about making time for their children. And part is the heightened accent on family values that has dominated the cultural skyline since the 1980s. Anecdotal evidence suggests that public events at synagogue (scholar-in-residence weekends, for example) are less attended than they used to be, not because synagogues do not provide the same or even better cultural fare than before, but because the new generation has less time and desire for public events of any sort. With no need to demonstrate public identity, people prefer privatized experience with families, with the accent on all three: "privatized," "experience," and "families."

What has become striking, then, is Judaism's turn to family events: a "tot Shabbat" in synagogue, which does attract great numbers of people; a return to an early Friday night service after which people go home for the traditional Shabbat dinner; and a new thirst for family ritual that reinforces the experience of living and growing up in a Jewish home. High on the list of family events is the Seder, of course; Chanukah, more than ever; and, increasingly, Shabbat. The change is evident in the explosion of family liturgies, first and foremost the Haggadah, which is republished in countless new formats every year. But Shabbat at home has made a recovery that could never have been predicted a decade or two ago.

This renewal of family ritual is evident even in Orthodox circles, where it might be expected that people know such things as how to make *Kiddush* or *Havdalah,* so that publishing home prayer books might be unnecessary. But serious Orthodoxy's recent phenomenal growth has drawn many Jews for whom family ritual is new. So the ArtScroll series has successfully marketed a host of paperback publications that provide texts, the requisite halakhah, and spiritual interpretations. These include even the *z'mirot* (pronounced z'mee-ROHT), Shabbat table songs that earlier generations knew by heart. On the liberal side of things, the Conservative movement in the United States now includes a complete Shabbat eve liturgy with transliteration of prayers for families who read no Hebrew. Reconstructionist Judaism provided its home liturgy in 1991, eight years before a new synagogue prayer book was even issued. And Reform Judaism has published not just one, but two prayer books for private devotion rather than public prayer.

We live in an age where family is being newly valued, and where the richness of Shabbat home liturgy is in greater demand than ever before. A volume of *My People's Prayer Book* given over to Shabbat at home is hardly an anomaly. It is a sign of the times. We offer it here with fervent prayers that it may make the Jewish tradition's age-old genius for the spirituality of home life come alive for a generation newly seeking it.

Introduction to the Liturgy of Shabbat at Home

Why Shabbat?

Lawrence A. Hoffman

SHABBAT AS SACRED CENTER

Take a look at any Jewish calendar and you will see how central Shabbat is to the Jewish conception of time. To begin with, no other days have proper names—they are called just *yom rishon, yom sheni* ("day one," "day two"), and so forth. Only day seven *(Shabbat)* gets its own name. By extension, Shabbat so dominates Jewish consciousness that the days before and after it, *yom shishi* ("sixth day," Friday) and *yom rishon* ("first day," Sunday), are sometimes called *Erev Shabbat* ("evening before Shabbat," pronounced EH-rehv shah-BAHT) and *Motsa'ei Shabbat* ("end of Shabbat," pronounced moh-tsah-AY shah-BAHT). But the latter two terms are used loosely. Because Hebrew days begin at sundown, *Erev Shabbat* may refer only to the few hours leading up to sundown, or even the evening service in the synagogue—even though, technically, most of that service occurs after Shabbat has actually begun. The same ambiguity applies to *Motsa'ei Shabbat*, which may designate just the evening following Shabbat (Saturday night), not any part of the next day. In any event, we see plainly that at least parts of three days in the week refer back to the only day worth noting, as far as Jews are concerned: Shabbat. No wonder home liturgies are provided for key moments in this period of time:

- Friday evening—*Erev Shabbat:* Most significant is the Friday evening home service that inaugurates the Sabbath, highlighted by (1) lighting Shabbat candles and (2) saying the *Kiddush* (pronounced *kee-DOOSH* or, commonly, KIH-d'sh), a prayer announcing the onset of sacred time, alongside (3) a sip of wine and its blessing. The whole thing is often called by the name *Kiddush;* to celebrate it is called "making *Kiddush.*"

- Saturday evening—*Motsa'ei Shabbat:* Another colorful event, *Havdalah* (pronounced hahv-dah-LAH or, commonly, hahv-DAH-lah, and meaning "separation"), concludes Shabbat, distinguishing it from *Motsa'ei Shabbat* that follows. *Havdalah* includes (1) wine, but also (2) smelling sweet spices, and (3) lighting and then dousing a colorful twisted candle with multiple wicks.

• Noontime on Shabbat day has its celebration too; this was just a blessing over wine at first but is now somewhat expanded into what is called (ironically, because it is really just a tiny ceremony) the "Great *Kiddush*" (*Kiddusha Rabbah*, pronounced kee-doo-SHAH rah-BAH but, commonly, kih-DOO-shah RAH-bah).

All three of these rituals were firmly in place by the time the Talmud was codified (about 550 C.E.), and the first two (*Kiddush* and *Havdalah*) are older still, taken for granted by the early part of the first century. Other ways of marking Shabbat developed later, especially a "third meal" *(s'udah sh'lishit)*, an extra meal late Saturday afternoon, and (in some Chasidic circles) a Saturday night celebration after sundown called *m'laveh malkah* (pronounced m'-lah-VEH mal-KAH or, commonly, MAH-l'v' MAL-kah, or m'LAH-v' MAL-kah), which means "accompanying the bride." In it, Shabbat, which is personified as a bride, takes her leave of us for a week, until she visits again.

The formal home liturgy includes the first three of these five rituals, and they are highlighted here. We have also dedicated a separate introductory essay to the fascinating subject of *s'udah sh'lishit,* which seems widespread enough to warrant inclusion, even though (unlike *Kiddush* and *Havdalah*) not all Jews keep it, and among those who do, its liturgy is highly variable.

It is helpful to think of liturgies as having either a weak or a strong structure. The prayers with strong structure are highly determined, strictly governed by Jewish law or custom, fairly universal in their usage, and open to relatively little change. They are tightly shaped, their pattern readily evident. By contrast, a weakly structured liturgy is mostly undetermined except for local usage and tends to attract all sorts of extra material over the course of time. It grows like Topsy, adding or subtracting prayers without any obvious structural plan. Using an architectural analogy, we could say that strong structure in liturgy is like a set of buildings shaped carefully so that they can be plunked down in the compact center of a city; squeezed on all sides, nothing much can be added later. By contrast, a weak structure is like urban sprawl. It begins with something relatively tiny, but then spreads out, attracting subdevelopments all over, until the original plan (if there even was one) is almost unnoticeable. The *Sh'ma* and Its Blessings and the *Amidah* (see Volumes 1 and 2) are strongly structured. The liturgy surrounding the reading of Torah (see Volume 4) is weakly structured. The home liturgy for Shabbat is also weakly structured. All three of its rituals began small but then proliferated into a more lengthy celebration with little structure overall.

Highly structured liturgies rarely grow very much. Their interest lies in their very structure, which bears its own message beyond whatever the prayer's words and music have to say. As we saw in earlier volumes of this series, the *Sh'ma and Its Blessings* (see Volume 1) provides a thumbnail sketch of the Jewish view of God: a single Deity who stands behind creation, revelation, and redemption and provides cosmic order, human purpose, and hope. The *Amidah* (see Volume 2) presents individual petitions, which add up to the classic Jewish doctrine of salvation.

Loosely structured liturgies may say a lot with their individual parts but have little structural integrity, because they have hardly any structure to start with. Because they act like a magnet, attracting liturgical additions like iron filings, their further fascination lies in the way they come to represent different eras in Jewish history. Our most strongly structured units (the *Sh'ma* and Its Blessings and the *Amidah*) were largely in place by the end of the second century; not much got added after that. The home Shabbat service is just the opposite. As a loosely structured liturgy, it has been expanded enormously.

We have divided the Shabbat home liturgy according to the times during the day when it is recited. We have omitted the relatively rare *m'laveh malkah* and provided a separate essay on the somewhat more traditional *s'udah sh'lishit*. But this book's focus is the three main elements that break up the twenty-four hour period from the time Shabbat arrives to the time it departs:

- *Erev Shabbat:* welcoming Shabbat with *Kiddush*
- Noontime on Shabbat day: *Kiddusha Rabbah*
- *Motsa'ei Shabbat:* bidding Shabbat farewell with *Havdalah*

All three of these parts developed in three stages:

1. They were begun in the classical rabbinic era, probably before the Mishnah was canonized (before 200 C.E.), but certainly before the finished Talmud came into being (circa 550 C.E.).

2. Medieval Jewish practice added its own ritual layers.

3. Of these later additions, one stands out: the mystical prayers of sixteenth-century kabbalists in the northern Israeli mountain town of Safed (pronounced TSFAHT). This mystical stratum is so pronounced on Shabbat that a failure to appreciate it would be to miss most of the significance that these prayers have had for Jews over the centuries. But mysticism is not easy to appreciate, and because the prayers assume a prior knowledge of it, we need to look next at Judaism's view of the esoteric.

THE ESOTERIC IN JEWISH PRAYER

The potential problem with studying the esoteric in any religion is that it is easy to learn all about it and still fail to understand it. Mystical descriptions of experience are, by definition, metaphoric. Having encountered something deeper than the run-of-the-mill events that constitute daily life, mystics must either declare their experiential breakthrough a delusion or find some language with which to think about it. Everyday pedestrian language which arises out of equally everyday pedestrian experience will not do, because whatever it is, a mystical experience is not just "everyday pedestrian."

Mystics are not the only ones to face this problem. Every specialized branch of knowledge develops its own vocabulary. Computer technology describes viruses, gigabytes, and hackers; corporate jockeying brings us hostile takeovers, magic bullets, and white knights. Scientists speak of photons, muons, and black holes. Sometimes the vocabulary helps us conceive of what is utterly beyond us, as when physicist Niels Bohr describes the atom as a tight nucleus around which electrons revolve, or Francis Crick and James Watson picture DNA as a double helix. The atom and DNA really do exist. But they cannot be seen. So people who have experienced their reality resort to imaginative representations of them, not because they really look that way, but because most of us need some kind of imagery with which to think. So too, mystics develop a specialized vocabulary, not because it does justice to experiences that transcend empirical evidence, but because they cannot think about those experiences without some conceptual scheme in mind. Describing their pictorial system is easy. Appreciating the fact that the system actually refers to something real is not—especially in our time, which is still so heavily impacted by the triumphalist science of the nineteenth century.

The nineteenth century suffered from a myopic view of reality. It made three grave errors. First, in keeping with the evolutionist perspective of the century, nineteenth-century thought assumed that human nature evolves through time from the primitive to the sophisticated. It followed that first- and second-century Jews who began rabbinic Judaism could hardly be adequate models for us today.

Second, nineteenth-century scholarship was a reaction to the Middle Ages, which were thought to be a backward slide from the high cultural watermark of Greco-Roman antiquity. To some extent, this evaluation of the Jewish past seems to contradict the first principle: the evolutionary climb of civilization. But it was possible to see evolution moving in a spiral advance that allowed for two steps forward and one step backward on occasion. So historians decided that the destruction of Rome, and with it the heritage of classical antiquity, initiated a lengthy "backward step," an era called the "Dark Ages." The Dark Ages were briefly interrupted by the Renaissance, but it did not come to an end until the "En*light*enment" (the opposite of the *Dark* Ages), which inaugurated modernity. It followed that medieval Jewish culture was a cultural retreat from the Rabbis who had inhabited the Roman Empire. Post-Enlightenment Jews were assumed to have more in common with the Rabbis of antiquity than they did with medieval commentators and legalists.

Now, assuming that medieval Jewry was too backward to serve as models for our own destiny; and assuming also that classical rabbinic Judaism was a good model, but not up to the level of spiritual attainment that marks our own era; it then follows that we should virtually ignore our medieval past but choose selectively from the classical era to find guidance for Jewish progress today. What remained to be decided was what criterion to use, and here the third error entered in.

The nineteenth century thought that the problem with the Dark Ages was its dependence on superstition, and it saw mysticism as superstitious through and through. When deciding what to value in antiquity, it followed that only insofar as the Rabbis were rationalists, not mystics, could they serve as reliable touchstones for us. By contrast, any rabbinic mysticism would be written off as evidence that even the Rabbis were still not up to the purely rationalistic standard of modernity. It was as if the Rabbis were mostly in touch with reason but still harbored some superstitious mystical silliness. The Middle Ages were "dark" because they mistakenly dropped rabbinic rationality and extended rabbinic mysticism into what became a dead end. Modernity reacted against medieval mysticism; it retraced a route back through the dead end to the main evolutionary pathway using what it could of the original rationalistic strain in its rabbinic past.

PARDES

A famous rabbinic tale, repeated in several sources, reports the case of four famous Rabbis who entered *Pardes*. As the Babylonian Talmud (Chag. 14b) describes it: "There were four who entered *Pardes*. Ben Azzai, Ben Zoma, Acher [Elisha ben Abuyah], and Rabbi Akiba…. Ben Azzai took one look and died…. Ben Zoma looked and went mad…. Acher left Judaism…. Only Rabbi Akiba departed unhurt."

All four of these Rabbis are well known from other contexts. Elisha ben Abuyah is an infamous apostate whose name the Rabbis never pronounce. Instead, they call him Acher, meaning "The Other." What religion he professed after leaving Judaism and why he left in the first place are matters of debate, but here his apostasy is explained by his entering *Pardes*. Two of the other Rabbis were similarly affected, in that they too "left" something. Ben Azzai "departed this earthly life," and Ben Zoma "took leave of his senses." Only Akiba emerged unscathed.

Rabbis and scholars—ancient, medieval, and modern—have discussed this intriguing tale at length. Not the least interesting observation is its literary form, with an extended metaphor of "entering and leaving." The four Rabbis enter a place called *Pardes* and must leave it. But three of the four leave more than *Pardes*. Each leaves behind a different characteristic that the ideal Rabbi was said to embody.

Sociologist Max Weber thought religions and cultures could be studied from the point of view of what he called their "ideal type," by which he meant the idealized identity toward which a member of that culture is expected to strive. For Chinese Confucianism, it was the sage; for classical Christianity, it was the ascetic and otherworldly monk; for the Rabbis, it was the Torah scholar—a Rabbi. Several specific characteristics made the Torah scholar what he was. He had to be a man, for instance, though we know of women who studied Torah and even attained mastery of it; the fact that they were women precluded their being considered Rabbis. Rabbis also, obviously, had to be living and sane. The Rabbi as scholar was, therefore, a (1) living (2) man (3) in full control of his sanity, (4) who had studied Torah and lived by it.

Pardes is the hypothetical place where Rabbis cease to be what they are. To the rabbinic mind, leaving one sex (2) for the other was impossible; but the three other vital parts of rabbinic identity could be abandoned, and *Pardes* is what caused Rabbis to abandon them. One Rabbi—Acher, "The Other"—becomes someone else altogether, no longer even a Jew, let alone a Torah scholar who not only knows what Torah says but also feels obliged to live by it (4). The two others leave life (1) and sanity (3) behind.

But Akiba is different. He is the Jewish Ulysses, the ideal type at its most heroic. The Greek ideal type was the wise and brave warrior, practically a god himself. In hero tales such as Homer's *Odyssey* and the Talmud's *Pardes*, the hero is lured into the ultimate challenge that only the best example of the ideal type would be expected to meet and surpass. Others fail the test because they are not fully the ideal. But the hero, a conqueror, overcomes unimaginable adversity. In the *Odyssey*, Ulysses returns from the Trojan War, already a warrior of stature. Homer's poem pits every known danger against him, but he arrives home safely. So, too, our four Rabbis are drawn to the ultimate rabbinic challenge, *Pardes*. Three of them fail. But what physical battle is to Ulysses, *Pardes* is to Akiba. Akiba survives the ultimate challenge that does in ideal types of lesser stature.

Pardes, then, must be some ultimate aspect of Torah learning that only the most adept can expect to master without taking leave of their senses, their learning, or their lives. And so it is: it is mysticism, the deepest level of Torah, that only the very few can hope to navigate successfully. The word means "garden," an allusion to the Garden of Eden, itself a perfect place that even Adam and Eve were not up to mastering. From *Pardes* (or, more precisely, from the Greek equivalent, *Paradeisos*), we get the English "Paradise."

Medieval tradition read more still into the word *Pardes*. In its Hebraic lettering, the vowels would have been missing. Only the four consonants *PRDS* would have been found. Each consonant was therefore likened to a deeper level of Torah insight.

Anyone can master the "P," which stands for *p'shat*, merely the literal surface level of what the Torah says. Deeper insight comes from the "R" and "D," which stand for *remez* ("hint") and *d'rash* ("exegetical interpretation"). *Remez* stands for such things as *g'matriyah*, the pursuit of deeper textual meaning by adding up the numerical value of the letters that comprise a Hebrew word and seeing what other words add up to the same value. *D'rash* is to Torah what rules of jurisprudence are to law: the application of generally recognized principles of interpretation to derive the meaning of a text (see Volume 5, *Birkhot Hashachar: Morning Blessings*, "The Thirteen Principles of Rabbi Ishmael," pp. 171–185). But not just any Rabbi can hope to enter the alluring but dangerous world of *sod* (from the "S"), meaning "secret." *Sod* is the final and ultimate meaning of Torah, the esoteric level available only to mystics.

Earlier generations found it easy to believe that religion leads ultimately to a revelatory experience of life's final meaning, its secrets or *sod*, if you like—the answers to such questions as "Where is God?" "What is the nature of human existence?" "Who am I?" and "Why do we suffer?" If religion cannot posit rationally acceptable answers, at least it guarantees the immediate experience of a transcendent reality that renders the questions moot. Such a transcendent experience is precisely what the errors of the nineteenth century threw into doubt. What past generations called "mysticism," emerging modernists called delusion. Instead of looking outward, they turned inward to find life's ultimate answers and came up with psychotherapy. So "therapy" and "mysticism" may address the same thing: navigating the uncharted depth of being. Therapists prefer the word "psyche." Mystics call it "the soul."

However much the two may respond to the same human striving, mysticism and therapy are not just different descriptions of the same thing. They presuppose radically different views of what constitutes the ultimate object of the search. Therapy digs deep into the "self," a concept that came into its own only in modern times, when medieval corporate identity—seeing oneself as a member of one's group—was replaced with rampant individuality. The religious journey into the "soul" does more than reveal a "self" unharnessed to anything beyond it. The soul is that part of ourselves that is most akin to the divine; it links our finite selves to the eternally transcendent. "Soul" is the uncharted region within us that is godlike. Like "mind," soul is beyond human chemistry, irreducible to materiality, unmappable as DNA or the genome.

To fully experience the soul is to go beyond it to the eternal: to be, as it were, party to the mind of God. The Rabbis identify two specific topics that typify such mystical search: how creation occurred (ma'aseh b'reishit) and the existence of God as only the angels know it (ma'aseh merkavah). These concerns were not banned, but investigating them was like entering Pardes; it was hazardous. We may at least dimly fathom the reality of these rabbinic warnings if, once again, we recall the parallel between religious mysticism and secular psychotherapy. Therapists too worry about causing their patients damage by rashly ripping away their defenses and revealing too quickly the full depth of the psyche. Call it what you will—soul, psyche, or something else entirely—there seems to be a level of insight to which we dearly aspire, but the discovery of which poses a threat to people unprepared for what they may find.

We return, then, to the nineteenth century's attitude toward mysticism. The nineteenth century has been called an era of scientific triumphalism, when people believed it was only a matter of time until a better telescope and microscope would reveal the infinitely large and the infinitesimally small. In such a world-view, there was no room for souls, mysticism, and the direct experience of God. It was relatively easy to understand the system of language that the mystics used, the way ordinary technicians working under Einstein understood scientific jargon. They could manipulate permutations of relevant symbols to produce meaningful combinations: a sentence about the universe in one case, an equation about relativity in the other. But they lacked firsthand knowledge of the experience toward which the language pointed.

The point of all this for us is that we will not understand Shabbat table liturgy unless we read ourselves back to the attitude toward mysticism that predated nineteenth-century blindness to the mystical. We should at least open ourselves to the possibility that mystical language, however odd, is a valid metaphorical way of discussing an ineffable experience. We want to be able to read and understand the sentences that mystics made about their experience, but even more, we want to let the language lead us to the experience itself.

If the word "mysticism" proves bothersome, call it what you will. Whatever you call it, this search for the *sod*—the ultimate significance of the universe and of our place within it—has always been part of rabbinic Judaism. Shabbat liturgy was designed to be read as a *sod,* a set of esoteric meanings written in metaphoric code and pointing to experience that language will never fully grasp.

THE *SOD* OF SHABBAT LITURGY

The particular group of mystics responsible for the final shape of Shabbat liturgy lived well after the Rabbis of late antiquity who entered *Pardes*. The Jewish mysticism that the Rabbis represented had not been altogether lost. It had continued in various forms and emerged in the thirteenth century, transformed into a set of overlapping doctrines that came to be called Kabbalah. Jewish émigrés who were expelled from Spain in 1492 brought Kabbalah with them to Safed, where a new layer of meaning was supplied by Isaac Luria. Shabbat liturgy has its ordinary surface level of *p'shat,* but it is intended to be read as a Lurianic *sod.*

To a great extent, Luria and his generation were able to find the *sod* they did because the events of their time predisposed them to it. They were victims of an existential reality born of their political condition. Expelled from Spain in 1492, and newly settled in the tiny town of Safed in the mountains of the Land of Israel, they were in the midst of reconstructing their lives in the reality of literal exile. Any immigrant community experiences such personal fragmentation. But that feeling was especially poignant for the exiles of sixteenth-century Safed. First, their families had lived in Spain for centuries (far longer than any of us have lived in North America!); they had been truly at home there. Second, they had not chosen to leave, but had been forcibly banished. Finally, the expulsion seemed especially cruel to them. Anti-Jewish riots in 1381 had led many upper-class Jews to avoid further persecution by converting to Christianity, but the exiles of 1492 had stubbornly remained Jewish. They were apparently being punished for their loyalty to God. Abandoned by God, half a world away from everything they had called home, unable even to visit the graves of grandparents and great-grandparents, they found themselves cast into a rugged mountain village with nothing to recommend it.

This existential fragmentation, however, was balanced by a spiritual breakthrough. Jewish philosophy in Spain was unable to explain what the émigrés were experiencing. Kabbalah, however, a rival doctrine, had an answer. It depended on an experience that mystics worldwide have described. Accounts differ, of course, but through all the diversity, a common thread runs through their narratives. It is best summed up by the phrase "mystical union," a sense of intimate unity with all that is, and just the opposite, therefore, of the fragmentation born of political exile. We think of this mystical goal as central to Eastern religions—as indeed it is—but it is not on that account absent from Judaism. Our problem has been the intellectual blinders that we looked at above: the unwillingness of rationalistic scholars to explore any evidence from the past that did not accord with the scientific models of religion that they, personally, considered "advanced."

Especially beyond their ken were practices we would consider mystical. To the extent that they could not miss them, they shunted them off to insignificance by declaring them marginal to mainstream Talmudism, footnotes to Jewish history, or sorry examples of how medieval Jews went wrong. The Jews in Safed were not hampered by these misconceptions. Part of their prayer life was aimed at attaining the very experience of mystical union that modern scholars would later ridicule.

Our first step at understanding the Lurianic contribution to Shabbat liturgy was a quick look at the historical circumstances that predisposed the community of Safed to find a mystical pattern to reality. Two further steps remain. In the face of nineteenth-century modernism, still very much with us, we need to recognize mysticism in general as a valid human experience. We shall see that the émigrés' personal familiarity with mystical union fit their existential need to find wholeness in a world of fragmentation. Once we recognize the validity of what the mystics knew as real, we can turn to the metaphorical system of language that they invented to describe it. It is that language that makes Shabbat liturgy so appealing.

Fortunately, though most of us are not exiles, mystical union is not an experience that is closed to us. How could it be, if it is innate to human nature? There are moments when we too can intuit the connectedness of all of life, the magnificence of the way natural laws explain the most diverse phenomena, revealing them, in all their differences, as parallel examples of the same thing.

Myla Goldberg's novel *Bee Season* pictures bar mitzvah boy Aaron Naumann remembering how he used to stare at the blinking red light on the wing of a plane he was in as it flew through a cloud. In that instant, he saw beyond the light and the cloud to the ultimate source of all being, the mystery behind the pure fact that anything exists at all. Just a light, we college-trained adults are likely to say, a mere cloud, mistaken by a child as the hand of God. So Aaron knows better than to tell anyone about his discovery. They will surely correct him, bring him into line with proper modern thinking—if need be, send him to a psychiatrist to correct his psychic imbalance. But Aaron will not give up. And then, on his bar mitzvah day, it happens:

> Alone on the *bima* speeding through the final *brachot* after completing his Haftorah portion.... Aaron can sense the approach of something larger, a sea swell building up to a huge wave. Then in a moment so intense Aaron has no idea he is still standing, it hits.
> Every person in the room becomes part of him.... He can suddenly see the Temple from forty-six different perspectives, through forty-six pairs of eyes. He is linked. He feels the theme and variation of forty-six heartbeats, the stretch and release of forty-six pairs of lungs.... He feels total acceptance and total love. (pp. 41–42)

True, Aaron Naumann is pure fiction. But his experience is not. In one way or another, it has been described by countless real people, many of them conditioned to discount the very possibility of it occurring. It may come through singing together at a rally, or through observing a sunset, the mystery of an insect's wing, or the grandeur of a meteor shower. For many of us, the sense of belonging to something far beyond ourselves does come—as it came to the exiles in Safed. They made spiritual history because instead of repressing the feeling as rationally impossible, they sought metaphors to do their experience justice.

Their existential condition and their spiritual breakthrough could have been seen by them as mutually contradictory. On the one hand, they were separated from their homes in Spain, a country their families had known for centuries; but on the other, like Aaron Naumann, they had momentarily experienced Being itself, so integrally interwoven with who they were that alienation was impossible. How could they be fragmented, separated from all they held dear—even from God, whose exiling them seemed a cruel trick—and at the same time be part of the "allness of it all," part, even, of God? Their answer is the essence of Lurianic Kabbalah. Both sensations are true. Fragmentation is the experience of an unredeemed world; mystical union is that same world experienced from the perspective of redemption. Because Shabbat is a "taste of the world-to-come," it could be the venue where wholeness replaces ordinary weekday fragmentation.

Applying new meanings to old words—as here, regarding Shabbat—is the cognitive side of mysticism. The experience of unification within the "allness" is the noncognitive reality to which the cognitive merely points. Aaron Naumann does not simply have a mystical experience. Once he has it, he yearns to express it in language that is too poverty stricken to do it justice. When he thinks Judaism may be unequal to the task, he finds his way to Hare Krishna, where his experience is confirmed by others and where also he is given a language to express it.

Aaron should have found the language he needed in Judaism. It is there, in the cognitive side of Kabbalah. The irony of *Bee Season* is the fact that Aaron's father, a cantor and student of Kabbalah, knows that language. But he has never had Aaron's experience, and Aaron is afraid to report it to a father who (Aaron thinks) is likely to discount it. So Aaron never gets the native Jewish language that would have justified his experience as real.

This kind of justifying language does more than say, in so many words, "Your experience is not delusional." It satisfies the mind's need to provide a logical explanation of how the experience operates. That is what science is, really: a set of mathematical statements that explain such experiences as motion, light, growth, and decay. So too, kabbalistic liturgy not only affirms the experience of mystical "allness," it also explains it in thoroughly logical terms.

We have so far considered the experiential aspect. Now we turn to the interpretive language for which Kabbalah is famous. We want to know how the language of Lurianic Kabbalah explained the existential situation of being an émigré in exile and, at the same time, the mystical experience of wholeness despite the patent condition of fragmentation. It is this mythic system of metaphor that constitutes the *sod* of Shabbat liturgy.

The key hypothesis of Lurianic Kabbalah is the parallel existence of different worlds. The number varies with the theorist, but at its simplest, it is assumed that our human world is mirrored by a world of God. The two, however, are actually the same, in that all existence is really a unified whole, intuited at the mystical moment of knowing we are part of the "all." What happens to Israel in this world happens simultaneously to God in the other one.

So, for example, the Talmud says that when the Temple was destroyed and Israel went into exile, God went with them. As Israel cried then, so too did God. In the kabbalists' time, it followed, God and Israel shared a common fate. God must feel the same alienation that the émigrés did. Needing a metaphor that aptly described the sense of aimlessness that total fragmentation implies, they pictured two lovers looking for each other in lonely solitude. God must be like that also, then. So God, they concluded, is best described as having a male and a female part; these two aspects of divinity make God like two lovers, searching each other out. On Shabbat, they find each other, just as the émigré community discovered total wholeness instead of the shattering fragmentation of the weekday world. Friday night liturgy became an exercise in celebrating their and God's wholeness.

If the image of fragmentation is two lovers adrift from one another, then Shabbat wholeness is best likened to the lovers' finding each other and celebrating a divine marriage, God's male and female sides coming together on their wedding night. The kabbalists did not shrink from the ultimate image of their metaphor: lovers joined in sexual intercourse. What better symbol is there for two becoming one? Shabbat became the night of a divine marriage; Shabbat dinner, the marriage feast. The ordinary householders of Safed would be the guests. They would greet the bride, God's female half, with *L'khah Dodi,* an invitation to "Come...and meet the bride..." (see full description forthcoming in Volume 8, *Shabbat in the Synagogue*). And as guests at a wedding do, they would toast the bride with *Eshet Chayil,* a paean of praise for worthy women, taken from the Bible (see *Eshet Chayil,* pp. 74–89).

But symbols often mean more than one thing, and sometimes their various meanings overlap, the way two ocean waves come together and superimpose their mutual strength upon each other. The *p'shat* (or surface) meaning was not untrue. *Eshet Chayil* could also be an ordinary husband praising his wife, or even Israel the People praising God, whom, the midrash said, Israel had "married" at Sinai. But to the kabbalists, all that mattered was the *sod*: the praise of God's feminine half, which was simultaneously (in our world of space and time) the Shabbat, come to join in intimate embrace for a magical twenty-four hours.

Shabbat at home had not always meant this. It had originated as something far less, and then grown in spurts until a final layer of Lurianic meaning gave it ultimate depth. As we have inherited it, Shabbat liturgy refers regularly to this Lurianic *sod*—but only if it is read with an eye to its hidden esoteric references.

The background given here outfits you to see Shabbat liturgy differently. In the next volume, we will turn to Shabbat in the synagogue. Here, our topic is Shabbat at home. Kabbalistic interpretation lies behind them both.

Shabbat Z'mirot

An Expanding Frontier of the Jewish Spirit

Lawrence A. Hoffman

Ashkenazi Jews call the "warm-up" section of psalms and songs that introduces the early morning synagogue service *P'sukei D'zimrah* (see Volume 3, *P'sukei D'zimrah: Morning Psalms*). The preferred title among Sefardim is *Z'mirot* (pronounced z'-mee-ROHT, "songs"; singular, *z'mirah,* pronounced z'-mee-RAH, though sometimes an alternative word from the same root, *zemer* [pronounced ZEH-mehr] is preferred). *Z'mirot* is also a generic name for songs in general, and is used to signify songs set aside for table singing during Shabbat meals.

On the one hand, *z'mirot* as Shabbat table songs are the most natural thing in the world: what could be more obvious than the attraction of stretching out a festive meal with song? On the other hand, singing Shabbat *z'mirot* is its own unique experience, going back many centuries, but not all the way to whenever it was that Jews first started meeting around the table for holiday celebrations. The difference between singing at meals in general and singing Shabbat *z'mirot* in particular is akin to the difference between prayer in general and meeting in synagogue, as we do, for specific Shabbat services. In both cases, if we do not recognize the difference, we so confuse the specific practices with the generalities of which they are indicative that we end up saying nothing significant at all about the very thing that interests us. Saying that Jews have always met God in prayer tells us nothing about what we now call synagogue services, and recognizing the relatively universal human custom of singing together after sharing a heavy holiday meal, especially with enough wine to last beyond dessert, says nothing about the unique home liturgical practice of including after-dinner songs at the Shabbat table. Still, the specific practice we call *z'mirot* did develop out of the general custom of mealtime singing, making it hard to differentiate between the two, except relatively arbitrarily. It helps to work backward.

Our *z'mirot* nowadays come packaged in a "canon." By "canon" in this instance, we mean a specific repertoire of songs generally appropriate, and even mandatory, for Shabbat table singing. A different canon of song is customary at each of the Shabbat meals—much the way a specific set of prayers demarcates each of the Shabbat (or, for that matter, daily) synagogue services. The canon for each meal is still relatively open; new songs come and old ones lapse, on occasion. Sefardim sing somewhat different songs than Ashkenazim. Reform Jews prefer a set that differs from the usual Orthodox repertoire. Israelis differ somewhat from North Americans. And any given home has its own favorites that need not accord with other homes next door or across the street. But in any case, a somewhat variable canon exists, and Jews who sing *z'mirot* feel obliged to choose, at least in part, from whatever collection it is that they consider canonical.

The sure sign of such a canon is the fact that prayer books customarily include the *z'mirot* that compose it as semi-mandatory material to be sung at the table. They are hardly halakhic staples—a far cry from Friday evening *Kiddush,* say, or the blessing for lighting candles. But they are not left entirely to choice either. They are recognized *minhag* ("custom"), recommended but not universally followed. People sing them because they add to the Shabbat experience, but if they are not sung, Shabbat has not necessarily been left wanting in any halakhic way. Still, prayer books carry them for those Jews who do want to sing them and want to know, therefore, what songs are customary and what the lyrics are.

A parallel case would be the songs that people often sing at the end of the Passover Seder. Many Jews would find the Seder lacking were they to do without songs such as *Echad Mi Yode'a?* ("Who Knows One?"), *Adir Hu* (usually translated, loosely, as "God of Might"), and *Chad Gadya* ("An only kid"). But popular as they may be, these and other similar songs are not required staples of the Seder. Most of them are relatively recent creations, from the seventeenth century on, added to the Haggadah to magnify the joy of the occasion. To be sure, they are consistent with the halakhic mandate "Expanding conversation about the Exodus from Egypt is praiseworthy." Similarly, Shabbat *z'mirot* satisfy the general halakhic principle of celebrating Shabbat with joy *(oneg)* and peace in one's home *(sh'lom bayit).* For centuries, however, both Seders and Shabbat meals were observed without such songs, and even today, what songs we sing, and even the choice to sing any at all, are optional, rather than hard and fast halakhic requirements.

What we want to know, then, is when specific sets of after-dinner songs for Shabbat became so popular that it was considered desirable, if not mandatory, to sing them, to the point where they were included in prayer books as part of the Shabbat meal liturgy.

With that goal in mind, we should discount most of the ancient references to Shabbat table songs, on the grounds that they represent singing in general, but not a canonical collection of songs considered semi-mandatory. The Mishnah, for example, refers obliquely to feasting without song after the Temple was destroyed (Sotah 9:11), and the Midrash contrasts Jewish table songs with pagan parallels, which Jews considered lewd (Song of Songs Rabbah 8:15). It may well have been that Jewish singing was customary until the Temple was destroyed; and it may be also that singing began again prior to the sixth-century midrashic account contrasting Jewish and pagan customs. It may also be that both accounts are just homiletical ways of indicating the tenor of the times: the tragedy of the Temple's fall, on one hand, and the ongoing rivalry between Judaism and paganism on the other. We know, for instance, that music figured prominently in other instances of pagan-Jewish conflict. The Rabbis looked askance at instrumentation at services, justifying it in many ways—including the need to mourn for the Temple's destruction. But historically, they were probably reacting to the entertainment style of pagan festive gatherings.

The first prayer books (*Seder Rav Amram* [ninth century, Babylonia] and *Siddur Saadiah* [tenth century, Babylonia]) make no reference to customary *z'mirot*. *Siddur Saadiah* does include a number of poems that might have been sung, and in general, we know of many other poems for holidays that were customary then, especially in the Land of Israel. These may have been sung also, and if so, they are a beginning of the custom that interests us. But the first clear reference to *z'mirot* comes from the eleventh-century French liturgical collection known as *Machzor Vitry*.

By the eleventh century, then, *z'mirot* were at least becoming the norm, and because at least one of the songs recorded there comes from the pen of a poet who lived a century earlier, we should begin to recognize the difficulty inherent in looking for a single clear date when *z'mirot* began.

In all probability, what we know as *z'mirot* are the result of several centuries of evolution. From the outset, the universal custom of singing at festive meals was common among Jews. Some of the poems from the geonic period (roughly 750–1034), especially in Eretz Yisrael, may have functioned that way. At least one poem, set to song by its author or by someone else later on, was known to Simchah of Vitry, who included it in his compilation called *Machzor Vitry*, along with the advice that "it is customary to include *z'mirot* after meals." The song from the prior century that he included was *D'ror Yikra*, attributed (possible incorrectly) to the famed Babylonian poet Dunash ibn Labrat (see *D'ror Yikra*, p. 127). It has stood the test of time and is included here as evidence of the earliest stratum of *z'mirot* in Jewish tradition.

The custom became well known thereafter and is recommended by other authorities in the centuries following. Poets ranged from those whom we hardly recognize today to the great bards of the Jewish People, Judah Halevi (1075–1141), for instance.

Still, the liturgical inclusion of Shabbat table melodies was not accomplished without controversy. Novelties in general polarize people to some extent, and *z'mirot* were no exception. Probably the most common objection was that the singing sometimes resembled anything but a pious Shabbat celebration. Medieval Jews used alcoholic beverages, especially wine and beer, the way we use water—a commentary from the time (Tos. to Taan. 12a) gives us some idea of the amount drunk when it recommends that on the day prior to Tisha B'av (a fast day commemorating the destruction of the Temple), Jews should reduce their usual intake of ten glasses of beer by half. By the end of a lengthy Shabbat meal, then, celebration could sometimes look like drunken revelry—to the point where Halakhah warns us to remain sober throughout Shabbat dinner.

Then, too, the songs were usually composed with models of the surrounding culture in mind. Dunash himself was party to an international dispute as to the propriety of composing Jewish songs in Arabic poetic meter. Songs were often

Jewish versions of common musical staples drawn from the general culture. The Passover song *Chad Gadya*, for instance, is quite like many folk compositions (such as the English "The House That Jack Built," and, even more, a German song, *"Der Herr, der schickt den Jockel aus"* [The man who chased away the fool"]). *Echad Mi Yode'a?* is a Jewish example of the common musical genre that builds a song on numbers. Rather than a Seder song, it was originally sung at wedding banquets, as a Jewish version of similar German songs.

And finally, even songs with specifically Jewish lyrics and themes were frequently sung to melodies that Jews absorbed from their environment—not an unusual practice, musically. *Hatikva*, the Israeli national anthem, is heavily dependent on *The Moldau* by Czech composer Bedrich Smetana (1824–1884). I will never forget the late Eric Werner, professor of Jewish music at the Hebrew Union College, sitting down at a piano and showing us how our standard *Birkat Hamazon* follows a variety of Polish folk melodies and dance tunes. Even the end of our *Alenu* melody *(bayom hahu...)* follows the melody for "The Farmer in the Dell."

For all these reasons, authorities were torn about the custom of *z'mirot*. *Z'mirot* were, after all, ways to celebrate the joy of Shabbat. In any event, the objectors ultimately failed to stop the custom. People like to sing. It may be as simple as that. And by the sixteenth century, singing *z'mirot* had become commonplace, at which time the second stage of their development occurred: the rise of Lurianic Kabbalah.

Although it is not the only form of Jewish mysticism, Kabbalah is the name we generally apply to its most well-known variety. It began in twelfth-century Provence, crossed the Pyrenees to Spain, and achieved its most significant literary status with the promulgation of the *Zohar* at the end of the thirteenth century. More than a single doctrine, Kabbalah is better described as a variety of approaches to Judaism, all of them mystical in one way or another and similar enough to be classified under a common title. Of the many schools of kabbalistic thought, the most famous is the one established by Isaac Luria (1534–1572). Luria was born in Jerusalem, the son of an Ashkenazi father and a Sefardi mother. When his father died, Luria's mother moved to Egypt, taking Luria with her. There, Luria grew to maturity, supported by his uncle, a wealthy tax farmer. Gifted with natural intelligence, Luria became a successful businessman in his own right but also distinguished himself as a student of Halakhah. He married his cousin and in 1569 or '70 moved back to Eretz Yisrael, where he studied briefly under a famous kabbalist, Moses Cordovero, and joined a circle of mystics in the mountain town of Safed. Near the end of 1570, Cordovero died and Luria emerged as the ideological leader of the circle. He wrote almost nothing himself; what we know of his ideas comes primarily through the work of his student, Chaim Vital.

For Luria and his circle, Shabbat represented an especially auspicious time to experience a taste of ultimate redemption. Friday night dinner particularly loomed as all-important because of the mystical doctrine that imputed both a masculine and a feminine side to God, which were presumed to join in sacred union on Shabbat (see pp. 18–22). This "divine marriage" was ritualized in a brilliantly conceived ceremony of *Kabbalat Shabbat* (see forthcoming Volume 8, *Shabbat in the Synagogue,* where it will be described in detail), which culminated in a "wedding feast" and featured the usual kind of singing for weddings but, in this case, songs of praise for the two gendered sides of God that joined in holy matrimony every Shabbat eve. The need for "wedding songs" spawned a new spate of *z'mirot,* many of which became standard parts of the growing *z'mirah* canon.

Luria himself wrote *z'mirot,* and the popular *Yom Zeh L'yisra'el* (which we include here) is said to be one of them. In actual fact, however, its composer was Isaac Handali, a relatively unknown poet in fifteenth-century Feodosiya (known also as Kaffa), a Crimean port city on the Caspian Sea, and one of the most ancient towns in the whole of the former Soviet Union.

Yom Zeh L'yisra'el appears in three different versions, one of which has five verses. In all probability, the fifth verse was added later, however, because the song as first published by Moses ben Jacob of Kiev (sixteenth century) has only the first four. But all five became canonical because of the acrostic *y.tz.ch.k.l.ch* formed by the initial y (from *Yom zeh*) of the refrain and the opening letter of each of the five verses. Taken together, the acrostic can be understood as a short form for "YiTZCHaK Luria CHazak" (Isaac Luria: Be Strong), suggesting the authorship of Luria—but mistakenly, as we saw.

As a composition from fifteenth-century Crimea, *Yom Zeh L'yisra'el* precedes Lurianic Kabbalah, and it has none of the mystical allusions found in poems emanating from Luria and his students. Just the opposite, however, is *Y'did Nefesh,* a composition by Elazar ben Moses Azikri (1533–1600). Azikri was a well-known kabbalist who figured marginally in a rampant political dispute of the time. For centuries, rabbinic ordination (*s'mikhah* [pronounced s'-mee-KHAH or, commonly, s'-MEE-khah]) had ceased. Rabbinic authorities were recognized by virtue of their knowledge, but even the great Moses Maimonides did not enjoy official ordination the way Rabbis in the Land of Israel had during the first several centuries of the rabbinic era. Indeed, in his Code of Jewish Law, Maimonides had ruled that ordination would be restored only in the Land of Israel and only at such time as an authoritative court of Jewish law composed of the finest scholars worldwide would be assembled there—clearly a reference to an ultimate situation that could come about only in a messianic age.

Partly in reaction to the Spanish expulsion, Lurianic Kabbalah had always emphasized a doctrine of the messianic end of days. In 1538, a rabbi, still unordained, named Jacob Berab decided to hasten the end of time by instituting ordination, a precondition, as he understood it, of the messiah's arrival. His plans were ultimately thwarted by a rival authority in Egypt, but not before Berab had awarded *s'mikhah* to four rabbis, including Joseph Caro, the author of the *Shulchan Arukh.* In turn, Caro ordained his own student, the grandson of Berab (Jacob Berab II), who ordained seven other men (the last of the ordaining chain), including Azikri.

Azikri would probably have remained a relatively unknown footnote to the entire ordination controversy had it not been for his diary, still extant in Azikri's own handwriting in the library of the Jewish Theological Seminary of America. Its author is revealed as spending much of each day in motionless silence contemplating the name of

God, to achieve what mystics called the state of *d'vekut* (pronounced d'vay-KOOT), literally, "clinging" to God, which meant the soul's temporary separation from the body and its loving embrace of God. Because the aspect of God being embraced was the *Sh'khinah,* the feminine principle of the divine, *d'vekut* has within it a sexual connotation, so that descriptions of *d'vekut,* or meditations designed to achieve it, are often couched in romantic poetry.

Y'did Nefesh, by Azikri, and the third of the *z'mirot* included here, is such a poem. It has four stanzas, the opening letters of which spell out the four-letter name of God. Azikri tells us that he meditated on the acrostic until he saw the four letters rise up off the page and form a single flame of fire before his eyes. The actual text of the poem begins in Azikri's usual handwriting, but shortly after, the script deteriorates and no longer follows the horizontal line with which it began—perhaps evidence that Azikri wrote it down while attaining the trance-like state he sought.

Lurianic Kabbalah, especially as carried by Luria's most prominent disciple, Chaim Vital (1542–1620), who recorded his teacher's practices and ideas, coincided with the invention of printing. As a result, kabbalistic thought traveled quickly throughout the Jewish world in printed volumes that invited easy access by students. Jacob Emden, for instance (1697–1776), applauded singing Shabbat *z'mirot* for its cosmic virtue. "[They are] words about Shabbat drawn from the Bible [*Tanakh*], talmudic laws and stories [*hilkhot v'aggadot hashas*], the *Zohar,* and midrashic literature. People who say them bring down good upon the world. God clings to them, attends to what they say, finds favor with them, and maintains the world that it be not destroyed."

By the eighteenth century, opinions like Emden's had become standard, especially in Chasidic circles, which popularized Lurianic Kabbalah to make it available to more than just the learned mystical adepts. According to his disciples, Rabbi Nachman of Breslov epitomized this Chasidic attitude, "admonishing us carefully over and over again to sing Shabbat *z'mirot.* His fierce anger was quickly evoked by anyone who ought to know better but who nonetheless would not make the effort to sing *z'mirot* on Shabbat and on Saturday night [*Motsa'ei Shabbat*] after Shabbat ended."

Chaim Nachman Bialik (1873–1934) was a poetic genius steeped in Chasidic thought and Jewish folklore from his formative days in Zhitomir, a center of Chasidism. At the same time, he was thoroughly conversant with the more academically formidable rabbinic tradition in general from his early adulthood spent in the yeshivah world of Volozhin in Lithuania, where, as a young man, he had discovered Zionism and the Jewish Enlightenment, a modernist reaction against traditional yeshivah culture. As a man of the common folk, a member of the talmudic elite, and a man of modern culture, he turned to poetry as well.

In 1889, Ahad Ha-am began publishing essays on his idea of Zionism as a means of Jewish national revival that went beyond politics to incorporate the historic cultural genius of the Jewish People, and two years later, captivated by Ahad Ha-am's proposed cultural revolution, Bialik left for Odessa, where a Hebrew renaissance was occurring in a circle of poets and writers, with Ahad Ha-am as its center. Despite temporary moves here and there, Odessa remained Bialik's home until 1921, when

Russian novelist Maxim Gorky convinced the Soviet government to permit several Jewish writers, including Bialik, to leave the country. From 1921 to 1924, Bialik joined an illustrious group of émigrés in Germany, where he became friends with Gershom Scholem (the founder of modern academic study of Jewish mysticism) and S. Y. Agnon (writer extraordinaire and future Nobel Prize winner in literature). By 1924, all three men had settled in Palestine, where Bialik spent his last decade as a writer, poet, lecturer, and translator.

From his Chasidic childhood, Bialik knew firsthand the central role of Shabbat *z'mirot*. He did not consciously write any new ones himself—indeed, he probably saw its musical canon as closed, and in any event, ever since his discovery of Zionism and the Enlightenment, he had slowly abandoned his traditional roots for the kind of secular Jewish nationalism that his cultural hero, Ahad Ha-am, espoused. Still, he remained enchanted with Shabbat memories, which were recorded in his poem *Shabbat Hamalkah*. The poem presupposes knowledge of the quintessential Shabbat song, *Shalom Aleikhem* (see p. 65), on which it is based. In the course of time, *Shabbat Hamalkah* became customary as a Shabbat song in many homes, an extension of the canon of *z'mirot* to reflect the Jewish spirit of modern times. We therefore include *Shabbat Hamalkah* as our fourth and final example of the *z'mirot* sung by the Jewish People to celebrate the joy of Shabbat.

S'udah Sh'lishit

A Rite of Modest Majesty

Michael Chernick

THE ORIGIN OF THE THREE SHABBAT MEALS

S'udah sh'lishit (pronounced s'-oo-DAH sh'-lee-SHEET), the third Shabbat meal, originated in early rabbinic attempts to set Shabbat apart from the other days of the week. From the Mishnah's description of life at the turn of the third century, it appears that in antiquity the average family ate two full meals per day. These meals centered around the consumption of bread. One meal was the equivalent of a breakfast eaten at home prior to work. The second meal was eaten after work, in the evening or at night, and again bread played a central role in the meal. Thus, *s'udah* was, by definition, a meal with bread. This meant the participants preceded the meal with the *Motsi* (Blessing over Bread) and completed it by reciting *Birkat Hamazon* (Grace after Meals).

People did not fast for the rest of the day; instead, they snacked. A "snack" meant any kind of eating in which either bread played no role or, if it did, people ate it hastily on the job without setting a table and sitting down together for a meal. Thus, for example, the Torah granted agricultural workers the right to eat some of the produce they were harvesting while on the job (Deut. 23:26). The produce itself was not bread. The Mishnah (B.M. 7:8) delineates how they could exercise this right. Other workers contracted for a midday food ration with their employers (7:1). This might include bread, but because it was eaten in an informal setting, it did not constitute *s'udah*. This, more or less, provides us with a sense of when and how Jews ate their weekday meals in antiquity.

The picture changes when it comes to Shabbat meals. On Shabbat, three meals were required: one on Shabbat evening, one during Shabbat morning, and the last during Shabbat afternoon. The emphasis on these three meals is clear from several Mishnaic rulings. The first discusses distribution of food to the poor. Whatever the distribution of money and other needs was on weekdays, for Shabbat a poor person received "food for three meals" on Friday. A second ruling considers the case of a householder who suffers a fire on Friday afternoon close to Shabbat or on Shabbat evening itself. An anonymous opinion allows the individual to save "food for three meals" from the blaze for himself and his animals. This opinion diminishes the amount that the householder may save as Shabbat proceeds, but R. Yose allows the rescue of "the food for three meals" anytime on Shabbat. A rule in the Tosefta (end of the fourth century), a compilation similar to the Mishnah, goes a bit further. It allows one who forgot that the bread he or she was baking for Shabbat was still in the oven to remove "three meals' worth" of it even if Shabbat had already begun. The person who did this had to use a tool not usually used for removing bread in order to maintain the sense of the sanctity of Shabbat and its distinction from the weekday.

What emerges is a clear concern that Jews prepare for the observance of Shabbat by organizing a food supply that would provide them with three meals. What is not so clear is why. The simplest answer is that an additional meal distinguishes Shabbat from the weekday in terms of menu. The basis of this distinction, at least according to Maimonides, is the requirement that people enjoy Shabbat in fulfillment of Isaiah's admonition, "If you call the Sabbath 'delight,'…then you can seek the favor of Adonai…." (Isa. 58:13–14; Maimonides, *Mishneh Torah,* "Shabbat Laws," 30:7). Eating better food than usual, more often than one did during the week, made Shabbat a day of greater physical joy. The presence of family, friends, or guests enhanced the meals by providing the kind of special socializing and community atmosphere that food seems to engender. The third Shabbat meal simply became another occasion for family, friends, and guests to gather for what has been called "table fellowship" because Shabbat rest provided more time for this kind of leisure activity.

THE THREE SHABBAT MEALS IN MIDRASHIC SOURCES

In one of our earliest rabbinic midrashic sources we find what we might call a "support midrash" for the three Shabbat meals. There is no known requirement found in the Torah to have three meals on Shabbat. It was just a desire to make the day special and enjoyable that generated the practice. However, the *Mekhilta,* an early rabbinic midrash of Exodus redacted in the late fourth century, sought to root this popular and accepted practice in an ancient event recorded in Exodus 16, the Torah's chapter about the manna. The chapter relates that the manna lasted only a single day during the week. A double portion of it, however, fell on Friday. This portion lasted throughout the entire Shabbat and, unlike the weekday portion, did not become inedible when Friday ended. Regarding this Shabbat portion of manna, Moses told the people: "Eat it *today,* for *today* is Shabbat unto Adonai; *today* you will not find it on the plain" (Exod. 16:25). The *Mekhilta* comments: "R. Zerika said: [From the fact that Moses repeated the word 'today' three times in his instructions about eating the Shabbat manna], we learn the requirement of the three Shabbat meals."

R. Zerika's remark certainly sought to give more obligatory force to the practice of eating three times on Shabbat, but his statement accomplished even more. It brought the rabbinic Jew's imagination back to the Exodus and the travels in the desert, and more specifically back to the manna experience. The Israelites, whose food was manna, were fed directly by God. With their very lives, they had to trust that God would not abandon them. By recalling the manna by using two loaves *(challot)* at each Shabbat meal (as a sign of the double portion Israel received for Shabbat), or by eating three meals on Shabbat, or by refraining from producing nourishment on Shabbat itself, rabbinic Jews expressed their faith that ultimately God alone was their trustworthy source of spiritual nourishment.

Possessing that spiritual nourishment and strength meant that one had a better chance of overcoming challenges and securing physical, not just spiritual, needs for oneself and one's family.

THE THREE SHABBAT MEALS IN JEWISH LORE

The requirement to eat three meals on Shabbat appears to be a specifically rabbinic Jewish institution. We know of no other early Jews—those in the Qumran community, for example—who practiced this observance. Therefore, it is not surprising that rabbinic Jews glorified this practice in aggadic (nonlegal) sources much as they emphasized it in their halakhic (legal) ones.

The major motif that emerges around the theme of the three Shabbat meals is that they provide sufficient merit to escape three calamities: the birth pangs of the messiah, judgment in Gehinnom (purgatory), and the war of Gog and Magog. The first is viewed as a period of internal Jewish spiritual, social, and economic catastrophe. The second refers to the belief that all of us owe some time in purgatory in order to be purified of our earthly sins. The third refers to a world cataclysm that will precede the messianic period.

Each of the three meals, it seems, is a protection against having to endure each of these three horrors. This was, of course, excellent motivation both for those who observed and for those who were lax about the three Shabbat meals. Its major message was that the enjoyment of Shabbat provided one with a taste of the perfection of the world-to-come. Thus, the reward for scrupulous observance of "the enjoyment of Shabbat" *(oneg Shabbat)* would ultimately be the experience of the wonderful perfection that would emerge at the "end of days," without any of the suffering that would precede it.

S'UDAH SH'LISHIT: LAW AND CUSTOM

S'udah sh'lishit presents an interesting case of custom overriding or modifying law. To illustrate this, let us review concisely some of the basic laws governing *s'udah sh'lishit* as outlined by the *Shulchan Arukh* (sixteenth century), considered by many the most authoritative code of Jewish law:

1. The timing of the meal is critical. To understand the issue, one must know that the afternoon prayers *(Minchah)* may be said as early as the sixth and a half hour

of the day (starting from dawn), but any time before the evening service *(Ma'ariv)*. That organization provides two blocks of afternoon time on Shabbat: the first, from the sixth and a half hour to whenever one chooses to say *Minchah;* and the second, from that time (whenever it is) to *Ma'ariv*. Early Ashkenazi practice prescribed eating this meal before either of these blocks, that is, *prior* to the earliest time when Shabbat afternoon prayer is permitted—before the sixth and a half hour of the day (starting from dawn)—and that custom, according to the *Shulchan Arukh*, was observed in France. But it became usual in all other Ashkenazi communities to eat *s'udah sh'lishit after* the earliest starting time for Shabbat afternoon prayers and, eventually, later still—preferably, as close to *Ma'ariv* as possible, but before sunset.

2. *Kiddush* is not required at *s'udah sh'lishit,* but two *challot* should be used at the meal.

3. One must include bread as part of *s'udah sh'lishit;* however, some say that one may use any food made from the five types of grain (which are used in bread making), for example, cake. Yet others say that one can use foods generally eaten with bread for *s'udah sh'lishit,* such as fish or meat, but one may not make *s'udah sh'lishit* only with fruit. There are even those who will allow a *s'udah sh'lishit* using only fruit, but it is best to follow the first opinion.

4. Women are obliged to eat *s'udah sh'lishit.*

What one notices is that the "laws" of *s'udah sh'lishit* are subject to quite a variety of opinions. This is probably due to the codifiers' desire to make sure that, one way or another, *s'udah sh'lishit* would be observed everywhere. For example, if people had eaten heavily earlier on Shabbat, a *s'udah sh'lishit prior* to the six-and-one-half hour mark would become onerous, not enjoyable. So it was rescheduled *after* that time, allowing a larger interval between Shabbat "brunch" and *s'udah sh'lishit,* until, eventually, the custom of eating later pushed *s'udah sh'lishit* as late in the afternoon as possible.

Similarly, with regard to the menu of *s'udah sh'lishit,* the *Shulchan Arukh* dropped its general preference for a single undisputed rule in favor of a variety of rulings. Again, this seems to be a way of facilitating people's observance of this Shabbat meal according to their needs and preferences. A wealthy individual might be able to afford a more elaborate *s'udah sh'lishit,* but those who spent a considerable amount of their earnings to make their Shabbat meals special would find making this third meal difficult. Simpler, less expensive foods would allow a poor individual to fulfill an obligation whose merits brought, as we have seen, considerable protection from evil times.

The one thing that is strikingly missing from the laws of *s'udah sh'lishit* as given in the *Shulchan Arukh* is the sense that it is a communal meal, eaten usually by a group of men outside of the framework of the home. At the outset it was not. Hence, the *Shulchan Arukh* declared women obliged to observe *s'udah sh'lishit* along with the other members of their household. As *s'udah sh'lishit* became more highly ritualized in the early sixteenth century, however, it became more and more a men's event. By the eighteenth century, its observance was a rarity among women. If women ate such a meal at all, it tended to take the form of a snack lacking the same ritual pageantry that men experienced.

S'UDAH SH'LISHIT AS RITE

At one time, there were no set songs or prayers for s'udah sh'lishit. It is clear, however, that the famous sixteenth-century Safed mystic Rabbi Isaac Luria began to create a rite for this Shabbat meal. His introductory poem "The Dwellers in the Palace" (B'nei Heikhala) invites those who seek the accessible mystical attributes of God to join the third Shabbat meal. The poem makes this invitation because this moment of the Sabbath is one in which only God's favor is present. No aspect of God's anger is allowed any influence as Shabbat begins to wane. At that time, God is most approachable and God's presence most felt, while the presence of evil is virtually gone. To this opening poem, later generations added Psalm 23 ("Adonai is my shepherd") and the magnificent hymn Y'did Nefesh ("My Soul's Beloved"), which speaks of the relationship between God and Jewry as the relationship between a beloved and his lover or child. These three elements have become standard liturgical pieces for s'udah sh'lishit, at least as far as the more "chasidically" oriented prayer books are concerned. Like so much of what is true about s'udah sh'lishit, however, what appears in texts is not always what actually happens, so there is a wide divergence of practice regarding the songs and prayers of s'udah sh'lishit. Further, Siddurim with less of a mystical tendency have left out these elements completely.

A CHASIDIC S'UDAH SH'LISHIT

The one community of Jewry where s'udah sh'lishit is scrupulously observed is in Chasidic circles. There, s'udah sh'lishit usually begins after a Shabbat afternoon prayer session that is held somewhat earlier than is the custom among other Jews. This is so because it is meant by Chasidim to be a moment of what I have called "modest majesty," and as such, it takes some time for its pageantry to be played out. It certainly includes two loaves of challah, usually accompanied by fish—herring and gefilte fish tend to be the favorites. Arbes (Yiddish for chickpeas; pronounced AHR-b's) are usually part of the menu, as is beer for the alcoholic element of the meal, though vodka is preferred among Russian Chasidim. These readily available foods point to the relative inexpensiveness and simplicity that considerably reduced the centrality of the purely physical at the meal. The main point of the Chasidic s'udah sh'lishit is its spiritual content.

Even before eating begins, the rebbe, or one of his representatives in a Chasidic community, begins a soulfully sung rendition of the kabbalistic poem "The Dwellers in the Palace," often using a composition by the rebbe or one of his teachers or ancestors. The Chasidim and their leader then sing other quiet *z'mirot* (Shabbat melodies) until a mood is set that opens the way for "saying Torah."

The idea of speaking words of Torah at the table has its roots in the Mishnah—*Pirkei Avot* 3:3—but the Chasidic version of this idea differs considerably from what the Mishnah imagined. Sometimes the "Torah" of the Chasidic *s'udah sh'lishit* takes the form of a story with an important moral. Sometimes it is a spiritualized or mystical reading of the portion of the week. Frequently it takes as its theme the sanctity of Shabbat and how Shabbat points to the redemption of Israel and the days of the messiah. Often, between one part of the rebbe's Torah and another, he or another Chasid begins a soft melody, usually without words (a *niggun*), to enhance the spiritual state of the group and the moment.

The Chasidic *s'udah sh'lishit* is not held privately in every Chasid's home. It is reserved for the Chasidic prayer house (pronounced KLOYZ) or the Chasidic *bet midrash*. Often it continues on beyond the actual end of Shabbat, in order to extend the ecstasy and spiritual "high" that the event engenders. Nevertheless, at some point the rebbe or his representative completes "saying Torah," and the words of Psalm 23 begin. The psalm is sung with deep feeling, trusting that God is the Chasid's shepherd, his source of protection. What more could one ask for than to dwell in God's house all the days of one's life? Once Psalm 23 is complete, the group says Grace after Meals *(Birkat Hamazon)*, recites the weekday evening prayers *(Ma'ariv)*, and returns home for *Havdalah* and the beginning of the workweek strengthened by their rebbe's Torah and their fellow Chasidim's company.

S'UDAH SH'LISHIT IN NON-CHASIDIC CIRCLES

A comparison of *s'udah sh'lishit* in mostly Lithuanian and anti-Chasidic or (at least) non-Chasidic circles differs notably from the Chasidic practice described above. This group, which is very committed to the study of the classical literature of the Jewish people, views the time allotted for *s'udah sh'lishit* as a period for more study. In these circles, there has even developed the attitude that one may fulfill the obligation of *s'udah sh'lishit* by studying and not eating at all. In many communities this has become the norm, and the period between late Shabbat afternoon *t'fillot* and the evening service for the exit of Shabbat is reserved for the *rav* (rabbi)—not the rebbe, with rebbe being the purely Chasidic title for its spiritual leader—to give a lesson (*shi'ur*, pronounced shee-OOR) in Talmud or some other classical Jewish work. In such congregations, an actual *s'udah sh'lishit* may, however, still be held on occasion, especially to celebrate the completion of the study of a tractate of Talmud or order of Mishnah. But in either case (with a meal or without), this form of *s'udah sh'lishit* is obviously more cerebral, touching the intellect more than the heart—a testimony to how varied Jewish practice can be and how many acceptable approaches to Jewish life are possible.

These varied approaches have even engendered a bit of Jewish humor. It is told that a Chasid was once asked why his group needed herring for *s'udah sh'lishit* when the "Litvaks" (Lithuanian Jewish non-Chasidim) spared themselves the expense by fulfilling their obligation through study. He replied, "What would happen if someone asked the *rav* a question that destroyed his lesson's entire thesis? You'd have no *s'udah sh'lishit!* But for us, herring remains herring!"

S'UDAH SH'LISHIT IN LIBERAL CIRCLES

Although mostly a phenomenon among traditional Orthodox and Conservative Jews, *s'udah sh'lishit* has made its way back into Reform and Reconstructionist circles as well. Usually *s'udah sh'lishit* in those communities is part of a *Shabbaton* (a full Shabbat day of study) or *kallot* (study retreats) of various sorts. In those settings, *s'udah sh'lishit* serves a function somewhere between the Chasidic and non-Chasidic event. Usually some food is served, but mostly in the form of a very light snack. There may be a song or two, but the main event tends to be a study session, unless the emphasis of the *Shabbaton* or *kallah* is focused in some other direction—for example, meditation or the arts. These *s'udah sh'lishit* events are often preludes to *Havdalah* and a main evening meal.

Clearly, this reclamation of *s'udah sh'lishit* by liberal Jews is part of an attempt, alongside organized study or spiritual events, to maintain the sense that the entire day is filled with the sanctity and consciousness of Shabbat. *S'udah sh'lishit* helps fill time that might otherwise lose the "feel" of Shabbat. Thus, *s'udah sh'lishit* in liberal contexts has become part of organized Shabbat events, rather than a personal private practice in homes and synagogues. As more people experience *Shabbaton* and *kallah* events, there may be a groundswell that brings *s'udah sh'lishit* back as part of the normative practices of liberal congregations and homes. Synagogue transformation may see a special place for *s'udah sh'lishit* as it tries to change and renew organized Jewish life. Only time will tell whether this historical, beautiful, and varied tradition will become an event marked by all sectors of the Jewish People each Shabbat.

Introduction to the Commentaries

How to Look for Meaning in the Prayers

Lawrence A. Hoffman

THE ART OF JEWISH READING

I remember the day I looked at a manuscript of a prayer book that no one could identify. It had been smuggled out of Russia (then the Soviet Union), and was obviously the liturgy for Rosh Hashanah, but who had written it? And when? It was handwritten, so the style told us much, but in addition, someone had written marginal notes in another handwriting, and yet a third person had written comments to the comments— a third unknown scholar of years gone by whose name we wanted to rescue from oblivion.

Standing before the massive volume, I reflected on the sheer joy of studying a traditional Jewish text. I had seen printed versions before, but never a handwritten one. What a wonderful habit we Jews developed once upon a time: writing a text in the middle of the page and then filling up the margins with commentaries. Every page becomes a cross section of Jewish history. Jewish Bibles come that way; so do the Talmud, the Mishnah, and the Codes. We never read just the text. We always read it through the prism of the way other people have read it.

To be a Jewish reader, then, is to join the ranks of the millions of readers who came before us, leaving their comments in the margins, the way animals leave tracks in the woods. Go deep into the forest, for example, and you will come across deer runs, paths to water sources carved out by hundreds of thousands of deer over time. The deer do not just inhabit the forest; they are part of the forest; they change the forest's contours as they live there, just as the forest changes them by offering shelter, food, and water. There is no virgin forest, really; it is an ecosystem, a balance between the vegetation and the animals who live there.

So, too, there are no virgin texts. They are also ecosystems, sustaining millions of readers over time. When we read our classic texts, we tread the paths of prior readers in search of spiritual nourishment. *My People's Prayer Book* is therefore not just the Siddur text; it is the text as read by prominent readers from among the Jewish People. You are invited to share our path, even to break new ground yourself, passing on to others your own marginal notes, should you wish.

THE LITURGICAL TEXT WE USE

Because home liturgy is not universally available in every prayer book, the Hebrew text of this volume draws on many sources. As with other volumes, we have depended primarily on the Siddur provided by the venerable Phillip Birnbaum. Back in 1949, Birnbaum labored over a Siddur that would contain the traditional liturgy in a modern scientific format. He combined the standard Ashkenazi rite with some modifications that had crept in and become popular in America. More than any other text, it is Birnbaum's that has met the test of time and that best represents the traditional liturgy most North Americans know best.

But his text was supplemented by selections from other prayer books, sometimes because Birnbaum chose to omit a passage that we preferred including or, equally as often, simply because the typesetting of another book seemed clearer and simpler to work with.

In any event, the final text was then translated by Joel M. Hoffman, in consultation with Marc Brettler. This translation strives to reproduce not only the content of the original Hebrew, but also its tone, register, and style, so as to bring to modern readers the same experience (to the greatest extent possible) that the original authors would have conveyed with their words. In terms of content, we assume that, by and large, words have meaning only to the extent that they contribute to sentences and concepts—as, for example, "by and large," which has nothing to do with "by" or "large."

We have tried to reproduce a tone and register similar to the original text: formal, but not archaic; prose or poetry, depending on the Hebrew. Where the Hebrew uses obscure words, we try to do the same, and where it uses common idiom, we try to use equally common idiom. Parallel structure and other similar literary devices found in the Hebrew are replicated as much as possible in this English translation.

We have not doctored the text to make it more palatable to modern consciousness. Blatant sexisms are retained, for instance, wherever we think the author intended them. We depend upon our commentaries to bridge the gap between the translation of the original and our modern sensibilities.

THE COMMENTARIES AND THEIR SOURCES

The heart and soul of *Minhag Ami* is its choice of commentaries that surround the prayer-book text. Translator Joel M. Hoffman explains his choice of words, provides alternatives, and compares his own translation with those of others. Marc Brettler comments particularly on the way the Bible is embedded in the Siddur.

Ellen Frankel ("A Woman's Voice") and Elliot N. Dorff provide theological reflections on what the prayers might mean, should mean, could mean, cannot mean, or have to mean (even if we wish they didn't). Alyssa Gray presents talmudic commentary, and Daniel Landes gives us the Halakhah of prayer, the rules and traditions by which this sacred liturgical drama has traditionally been carried out. Lawrence Kushner and Nehemia Polen supply a kabbalistic commentary, adding wisdom from the world of Chasidic masters, and David Ellenson surveys liberal prayer books of the last two hundred years to see how their writers agonized over attempts to update this book of Jewish books for modern times. My own contribution is, primarily, a summary of what we know about the historical development of the liturgy: when prayers were written and what they meant in the context of their day.

This book is enhanced by help from Tamar Sarah Malino, whose rabbinic dissertation *Shabbat Zemirot and Their Commentaries* (New York: Hebrew Union College, 2001) was consulted and whose compiled version of *Yom Zeh L'yisr'ael* is used here. Joel Hoffman expresses gratitude to Marci Bellows, Jonathan Crane, Ilyse Glickman, Rebecca Gutterman, Jeremy Master, Michael Pincus, Linda Steigman, Benjamin Sternman, Taron Tachman, Scott Weiner, Shoshanah Wolf—members of his class at Hebrew Union College who contributed to the translation of *Y'did Nefesh*.

Most of all, this volume in our series has been enhanced greatly by an introductory essay by Michael Chernick on the custom of adding a "third Shabbat meal" *(s'udah sh'lishit)*. By choosing to include this topic, we made the calculated decision that more than a set of words, liturgy is the acted-out ritual of a community. The *s'udah sh'lishit* has no standardized liturgical text; but as a common ritualized practice of Shabbat, it is a liturgy no less than those occasions that revolve about a stipulated text.

The halakhic commentary deserves its own introduction here, if only because its nature is not easily accessible to most Jewish readers. Halakhah (Jewish law) is essential to Judaism. Frequently misunderstood as mere legalism, it is actually more akin to Jewish poetry, in that it is the height of Jewish writing, the pinnacle of Jewish concern, sheer joy to create or to ponder. It describes, explains, and debates Jewish responsibility, yet is saturated with spiritual importance. Jewish movements can be differentiated by their approach to Halakhah, but Halakhah matters to them all.

The topic of Halakhah is the proper performance of the commandments, said to number 613, and divided into positive and negative ones, numbering 248 and 365, respectively. Strictly speaking, commandments derived directly from Torah *(mid'ora'ita)* are of a higher order than those rooted only in rabbinic ordinance (called *mid'rabbanan*), but all are binding.

The earliest stratum of Halakhah is found primarily in the Mishnah, a code of Jewish practice promulgated about 200 C.E. The Mishnah is the foundation for further rabbinic discussion in the Land of Israel and Babylonia, which culminated in the two Talmuds, one from each center, called the Palestinian Talmud (or the Yerushalmi) and the Babylonian Talmud (or the Babli). Although dates for both are uncertain, the former is customarily dated at about 400 C.E., and the latter between 550 and 650.

With the canonization of the Babli, Jewish law developed largely by means of commentary to the Talmuds and responsa, applications of talmudic and other precedents to actual cases. These are still the norm today, but they were initiated by authorities in Babylonia called Geonim (sing., Gaon) from about 750 to shortly after 1000. By the turn of the millennium, other schools had developed, in North Africa in particular, but also in western Europe. Authorities in these centers are usually called Rishonim ("first" or "early" [ones]) until the sixteenth century, when they become known as Acharonim ("last" or "later" [ones]).

The first law code is geonic (from about 750), but it was the Rishonim who really inaugurated the trend toward codifying, giving us many works, including three major ones that are widely cited here: the *Mishneh Torah,* by Maimonides (Moses ben Maimon, 1135–1204), born in Spain but active most of his life in Egypt; the *Tur,* by Jacob ben Asher (1275–1340), son of another giant, Asher ben Yechiel, who moved to Spain from Germany, allowing Ashkenazi and Sefardi practice to intertwine in his son's magnum opus; and the *Shulchan Arukh,* by Joseph Caro (1488–1575), who is technically the first generation of the Acharonim, but who wrote influential commentaries on both the *Mishneh Torah* and the *Tur* before composing what would become the most widely used legal corpus ever.

Several commentaries here draw centrally on these sources, and not just for halakhic guidance, but for historical information as well. Most of what Jews have written through the ages has been halakhic in nature, so reconstructions of Jewish ritual at any stage of its development and even the theological assumptions that underlay Jewish practice must often be reconstructed from legal sources that purport only to tell us what to do, but end up telling us why as well.

There is no way to convey the richness of even a single one of these works, let alone the legion of other sources in Jewish tradition on which *My People's Prayer Book* draws. Suffice it to say that the commentaries that follow access some sixty or so of the greatest works of our people, from the close of the geonic era (1034) to the present.

The authors of the commentaries represent a similar panoply of contemporary scholars, all students of the prayer-book text and all committed to a life of prayer, but representative of left, right, and center in the Jewish world. They represent all of us, all of *Am Yisrael,* all of those God had in mind when God said to Ezekiel (34:30): "They shall know that I, Adonai their God, am with them, and they, the House of Israel, are My people." Unabashedly scholarly and religious at one and the same time, *Minhag Ami,* "A Way of Prayer for My People," will be deemed a success if it provides the spiritual insight required to fulfill yet another prophecy (Isa. 52:6), that through our prayers

> My people [*ami*] may know my name
> That they may know, therefore, in that day,
> That I, the One who speaks,
> Behold! Here I am.

1 | *Welcoming Shabbat*

A. *HADLAKAT NEROT* ("CANDLE LIGHTING")

[1] Blessed are You, Adonai our God, ruler of the world, who sanctified us with his commandments and commanded us to light a Shabbat candle.

בָּ֫רוּךְ אַתָּה, יְיָ אֱלֹהֵֽינוּ, מֶֽלֶךְ הָעוֹלָם, אֲשֶׁר קִדְּשָֽׁנוּ בְּמִצְוֺתָיו וְצִוָּֽנוּ לְהַדְלִיק נֵר שֶׁל שַׁבָּת.

BRETTLER (BIBLE)

[1] *"Light a Shabbat candle"* The Bible knows of a Tabernacle candelabrum that was replenished with oil twice daily (Exod. 27:20–21), so that it would always remain lit (Exod. 27:20), but lighting Shabbat candles goes unmentioned. Fire, however, is expressly prohibited as Shabbat labor (Exod. 35:3): "You shall kindle no fire throughout your settlements on the Shabbat day."

DORFF (THEOLOGY)

[1] *"Who sanctified…and co-mmanded us"* In the Torah, God does not command Shabbat lights. Noting the same problem with Chanukah lights, the Talmud (Shab. 23a) cites Deuteronomy 17:11, where we are told to obey the authorities of future generations. Deuteronomy 17:11 is one of several passages (see also Deut. 27:11; 30:11–12) from which the Rabbis deduced their right to *(p. 44)*

ELLENSON (MODERN LITURGIES)

[1] *"To light a Shabbat candle"* Although part of the traditional Jewish home ritual for Shabbat, this blessing appears in no Reform prayer books of the nineteenth century, because these books were principally intended for synagogue, not home-based, *(p. 45)*

FRANKEL (A WOMAN'S VOICE)

Hadlakat Nerot ("Candle Lighting") For centuries, Jewish tradition has linked three core *mitzvot* with women's lives: *challah* (separating out a portion of dough as a memorial symbol of Temple sacrifice), *niddah* (observing the laws of "family purity," specifically, conjugal separation during menstruation), and *hadlakat nerot* (lighting candles on the Sabbath and holy days). The initial letters of these three words form the acrostic ChaNaH (Hannah), a biblical figure *(p. 46)*

A. *HADLAKAT NEROT* ("CANDLE LIGHTING")

[1] Blessed are You, Adonai our God, ruler of the world, who sanctified us with his commandments and commanded us to light a Shabbat candle.

GRAY (TALMUD)

[1] *"Commanded us to light a Shabbat candle"* Lighting Shabbat candles is influenced by talmudic law and medieval *minhag* (custom). The Talmud establishes obligatory Shabbat lights (M. Shab. 2:6–7; Shab. 25b), but only for the utilitarian end of providing peace in the home *(sh'lom bayit)* by providing light for a comfortable Shabbat meal (Shab. 23b; 25b; Tosafot to Shab. 25b). Only in the Middle Ages (in Ashkenaz, at least), did Shabbat lights come to be viewed not *(p. 48)*

KUSHNER & POLEN (CHASIDISM)

Hadlakat Nerot ("Candle Lighting") It is difficult to imagine a more primal ritual than the lighting of a candle. The simple mystery of a tiny flame—invisibly joined to a wick, bestowing light and continuously flickering upward—evokes a sense of the numinous in all spiritual traditions. The flame of a candle strikes us at once as a perfect metaphor for a soul (even one that has departed) yearning or, in the case of the Sabbath candles, renewed and reconnected to *(p. 49)*

¹בָּרוּךְ אַתָּה, יְיָ אֱלֹהֵינוּ, מֶלֶךְ הָעוֹלָם, אֲשֶׁר קִדְּשָׁנוּ בְּמִצְוֹתָיו וְצִוָּנוּ לְהַדְלִיק נֵר שֶׁל שַׁבָּת.

LANDES (HALAKHAH)

Hadlakat Nerot ("Candle Lighting") [1] Shabbat arrives automatically with sunset, but, paradoxically, most halakhic authorities believe that our human role in accepting it can "make" it come earlier. In the opinion of many, such "acceptance" occurs through verbal declaration—"I take responsibility for 'the holiness of the Shabbat' [*k'dushat shabbat m'kabel ala'i*]." Some regard mere thought, unarticulated in speech, as enough (*Mishnah B'rurah*, O. Ch, *(p. 49)*

L. HOFFMAN (HISTORY)

¹*"Who has commanded us to light"* Kindling Shabbat lights goes back to rabbinic times. The Mishnah lists it along with two other *mitzvot* for which women are obliged on pain of dying in childbirth should they fail in their responsibilities. This emphatic demand may have been motivated by the fact that kindling Shabbat lights was a point of controversy between Pharisees (the group whom the Rabbis saw as their immediate predecessors) and Sadducees (their rival party). At issue was the interpretation of Exodus 35:3, "You shall kindle no fire throughout your settlements on the Sabbath day." The Pharisees held that *(p. 53)*

J. HOFFMAN (TRANSLATION)

¹*"Blessed"* Ideally pronounced "bless-ED." The word *barukh* in Hebrew is the passive form of a verb that never appears in the active voice, making it difficult to translate. We discuss this issue more fully in Volume 1, *The Sh'ma and Its Blessings.*

¹*"Light"* Others, "kindle," but "kindle" seems too rare an English word for the common Hebrew word.

¹*"Candle"* The singular here is surprising; most translations emend "candle" to "[the] candles," in the form of "…the Shabbat candles." But the Hebrew is clearly singular, and does not contain the definite article "the." Also, the Hebrew word *ner,* while currently denoting a candle, predates *(p. 55)*

DORFF (THEOLOGY)

link novel practices with Torah, even if the Torah never actually mentions them. They thus maintain that Chanukah lights—and, by extension, Shabbat lights also—go back to an implicit commandment in Torah. (Sifre Numbers 134; Sifre Deuteronomy 154; B.B. 59a–59b; cf. Elliot N. Dorff and Arthur Rosett, *A Living Tree: The Roots and Growth of Jewish Law* [Albany: SUNY Press, 1988], pp. 187–198, 213–223.)

Shabbat lights have theological consequences. The sun sets every Friday evening, whether or not we light candles. A commandment to light them, however, implies that God alone cannot bring Shabbat. But neither can we. Saying the same blessing any other night, for instance, is useless. Apparently, to make Shabbat happen, we need God, and God needs us. God arranges a sunset every Friday, which we recognize with Shabbat lights, making Shabbat a cooperative effort between Jews and God.

Similarly, for life in general, Judaism holds that we may not do whatever we wish; we share this world with God. But God chose not to run the world alone either; instead, God seeks human help. When we say that God "hallows us" through commandments, we mean that we become holy by serving divine ends. That is why the Talmud (Shab. 119b) rules that saying *Kiddush* on Friday night makes us "God's partner in creation." This divine-human partnership is at the heart of our relationship with God.

[1] *"To light"* Several simple rules govern the timing for lighting candles:

1. Lighting should be close to sunset so as to demonstrate the purpose of honoring Shabbat. When the day is exactly twelve hours long (the equinox), with sunset at 6:00 P.M., the earliest one may light candles is 4:45 P.M. (*Shulchan Arukh,* O. Ch. 263:4). At that time, 1¼ hours (6:00 − 4:45 = 1¼ hours) is 10.4% (= 0.104) of the day (1.25/12). So for other times in the year, multiply the number of daylight hours by 0.104, and you will have the amount of time before sunset at which you may light candles at the earliest. For example: if some Friday during the winter, the sun rises at 7:15 A.M. and sets at 4:05 P.M., there would be 4 hours (= 240 minutes) and 45 minutes of daylight in the morning (240 + 45 = 285 minutes); and 4 hours and 5 minutes in the afternoon (240 + 5 = 245 minutes), for a total of 530 minutes of daylight. Multiply 530 by 0.104, and you find that 55.12 minutes before sunset, or approximately 3:10 P.M., is the earliest time for lighting.

   During the summer this presents a problem for families with children whose bedtime is early. When children are old enough to understand something about Shabbat, families frequently sing Shabbat songs at an early dinner, but wait to light the candles and say *Kiddush* until the proper time.

2. Candles must be lit no later than eighteen minutes before sunset, lest a mistaken calculation cause an inadvertent violation of the prohibition against igniting a Shabbat fire.

3. Candles must burn until nightfall so that their connection to Shabbat is evident (*Shulchan Arukh,* O. Ch. 263:9). That is why Shabbat candles are thicker than Chanukah candles, which (except for Shabbat) are lit after dark and need not last as long.

Shortly before lighting candles, some families have each family member put money in a box for *tzedakah* (charity). As we conclude our week of earning money for ourselves, we give some charity—typically to the synagogue, Israel, or the poor—conscious of the fact that everything ultimately belongs to God (Deut. 10:14; Ps. 24:1).

[1] *"A Shabbat candle"* As night falls, taking with it daytime light and warmth, human beings have always created their own light and heat through fires and now through electricity. Shabbat candles also provide light, but they are not intended to serve purely pragmatic ends. (The Rabbis actually forbade reading by Shabbat lights, lest we be tempted to add oil to lengthen or enhance their brightness and thereby violate the ban against creating Shabbat fire [M. Shab. 1:3; Shab. 12a–13a, 149a; Maimonides, "Laws of the Sabbath" 5:14; *Shulchan Arukh,* O. Ch. 275:1–4]). They mark Shabbat as a day that connects us with God and with each other.

Symbolically speaking, Jewish tradition likens light both to Torah (Prov. 6:23; Ket. 111b) and to our *n'shamah,* our "human life-breath" (Prov. 20:27). Lighting candles reaffirms our commitment to Torah precisely as we begin to inhale the special renewal that is the Shabbat.

Our current blessing speaks of "lighting a Shabbat candle [singular]," but the Rabbis (*Shulchan Arukh,* O. Ch. 263:1) set a minimum of two to indicate that we intend to fulfill both Decalogue versions of the commandment: "to remember the Sabbath day" (Exod. 20:8) and to "observe" it (Deut. 5:12). But more than two candles are permissible (Moses Isserles, *Shulchan Arukh,* O. Ch. 263:1), so some people light extra candles for each family member and, possibly, an additional candle for the six million who perished in the Holocaust.

———◆———

ELLENSON (MODERN LITURGIES)

use. The original edition of the *Union Prayer Book* (*UPB*) from 1895 is no exception. Most Reform Jews of that era would have welcomed Shabbat in their homes according to the traditions that were commonplace in Europe and would have expected no liberal prayer book to help them do so.

By 1921, however, the balance between synagogue and home liturgy was shifting in favor of the synagogue, where a late Friday night service was becoming the norm, so much that rabbis wanted to begin it in the same way that Shabbat was begun at home: with the lighting of candles. So the *UPB* of that year introduced the Friday night synagogue service with the instructions, "The ceremony of ushering in the Sabbath is begun by the kindling of the lights."

Nevertheless, in 1921, the blessing over those candles was not yet present. Only in the 1940 edition did the blessing make its way into the *UPB.* Today, the blessing over the Sabbath candles is found in all non-Orthodox prayer books, sometimes intended for the synagogue service, but sometimes meant also as a guide for home celebration.

It was in the 1940s, too, that Abraham Binder, music director of Stephen Wise Free Synagogue and prominent composer of Jewish music, took the traditional musical mode (or *nusach*) for *Kabbalat Shabbat* (the service inaugurating Shabbat) and shaped it into the melody for candle lighting that has since become universal in Reform circles.

By then the custom of inaugurating the Friday evening service with the lighting of Shabbat candles was almost universally observed, as it still is today, in Reform temples. The result of this growing emphasis on synagogue ritual meant that the *Kiddush* as well as the candles were placed in the Reform prayer book. The synagogue began taking the place of the home.

In an attempt to restore Shabbat to Reform Jewish homes, the *Gates* series of Reform prayer books (beginning in 1975 with *Gates of Prayer*) initiated a separate home prayer book called *Gates of the House* (1977)—revised as *On the Doorposts of Your House* (1994). Since then, candle lighting has remained a central synagogue ritual, but it has largely returned to Reform home ritual as well.

[1] *"Who...commanded us"* In her *Book of Blessings*, Marcia Falk takes issue with the very concept of divine commandment, central though it may be to classical rabbinic Judaism and the liturgy that the Rabbis devised. As a feminist, she believes that saying God "commanded" reinforces the very "hierarchical structure of power and authority in the world" that Falk thinks feminists should oppose. So here, as in all her blessings, Falk shifts the emphasis from God to the "the human community" and the place of the self within it. Believing that the metaphors of "heart" *(lev)* and "spirit" *(nefesh)* best capture these notions of "community" and "self," she employs "these words"—heart and spirit—as the "central images" in all her blessings. Therefore, her blessing for the lighting of Shabbat candles reads, "May our hearts be lifted, our spirits refreshed, as we light the Sabbath candles."

———◆———

FRANKEL (A WOMAN'S VOICE)

who became a favorite character in Jewish women's devotional prayers. Significantly, two of these three *mitzvot* are associated with the observance of Shabbat. Even more significantly, all three are positive time-bound commandments, despite the fact that rabbinic law holds women exempt from them because (it is usually explained) they might interfere with the special demands that are placed on them by children and domestic duties. But lighting candles requires almost split-second timing; striking the match a minute too late would violate the sanctity of the holy day.

Why are these three *mitzvot* assigned specifically to women? Why is it their duty to welcome the Sabbath back into the family home and to welcome their husbands back into their beds? Why are they designated sentries of these particular sacred borders?

The Rabbis of antiquity understood that women were attuned to different rhythms than men. In the traditional home, women have been responsible for managing the elaborate cycles of observance: Sabbath and festival meals prepared and served, children scrubbed and dressed, relatives and guests accommodated, the elderly and unfortunate taken into account. And through the laws of family purity *(tohorat hamishpachah)*, they also managed the cycles of fertility and birth. Without them, the Jewish family would quite literally fall apart. (Of course, in modern times, the changed and changing rhythms of women's lives have challenged many of these rabbinic assumptions.)

Understanding the tremendous responsibility inherent in these three "women's *mitzvot*," Jewish women have for centuries focused much liturgical creativity on them. The first *t'khinah* literature (pronounced t'KHEE-nah, known also in the plural as *t'khin's,* pronounced t-khee-n's), Yiddish devotional prayers written by European Jewish women beginning in the seventeenth century, contains many prayers meant to be recited before performing these three activities. Here is an excerpt from a *t'khinah* to be recited before lighting candles, composed in the late eighteenth century by Shifra bat Yosef of Brody. Note the wealth of kabbalistic allusions as well as the independent spirit of its author:

> The *mitzvah* of Sabbath candles was given to the women of the holy people that they might kindle lights. The sages have said that because Eve extinguished the light of the world and made the cosmos dark by her sin, [women] must kindle lights for the Sabbath. But this is the [real] reason for it. Because the Tabernacle of Peace [the *Sh'khinah*] rests on us during the Sabbath, on the [Sabbath-]souls, it is therefore proper for us to do below [on earth], in this form, as it is done above [within the Godhead], to kindle the lights. Therefore, because the two souls shine on the Sabbath, they [women] must light two candles. (From Chava Weissler, *Voices of the Matriarchs,* [Boston: Beacon Press, 1998], p. 62)

The brief moment of silence traditionally observed at *licht bentschen* (pronounced LIKHT behn-ch'n), when a Jewish woman—eyes closed, hands circling the flames, suspended momentarily between the whirlwind preparations for the Sabbath and the relentless demands of serving the meal—prepares to recite the blessing over the candles, has often been a rare island of calm in an otherwise stressful life. It is at this time that many women feel closest to God and to their families. That may be why they have prayed most intensely at this moment for divine protection, the probable origin of the circling hands and compassion for their loved ones. Here is an excerpt from another *t'khinah* to be recited before lighting the candles, this one written about a century ago in the United States as new pressures began to encroach upon Jewish life:

> The persecutions we have endured in other lands have driven us here to America, a refuge for the persecuted and suffering. Making a living here is very hard and [because of our many sins] Jewish children have no choice but to desecrate the *Shabbos* and *yom tov.* I accuse no one, heaven forbid, of doing this simply to anger You, to blaspheme your holy name. But time and circumstances have brought this about.

> I beg of You, God of Abraham, Isaac and Jacob, guard and protect me, my husband, and children from *chillul* ["desecration of"] *Shabbos* and *yom tov.* Permit us to gain our *parnoso* ["livelihood"] easily and without sorrow, without transgression, so that

because of the need for a livelihood we shall not be compelled to profane the *Shabbos* or *yom tov* and be able to rest on the holy days and serve You wholeheartedly. (From Norman Tarnor, *The Book of Jewish Women's Prayers* [Northvale, N.J.: Jason Aronson, 1995], pp. 46–47)

Hadlakat nerot—a deceptively simple act: lighting two candles and chanting a line of Hebrew. But in reality this ritual carries great spiritual significance, marking a pivotal moment in the life of the Jewish family and the divine-human connection.

———◆———

GRAY (TALMUD)

just as utilitarian, but also as marking the special sanctity of Shabbat.

Seeing Shabbat lights as merely utilitarian, the Talmud mandates no blessing *(b'rakhah)* over them. The *b'rakhah* is medieval (or perhaps geonic), and it is problematic, for how can God be said to have commanded this utilitarian act that is not mentioned in the Torah? One answer is that Deuteronomy 17:11 commands us to heed the words of the sages of each generation. Thus, although God did not expressly command Shabbat lights, God did command adherence to rabbinic judgment in every era, even the one in which such lights became known as a commandment (Maimonides [1135–1204], "Blessings" 11:3).

But still, the blessing occasioned controversy. Meshullam of Melun (outside Paris, twelfth century) argued against it altogether, a position that aroused the ire of the great Rabbenu Tam (Jacob Tam, twelfth century), who insisted on the *b'rakhah* (*Sefer Hayashar*, Responsa 48; *Tur*, O. Ch. 263); his view was ultimately codified by Joseph Caro (1488–1575; *Shulchan Arukh*, O. Ch. 263:5) and became our practice.

Question arose also as to whether the *b'rakhah* should be recited before or after the actual lighting. Generally, talmudic law mandates blessings before performing the act over which they are said (Pes. 7b). But the talmudic law could be problematic in the case of Shabbat lights. It is arguable that the recitation of the blessing is a personal acceptance of Shabbat. Once Shabbat is personally accepted, no light can be kindled (Exod. 35:3). Some medieval scholars noted that women (who typically lit the candles) had the custom of first lighting them, then waving their hands over them and/or hiding their faces, and then reciting the blessing. The rationale behind this solution was explained by R. Joseph b. R. Moshe (a student of the great R. Israel Isserlein, 1390–1460, Germany). The talmudic rationale for the *mitzvah*, he knew, was *sh'lom bayit*, "peace in the home" (Shab. 25b). Because candles can bring neither peace nor joy if they are not seen, it followed that the candles were "technically" alight with *shalom* and *oneg* ("peace and joy") only after the blessing was said and the eyes uncovered. The women themselves had thus invented a way to fulfill the Talmud's requirement (Pes. 7b) to recite blessings prior to the performance of *mitzvot*, without, however, letting the light itself count until afterward. Moses Isserles (R'ma, 1530–1575, *Darkhei Moshe* to the

Tur, O. Ch. 263) quoted a similar understanding in the name of Jacob Weil (Germany, d. before 1456).

Eliezer b. Joel Halevi (Ravya, twelfth–thirteenth centuries) is the first to record the practice of lighting two candles, which, he says, corresponds to the two biblical commands to "remember" *(zakhor)* the Sabbath day and to "guard" *(shamor)* it.

———◆———

KUSHNER & POLEN (CHASIDISM)

its source on high. On the Sabbath each Jew, it is said, receives a *n'shamah y'teirah,* an extra soul. And any Jew who has ever watched the Sabbath lights reflected in his or her mother's eyes knows this must be true.

Rabbi Levi Yitzhak of Berditchev, in his *K'dushat Levi (Hanukah,* second entry), reminds us that Shabbat candles are indeed the first *mitzvah* of Shabbat—even before the *Kiddush* (or sanctification itself)—because, once lit, the Sabbath has begun. And to light them, effectively, brings light down from above.

And, according to some, that light even obliterates the darkness of night: Rabbi Sh'lomo Lieb of Lentchna once told his friend Rabbi Yitzhak of Vorki, after sharing a Sabbath meal, that the reason we do not customarily say "Good evening" on Shabbos (Yiddish for Shabbat, pronounced SHAH-b's), is that on Shabbos there is simply no darkness. And therefore, because there is neither night nor evening, it's all light.

———◆———

LANDES (HALAKHAH)

261:21, Israel Meir Hakohen Kagan, 1838–1933, Radom, Poland). Others require a specific ritual act: reciting the Friday night *Amidah* or *Kiddush,* for instance, both of which evoke *k'dushat hayom* (pronounced k'-doo-SHAT hah-YOHM), "the holiness of the [Shabbat] day" (RYTbA, Yom Tov Asevilli, 1250–1330, Spain, *novellae,* Shab. 35a; Taan. 12a; Eruv. 40a); or lighting Shabbat candles, unless accompanied with a specific intention not to make Shabbat until later (O. Ch. 263:10). Still others add increasingly earlier sections of the evening liturgy, such as *Bar'khu* (the communal call to prayer, pronounced bah-r'-KHOO), Psalm 92 ("A psalm...for the Sabbath day"), or, especially, the last paragraph of *L'khah Dodi* (pronounced l'-KHAH doh-DEE), "Come O bride, come O bride" *(Bo'i khallah, Bo'i khallah,* pronounced *boh-EE khah-LAH boh-EE khah-LAH)*—the line in the Friday night synagogue prayer that invites Shabbat to commence.

The personal acceptance of Shabbat entails Shabbat's actual presence with all its prohibitions. If, however, the community has not similarly accepted Shabbat early, rabbinically forbidden work for the purpose of a *mitzvah* may still be done. (On

Shabbat prohibitions, see the classic "handbook," Y'hoshua Y. Neuwirth [Jerusalem, contemporary], *Sh'mirat Shabbat K'hilchatah*).

But why begin Shabbat early, particularly on famously "short Fridays" in winter, when it is a struggle just to make Shabbat on time?

The desire derives from the rabbinic understanding of Leviticus 23:32, "You shall practice self-denial on the ninth of the month." But Yom Kippur, the fast day referred to, falls on the tenth day of Tishrei, not the ninth. So the Talmud (R.H. 9a) concludes that the commandment to fast begins earlier than sunset. The Rishonim (early authorities) generalize this lesson of *tosefet k'dushah* ("adding holiness," pronounced toh-SHE-feht k'-doo-SHAH) to Shabbat, so that Shabbat arrives earlier and ends later than the bare twenty-four hours of the seventh day. Maimonides (1135–1204, Egypt) evidently disagrees, omitting this practice from his code (Vidal of Tolosa, fourteenth-century Spain, *Maggid Mishneh*, "Laws of Rest on the Tenth," 1:6); the vast majority of Rishonim, however, affirm it as a *mitzvah* with Torah status.

Although Shabbat is a "positive commandment dependent on time" (*mitzvat aseh shehaz'man g'ramah*, pronounced meets-VAHT ah-SAY sheh-hah-z'-MAHN g'rah-MAH), it is equally incumbent upon men and women (*P'ri M'gadim*, commentary on *Piskei HaRosh* [Asher ben Yechiel], by Yom Tov Lipmann Heller, early to mid-seventeenth century, Bavaria, Poland, 608:1). It is better seen theologically as a *mitzvah l'ma'alah min haz'man* (pronounced meets-VAH l'-MAH-ah-lah meen hah-z'-MAHN), "a commandment that transcends time" (R. Yechiel Yaakov Weinberg, 1885–1966, Germany and Switzerland, *S'ridei Esh*, 2:20). The concept of *tosefet k'dushah* combines objective reality and personal subjective meaning to demonstrate the human partnership with the divine in the creation of holiness. In moving up the time for Shabbat candles and *Kiddush* and in moving back the time for *Havdalah*, the God-intoxicated individual, family, and community can enlarge Shabbat beyond twenty-four hours.

Halakhically, this is a positive *mitzvah*; theologically, it is transcendence; philosophically, it is a miracle; experientially, it is heroic!

Hadlakat Nerot ("Candle Lighting") *[2] Hadlakat nerot* (pronounced hahd-lah-KAHT nay-ROHT; Shabbat candle lighting: in Yiddish, *licht bentschen*, pronounced LIKHT BEHN-sh'n) is the last act of Shabbat work (*m'lakhah*, pronounced m'-lah-KHAH) performed in the house as Shabbat commences. Kindling fire thereafter is directly forbidden in the Torah (Exod. 35:3).

Although a simple act, *hadlakat nerot* is profoundly moving. Its power is purely exoteric; there is no mystical "hidden" meaning. It epitomizes three halakhic values: *kavod Shabbat, oneg Shabbat,* and *sh'lom bayit.*

Kavod Shabbat (pronounced ka-VOHD shah-BAHT) and *oneg Shabbat* (pronounced OH-nehg shah-BAHT), respectively, "honor" and "joy" of Shabbat, the two primary rabbinic commandments of the day, parallel the Torah commandments of *shamor* (pronounced shah-MOHR, "keep [Shabbat]") and *zakhor* (pronounced zah-KHOR, "remember [Shabbat]"), both from Isaiah 58:13, "Call Shabbat 'joy'; [call]

Adonai's holy day 'honored.'" *Kavod* ("honor") refers to matters that honor Shabbat but are prepared prior to it; *oneg* ("joy") denotes matters that partake of the day itself (Gra, Elijah of Vilna, 1720–1797, O. Ch. 52a, regarding Maimonides' "Laws of Shabbat" 30).

Kavod Shabbat ("honor of Shabbat"), therefore, includes dressing in clean and distinctive Shabbat attire; allowing time to prepare oneself properly for Shabbat, and not eating so close to Shabbat that when it arrives, you are not hungry enough to enjoy the food.

Whether hungry or not, one sets a proper table within a cleaned and ordered house and lights candles prior to Shabbat to create a proper Shabbat mood (Maimonides, "Shabbat" 30:5). This last *mitzvah* is best done personally, especially if one normally assigns such ordinary household work to others. "The *mitzvah* devolves upon [the householder] more than any agent" (Kid. 41a).

Hadlakat nerot is true "honor of Shabbat, for there can be no important meal without light" (Rashi to Shab. 25b). It is an instance of *kavod Shabbat,* but it leads also to *sh'lom bayit* (pronounced sh'-LOHM BAH-yit, "peace of the home"). The Talmud (Shab. 25b) cites Lamentations 3:17, "My life was bereft of peace [*shalom*]," as referring to the neglect of "kindling Shabbat light." As Rashi explains: "Where there are no candles, there is no peace, for people stumble as they walk in darkness." *Sh'lom bayit* connotes an atmosphere of warmth, light, trust, and concern among all household members. Although important all week, it is especially crucial on Shabbat. *Shomer Shabbat* (pronounced shoh-MAYR shah-BAHT, but commonly SHOH-mayr SHAH-b's), "the keeper of Shabbat," implies an ethic that is patent in the exhortation: "Everyone should be very careful to be at peace with one's spouse, for this is the essence of preparing for Shabbat, and one who does not do so destroys one's house, blemishes the soul and causes only evil to oneself" (*Sefer Shomer Shabbat,* quoted by the Menachem Tziyon, Rabbi Menachem B. Sacks, 1893–1987, Jerusalem, Chicago).

Kavod Shabbat and *sh'lom bayit* are incumbent on everyone, but given the classic role of the woman as the "essence of the home" (*akeret habayit,* pronounced ah-KEH-reht hah-BAH-yeet), the honor of this commandment is given particularly to her (though if there is no "woman of the house," it is done by a man). In recent times, the late Rebbe of Lubavitch urged all women in the house, including children, to light Shabbat candles, but the prevailing custom has been for married women—or the "homemaker" (*baleh busteh,* pronounced bah-l'-BUS-tah [where the "u" in BUS rhymes with the "ou" of "could"]) even if not married—to light them. Men should help prepare the candleholder (in traditional Ashkenazi homes known as the *lichter,* pronounced LICH-t'r) and candles. Some men light the candles for an instant and blow them out, in order to create carbon wicks that flame up easily when the woman lights them.

As a practical consequence, electric lights should be left on wherever people may be during Shabbat (e.g., in a bedroom closet). Shabbat candles should be on or near the Shabbat table (O. Ch. 263; See *Mishnah B'rurah* 2 and 45).

The general halakhic principle is that a blessing over an act precedes the act itself (*over la'asiyatan,* pronounced oh-VEHR lah-ah-see-yah-TAHN). Maimonides ("Shabbat" 5) and possibly the *Shulchan Arukh* (O. Ch. 263:10), therefore, rule that the blessing "to light a Shabbat candle" should precede the actual act of lighting. Ovadia Yosef (contemporary authority in Israel, *Yabe'a Omer* 216, 6:48; *Y'chaveh Daat* 2:33) and his student Tzion Biaroh (*Sha'arei Tzion* 1:9) call this normative "for Sefardim and all who live in Israel."

Alternatively, candles should be lit before the blessing is recited, a reversal of normal procedure, based on the reasoning that saying a blessing with the words "to light a Shabbat candle" itself implies accepting Shabbat, so that Shabbat commences with the blessing, after which no light may be kindled (*Tur,* R. Moses Isserles, 1530–1572, Cracow, O. Ch. 263; and R'ma, ad loc.).

The second opinion is the general *minhag.* After lighting candles, one places a hand before the eyes, blocking them from view, so as to avoid enjoying them until after the blessing is made. Only after making the blessing are hands lowered to admit the light to consciousness. Some women pause then to pray personally for household members and for *sh'lom bayit* in general.

An implication of this custom of blocking the candles from view after lighting them is that the lit candles are part of *oneg Shabbat.* We saw earlier that *oneg* is the actualization of Shabbat itself (in contrast to *kavod,* which refers to preparing for it). Maimonides regarded candle lighting as part of *kavod Shabbat,* because it proceeds Shabbat's arrival. But he also explicitly states ("Shabbat" 5:1) that it is a fulfillment of *oneg Shabbat* ("even if a person has nothing to eat, he should beg door to door to buy oil for [Shabbat] light, because this is within the category of *oneg Shabbat*"). Maimonides, evidently, has it both ways: *hadlakat nerot* is both *kavod* and *oneg!*

To understand this, consider further *oneg Shabbat.* It includes the consumption of fine foods and drink for all Shabbat meals and a distress-free attitude during the day. The height of *oneg Shabbat* is marital intimacy (Ket. 62b), because Shabbat eve is "a night of pleasure, rest, and bodily enjoyment" (Rashi, Solomon ben Isaac, 1040–1105, France). But in the final halakhic analysis, sex, and even eating, are discretionary acts—one need not eat if suffering from indigestion, for instance. Candle lighting, however, is not only a *mitzvah* but a *chovah* (pronounced choh-VAH), an absolute obligation: it is always obligatory, even when, as on Yom Kippur, sensual gratifications such as sexual relations and eating are forbidden ("Resting on the Tenth Day of Tishrei," chap. 3).

So the actual lighting of candles—which establishes, in advance, a Shabbat mood conducive to *sh'lom bayit*—fulfills the obligation of *kavod* ("honoring") Shabbat. In a sense, only the person lighting candles directly fulfills the *mitzvah* of *kavod.* But just enjoying the light accomplishes *oneg* ("joy of") Shabbat, and "both men and women are thus obligated to have lights burning in their home on Shabbat" ("Shabbat" 5:1), no matter who does the actual lighting. The sensual and spiritual dimensions of *oneg Shabbat* thus merge together.

In summary, once the candles are lit, it is customary for the one lighting to have accepted Shabbat and meritorious if the entire household does also (R'ma 263:10;

Mishneh B'rurah 42–44). Candles are lit during twilight *(bein hash'mashot)* in accord with the principle of *tosefet* ("adding on to") Shabbat. Lighting them fulfills the *mitzvah* of honoring Shabbat; enjoying their light accomplishes Shabbat "joy."

———◆———

L. HOFFMAN (HISTORY)

even though no *new* light could be kindled, lights already begun could be allowed to burn down. The Sadducees believed that even fires already lit were prohibited and had to be doused before Shabbat set in. Kindling light in one's home, where it would be clearly visible from the street, would have demonstrated allegiance to the Pharisees rather than the Sadducees.

The custom was, therefore, politically motivated, but not yet considered a *mitzvah,* a "commandment," for which a blessing was required. Women simply lit candles before sundown, and when their husbands came home from the synagogue services Friday evenings, they found them burning.

An actual blessing over Shabbat lights is not attested to until relatively late, after the period of codification of the Talmud (traditionally dated mid-sixth century). What makes the new blessing striking is that rabbinic tradition had by then prohibited the creation of any blessings not found in the Talmud. Post-talmudic Jewish authorities in Babylonia from, roughly, 750 to 1034 (the Geonim) had, therefore, to justify their invention of a blessing for Shabbat candles by giving it, somehow, a talmudic mandate.

With no firm halakhic precedent to draw on, the Geonim reverted to homiletical explanations drawn from Talmud. Primarily (Shab. 25b), there is Samuel's declaration of Shabbat lights as an obligation *(chovah)*—though not necessarily a *mitzvah* (the two are not the same). Elsewhere (Shab. 34b), Job 5:24 ("You shall know that your tent is in peace") is said to imply light in one's home.

In the end, however, we still find ourselves asking how we know it is a commandment (a *mitzvah*). Our first known prayer book, *Seder Rav Amram* (ninth century), replies:

> Rav Avya said [from Deut. 17:8, 11], "If a case is too baffling for you to decide…you shall promptly repair to the place that Adonai your God will have chosen…[and] act in accordance with the instructions given you." Rav Nachman bar Isaac said [from Deut. 32:7], "Remember the days of old, consider the years of ages past; ask your father, he will inform you, your elders, they will tell you."

These are hardly convincing. If we rely on the first verse, we must assume that the question of lighting candles is "a case that is too baffling," demanding the opinion of later authorities, which is to say, the author of the responsum who says we should do it. This is clearly circular reasoning. It amounts to further instruction, not demonstration. If we use the second verse, it is because we assume that candle lighting is quite ancient, so that even though no scriptural warrant is available, it is still a valid "commandment" carried by oral, if not written, law. That too is highly dubious.

The real reason Amram chooses these verses is that the Talmud cites them to justify Chanukah lights, over which a blessing is said even though they too are not biblically mandated. What goes for Chanukah, Amram seems to believe, must go for Shabbat.

Later, Hai Gaon (999–1034) repeats Amram's logic and adds the Mishnah that compels women to light candles on Shabbat, which, of course, is where we began. The issue still remains: granted, women have been lighting candles for centuries as an obligation; still, how do we know that the practice is a "commandment" demanding a blessing that says God "has commanded us" to light them?

Put otherwise, we might ask: why did the Geonim invent the blessing and then go to such lengths to justify it, especially because people had been lighting candles for centuries without one?

Their decision was a response to their own ideological conflict. In the eighth century, someone named Anan ben David challenged the authority of rabbinic interpretation, arguing that Jews should look directly in the Bible to ascertain what God wanted. Anan argued that the ancient Sadducees, not the Pharisees from whom rabbinic Judaism claimed to be descended, had understood the biblical injunction correctly. His followers, known as Karaites (from the Hebrew k'ra, meaning "scripture"—they were scriptural literalists), thus rejected the obligation to light Shabbat candles in their homes.

The Geonim responded by instituting a blessing over these lights, affirming not only that candle lighting was more than an ancient obligation, but also that it was a genuine mitzvah ("commandment") that now had its own blessing.

The blessing did not catch on universally all at once. Saadiah Gaon, who authored our second known prayer book (about 930), says, "On Friday before sunset, it is necessary to kindle Shabbat light, over which most of us say, '…to kindle Shabbat light.'" Clearly the blessing was still not universal, but only a custom for "most of us." A century later, Jews in Provencal were still not saying it, and the famous Rabbenu Tam (Jacob ben Meir, 1100–1171) actually cites an argument against it.

Even where it did catch on, however, it is not altogether clear that the candles over which the blessing was said were the ones that women were already lighting at home. Amram says only (section 2:1), "We enter the synagogue [!].… The person who lights Shabbat candles must say the blessing, 'Blessed…who has commanded us to kindle Shabbat light [ner shel shabbat].'" Saadiah also means a light kindled in the synagogue, because immediately after mandating this blessing, he tells people to "say" the Shabbat evening (Ma'ariv) service. His verb "to say" is in the masculine plural, because he has in mind men who attend synagogue, not women waiting at home.

Women probably still lit candles at home, as they had since the second century, but without a blessing. At the same time, it was becoming customary for men to light candles as well—but in the synagogue and with a blessing.

Only in the eleventh century do we find a responsum, by the same Hai Gaon mentioned above, describing a "householder" who lights candles (Sha'arei T'shuvah,

Leiter, 91). These must be home lights, although it still seems to be men, not women, who said the blessing. We hear also now of more than one light being kindled (cf. *T'shuvot Hageonim,* Musafiya, 82). But the current idea that the two lights represent the two *mitzvot* surrounding Shabbat ("keep" and "remember") seems still to be unknown. Alyssa Gray (see Gray, "Commanded us to light a Shabbat candle") dates that custom to Eliezer b. Joel Halevi (Ravya, 1140–1225)

As we see, women have been lighting candles from the beginning. The Talmud explains their assignment in two ways. On the positive side, God is said to have told women, "I created you with a soul called 'Light.' Therefore you have the duty of kindling Shabbat light." But the Talmud also says Eve extinguished Adam's light, bringing death to the world, so women must kindle a new light weekly. (See traditionalist-feminist reaction to this and other negative claims in Frankel, *Hadlakat Nerot* ["Candle lighting"]). The *Zohar* believes women light candles to guarantee that they have children who grow up to be great lights of Torah.

———◆———

J. HOFFMAN (TRANSLATION)

the invention of wax candles. When the prayer was written, a *ner* was an oil lamp. Nonetheless, because *ner* was such a familiar concept for the original authors of the prayer, we use a familiar concept in translating it.

———————◆ ◆ ◆———————

B. *Birkat Banim* ("Blessing of Children")

[For sons, say]:

¹ May God make you like Ephraim and Manasseh.

[For daughters, say]:

² May God make you like Sarah, Rebekah, Rachel, and Leah.

[For both sons and daughters, continue]:

³ May Adonai bless you and keep you.

⁴ May Adonai shine his face toward you and treat you graciously.

⁵ May Adonai lift his face toward you and grant you peace.

[For sons, say]:

יְשִׂמְךָ אֱלֹהִים כְּאֶפְרַיִם וְכִמְנַשֶּׁה.¹

[For daughters, say]:

יְשִׂמֵךְ אֱלֹהִים כְּשָׂרָה רִבְקָה רָחֵל וְלֵאָה.²

[For both sons and daughters, continue]:

יְבָרֶכְךָ יְיָ וְיִשְׁמְרֶךָ.³

יָאֵר יְיָ פָּנָיו אֵלֶיךָ וִיחֻנֶּךָּ.⁴

יִשָּׂא יְיָ פָּנָיו אֵלֶיךָ, וְיָשֵׂם לְךָ שָׁלוֹם.⁵

BRETTLER (BIBLE)

[1] *"Ephraim and Manasseh"* From Genesis 48:20, where Jacob blesses Joseph's two sons. The patriarchs—or at least Judah, or Reuben, Jacob's first-born—might seem more likely sources of blessing for us. We get Ephraim and Manasseh instead, because the Bible introduces their blessing with the promise, *"By you* shall Israel invoke blessings...."

[2] *"Sarah, Rebekah, Rachel, and Leah"* Unlike the three patriarchs, the four matriarchs are never mentioned together in the Bible. *Imahot* (matriarchs) as a category is post-biblical. This blessing is otherwise odd as well, in that at least two of the four (p. 60)

DORFF (THEOLOGY)

[1–2] *"May God make you like..."* Together or separately, parents put their hands on each child's head, and then recite the appropriate line for sons or daughters followed by the Priestly Blessing (see Volume 2, *The Amidah*, pp. 176–183). Some families bless children immediately (p. 60)

ELLENSON (MODERN LITURGIES)

Birkat Banim ("Blessing of Children") In keeping with the often heralded "return to tradition" that marks so much of contemporary liberal Judaism worldwide, the Priestly Blessing applied to children at home has begun to reappear in present-day (p. 61)

FRANKEL (A WOMAN'S VOICE)

Birkat Banim ("Blessing of Children") The sources of these three blessings—Jacob's blessing over his grandsons, Ephraim and Manasseh; an invocation of the matriarchs, Sarah, Rebekah, Rachel, and Leah; and *Birkat Kohanim,* the magical Priestly Blessing—are among the oldest words in our liturgy. Even today, when recited by parents, these words take on fresh currency and power.

For some families, however, these blessings evoke pain: the physical (p. 63)

B. BIRKAT BANIM ("BLESSING OF CHILDREN")

[For sons, say]:

[1] May God make you like Ephraim and Manasseh.

[For daughters, say]:

[2] May God make you like Sarah, Rebekah, Rachel, and Leah.

[For both sons and daughters, continue]:

[3] May Adonai bless you and keep you.

GRAY (TALMUD)

Birkat Banim ("Blessing of Children") Blessing children arose naturally as a sign of *sh'lom bayit* ("peace in the home"), the hallmark of Shabbat. The citation of Ephraim and Manasseh, Joseph's two sons, is particularly poignant. Sold by his brothers into slavery, Joseph had not seen his father for years. Genesis ends with them finally being reunited and Jacob joyfully blessing not only Joseph, but Joseph's children as well, the grandchildren whom he never expected to meet. (p. 63)

KUSHNER & POLEN (CHASIDISM)

Birkat Banim ("Blessing of Children")
Professor Isadore Twersky of Harvard
University, the Talner rebbe of Boston,
once cited Maimonides' son, Avraham
Maimuni, saying that when Isaac
blesses Jacob (Gen. 27:28): "*And* may
God give you of dew of heaven, of fat of
earth…" the word "And" implies that
something has already been spoken
before the recorded words of the
blessing. The actual words of blessing,
he concludes, therefore are always
preceded by something ineffable. *(p. 63)*

[For sons, say]:

יְשִׂמְךָ אֱלֹהִים כְּאֶפְרַיִם וְכִמְנַשֶּׁה.¹

[For daughters, say]:

יְשִׂמֵךְ אֱלֹהִים כְּשָׂרָה רִבְקָה רָחֵל וְלֵאָה.²

[For both sons and daughters, continue]:

יְבָרֶכְךָ יְיָ וְיִשְׁמְרֶךָ.³

LANDES (HALAKHAH)

Birkat Banim ("Blessing of Children")
To show complete devotion, parents are
to put both hands on their children,
just as the *kohanim* ("priests") do when
they bless the people (*Birkat Kohanim*,
the "Priestly Blessing" in the *Amidah*;
see Volume 2, *The Amidah*, pp. 176–
183). Parents say the blessing as a
continuation of the patriarchal blessing
in Genesis 48:20, for, as *kohanim*, they
too transmit blessings from God. In
some communities, children kiss their
parents' hands upon the   *(p. 64)*

J. HOFFMAN (TRANSLATION)

Birkat Banim ("Blessing of Children")
The Hebrew word *banim* means
"children." Because it also means
"sons," some people add *banot*
("daughters") here, making this the
"blessing of sons and daughters." We
prefer to group them together in
English as we do in Hebrew, referring
collectively to the "blessing of
children."

Other examples where *banim*
clearly means "children" and not "sons"
include the *Avot* (Volume 2, *The
Amidah*, pp. 60–61), where we translate
"*banim* of their *banim*" as
"descendants" and certainly
not "male descendants."

¹⁻² *"Make"* Literally,
"put."

³ *"May Adonai bless you
and keep you"* See Volume 5,
*Birkhot Hashachar: Morning
Blessings*, pp. 122–123,
where we discuss the poetic
impact of the original
Hebrew.

◆◆◆

4 May Adonai shine his face toward you and treat you graciously.

5 May Adonai lift his face toward you and grant you peace.

⁴יָאֵר יְיָ פָּנָיו אֵלֶיךָ וִיחֻנֶּךָּ.

⁵יִשָּׂא יְיָ פָּנָיו אֵלֶיךָ, וְיָשֵׂם לְךָ שָׁלוֹם.

BRETTLER (BIBLE)

matriarchs (Sarah and Rachel) did not enjoy particularly good fortune. The blessing is, therefore, late in origin and modeled after the corresponding male biblical version ("May God make you like Ephraim and Manasseh").

³ *"May Adonai bless you"* According to the Torah, this blessing (from Num. 6:24–26) was to be recited by "Aaron and his sons" (Num. 6:23)—that is, by priests—though when and where are not specified. It is here democratized to a familial, non-priestly setting. The paraphrase of this blessing in Psalm 67:2, "May God be gracious to us and bless us; may He shine his face at us," as well as elsewhere (e.g., Pss. 4; 6; 119:130–135; Mal. 1:6–2:9), suggests that it was widely known in the biblical period. It is compactly structured, with each verse longer than the one before it, as if to suggest the growing outpouring of divine blessings. We know of several Mesopotamian parallels, and a slightly shorter version, written on silver (probably an amulet) in the seventh or sixth century B.C.E., was found in a burial trove in Jerusalem.

⁴ *"May Adonai shine his face"* These verses are strikingly anthropomorphic: Adonai shines his face on and lifts it toward the blessing's recipient. Biblical texts are comfortable with anthropomorphisms, and even rabbinic culture, which is often thought to reject them, frequently views God in human form.

⁵ *"May Adonai...grant you peace"* Shalom, usually translated as "peace," is better understood—both in its original context, and (especially) in its familial setting here—in the sense of "(personal) well-being."

DORFF (THEOLOGY)

after candle lighting; others do it when they return home from synagogue but before sitting down for dinner; yet others do it after reciting *Eshet Chayil* ("A Worthy Woman"—see p. 74). Sometimes the mother blesses the children immediately after lighting candles, and the father does so after reciting *Eshet Chayil.* When children marry, it is permissible, even desirable, for parents to bless their children-in-law too.

^{1–2}*"Ephraim and Manasseh…Sarah, Rebekah, Rachel, and Leah"* The formula for sons follows Jacob's blessing of his grandsons, Ephraim and Manasseh, said here to fulfill the promise of Genesis 48:20: "So shall Israel be blessed." The intent was clearly to provide models for children to emulate. For daughters, the model is the matriarchs. Some object that praying for our children to be like ancient worthies pressures them unduly to strive to be better than they are. But the formula asks nothing from the children alone; rather, God is to make them as worthy as our ancestors. Also, they need not be perfect, like God, but only as meritorious as our ancestors, who, though estimable, were hardly faultless. Most importantly, providing a model toward which to aspire may become a self-fulfilling prophecy. Telling children, for example, "You are the kind of person who cares for others" (when that is not obviously true) helps them see themselves differently; liking what they see, they may strive to become what they have been told they already are.

^{3–5}*"May Adonai…"* Because we are commanded to emulate God, our understanding of what God is being asked to do here has consequences for human behavior. (For a fuller discussion, see my commentary in Volume 5, *Birkhot Hashachar* [*Morning Blessings*], pp. 122, 129–130.)

1. [In general,] may Adonai give you all life's good and keep you from the bad. (Consequence: we should strive to bring people blessing, not trouble.)
2. [When your relationship with God is good,] may Adonai smile on you and give you more than you deserve. (Consequence: we should treat others graciously even beyond what they deserve.)
3. [When your relationship with God is bad,] may God face you [rather than turn his back on you] and make peace with you. (Consequence: when we quarrel with others, we should look them in the face and make peace.)

On ordinary weekday nights, dinner may be so rushed that families do not even eat together; but with everyone at home together, Shabbat, as it were, stops the world. So while blessing our children is always in order, it is especially apt on Friday evening. Pausing to put our lives in perspective, we better appreciate the blessing of children, whom we bless in return.

———◆———

ELLENSON (MODERN LITURGIES)

Reform liturgy. We find it first in American Reform's *Gates of the House* (1977) and British Reform's *Forms of Prayer for Jewish Worship* (1977); then, some time later, in *On the Doorposts of Your House* (1994), the American Reform Movement's revision of *Gates of the House;* and in the British Liberal *Lev Chadash* (1995). In all these publications, parents are invited to bless their children at the Shabbat table.

As we see here, the normal introductory formula asks that sons be blessed in the name of Ephraim and Manasseh, and girls in the name of Sarah, Rebekah, Rachel, and Leah. There seems to have been some hesitation to imagine our own children blessed exactly like the biblical worthies, however, since *Lev Chadash* omits this introductory formulae altogether, jumping directly to the blessing ("May God bless you….") and mentioning neither matriarchs nor patriarchs. Similarly, American Reform volumes, which include the preamble, alter the English to ask only that "God inspire you to live in the tradition [!] of [the matriarchs and patriarchs]." The notion of "tradition" plays a role in other books too, as in *Lev Chadash,* which urges, "A noble heritage has been entrusted to us; let us guard it well."

Marcia Falk *(The Book of Blessings)* expressly objects to the "specificity" of a formula that seems "restrictive rather than expansive." Preferring that parents wish only that their own child become "her or his best self," she recasts the blessing "to provide affirmation for the child and to foster awareness in the giver of the blessing." In place of the standard blessing, she proposes, "Be who you are—and may you be blessed in all that you are."

The American Conservative Movement *(Siddur Sim Shalom,* 1998) adds further specificity, but gendered differently for boys and for girls:

> May you be blessed by God as were Ephraim and Menasheh,
> who understood that wherever they lived
> their Jewishness was the essence of their lives,
> who loved and honored their elders and teachers,
> and who cherished one another
> without pettiness or envy,
> accepting in humility the blessings that were theirs.

> May God bless you
> with the strength and vision of Sarah,
> with the wisdom and foresight of Rebecca,
> with the courage and compassion of Rachel
> with the gentleness and graciousness of Leah,
> and their faith in the promise of our people's heritage.

For its public synagogue ritual, this Conservative Movement liturgy provides no transliteration, because the editors assume competence in Hebrew. But virtually all of the home service for Shabbat eve, including such staples as the blessing for candle lighting and *Shalom Aleikhem,* comes with transliteration. The blessing of children is an exception. There, parents are expected to know by heart or to be able to read in Hebrew the Priestly Blessing.

———◆———

FRANKEL (A WOMAN'S VOICE)

or emotional loss of children, the sting of barrenness, the lack or loss of a partner. In some families, children are not blessed but tolerated or abused. In others, parents are not permitted to bless but are blamed or rebuffed. Despite the risks of having children, the tradition teaches us that the blessings beckon more urgently than the risks. And so we bless our children with the words of our ancient forebears, who knew plenty of heartache from their own offspring.

◆

GRAY (TALMUD)

A suggestion of such a blessing may be seen in the Talmud (Shab. 23b), where Rav Huna says, "Anyone who customarily kindles Shabbat light will have children who are Torah scholars." Medieval authorities expressly connect Shabbat light to the blessing of children. Abraham b. Azriel of Bohemia (*Sefer Arugat Habosem,* twelfth century), for instance, thought the two Shabbat candles symbolize husband and wife, who hope to merit giving birth to a son and daughter. This same link was elaborated nearly half a century later in the commentary to the Torah portion *Yitro,* by Bachya ben Asher (thirteenth century, Spain). When a woman lights Shabbat candles, Bachya says, she should pray for children enlightened in Torah. Such a prayer is particularly efficacious then, because God hears prayer more readily when it is offered in the context of performing another *mitzvah* (in this case, candle lighting). Jonah Gerondi too (*Epistle Concerning Repentance,* "Day 7": thirteenth century, Spain) directed women to pray for children who are successful in Torah as they kindle Shabbat lights.

3–5 "May Adonai…grant you peace" This threefold Priestly Blessing with which God commanded Aaron and his sons to bless the Israelites (Num. 6:22–27) constitutes God's own example of an efficacious blessing, so it is particularly apt for Shabbat, when God too observed the primal day of rest (Gen. 2:2–3). In particular, the Priestly Blessing closes with the prayer that God's face be lifted and provide peace, an allusion to *sh'lom bayit* (Shab. 23b).

◆

KUSHNER & POLEN (CHASIDISM)

Each blessing begins with something inchoate that can only be inferred or intuited because it is so subtle and sublime. Isaac says earlier in the Genesis story (27:4), "…that *my soul* may bless you…." This reminds us that the main idea of blessing must come from the soul. As Twersky said, the blessings from parent to child are simply too delicate for words.

Johannes Pedersen, in his monumental, four-volume work, *Israel: Its Life and Culture* (Oxford University Press, Branner Ogkorat, Copenhagen, 1926, vols. I–II, 198–200), offers a similar and extraordinary insight into the nature of blessing: "The act of blessing another," he says, "means to communicate to [someone] strength of soul, but one can communicate to [another] only of the strength one has in oneself. [One] who blesses another gives [that person] something of his [or her] own soul…. The strength of the word of blessing depends upon the power that the word possesses to hold the real contents of a soul. By means of the word something is laid into the soul of the other…."

Thus, in the case of parents blessing children at the Sabbath table, the core of every blessing is the soul-pride, the sweetness, the *naches* (pronounced NAH-kh's) the parent has received from his or her child over the past week. And, in addition to the formulaic "…like Ephraim and Manasseh" etc., parents effectively return the *naches* in words of blessing. The litmus test of the blessing is that it should make the child smile.

Several commentators have attempted to explain why, of all the possible ego models, Ephraim and Manasseh are mentioned by name in the blessing of children. Rabbi Yehuda Aryeh Lieb of Ger (d. 1905), author of *S'fat Emet* (I, p. 282; 5661), suggests that the reason is that these two sons of Joseph were effectively moved up one generation and treated as children. And this, in turn, reminds us of the direct relationship grandchildren enjoy with their grandparents. Through this grandchild-grandparent bond, we (all) possess an unmediated relationship with our ancestors. Thus, the blessing evokes a direct line to all previous generations. Others have noted that Ephraim and Manasseh, as the first ones born in exile, are symbols of Jewish survival in alien lands. And still others have suggested that Ephraim and Manasseh are mentioned by name because they are the very first set of brothers in the Hebrew Bible who get along with one another.

LANDES (HALAKHAH)

conclusion of the blessings, imbued with the idea of *k'vod av v'em,* "honor due to father and mother," and love for the spirit of God that has hovered on their parents' fingers.

At the time of blessing, parents should consider the fact that during the week it is natural to become upset with children's misbehavior. This blessing should awaken parental commitment to avoid any further "curse" to their children from this point onward.

C. *SHALOM ALEIKHEM* ("PEACE TO YOU")

[1] Peace to you, angels of service, angels on high, from the king over the kings of kings, the Holy One blessed be He.

[2] Come in peace, angels of peace, angels on high, from the king over the kings of kings, the Holy One blessed be He.

[3] Bless me with peace, angels of peace, angels on high, from the king over the kings of kings, the Holy One blessed be He.

[4] Go in peace, angels of peace, angels on high, from the king over the kings of kings, the Holy One blessed be He.

[1] שָׁלוֹם עֲלֵיכֶם, מַלְאֲכֵי הַשָּׁרֵת, מַלְאֲכֵי עֶלְיוֹן, מִמֶּלֶךְ מַלְכֵי הַמְּלָכִים הַקָּדוֹשׁ בָּרוּךְ הוּא.

[2] בּוֹאֲכֶם לְשָׁלוֹם, מַלְאֲכֵי הַשָּׁלוֹם, מַלְאֲכֵי עֶלְיוֹן, מִמֶּלֶךְ מַלְכֵי הַמְּלָכִים, הַקָּדוֹשׁ בָּרוּךְ הוּא.

[3] בָּרְכוּנִי לְשָׁלוֹם, מַלְאֲכֵי הַשָּׁלוֹם, מַלְאֲכֵי עֶלְיוֹן, מִמֶּלֶךְ מַלְכֵי הַמְּלָכִים הַקָּדוֹשׁ בָּרוּךְ הוּא.

[4] צֵאתְכֶם לְשָׁלוֹם, מַלְאֲכֵי הַשָּׁלוֹם, מַלְאֲכֵי עֶלְיוֹן, מִמֶּלֶךְ מַלְכֵי הַמְּלָכִים הַקָּדוֹשׁ בָּרוּךְ הוּא.

BRETTLER (BIBLE)

Shalom Aleikhem ("Peace to You") *Aleikhem* is more literally translated as "upon you."(It uses the preposition *al*, meaning "upon.") *Shalom aleikhem*, then, is built on a paradigmatic biblical wish, *shalom al yisra'el* ("Peace be upon Israel"), found in Psalms (125:5; 128:6) and also on a sixth-century C.E. synagogue mosaic at Jericho. The song assumes a highly developed angelology, not attested to in the Bible, but found in early post-biblical works, including some Dead Sea Scrolls. It is thus not surprising that the terms "angels of service" and "angels on high" are lacking in the Bible. The *malakhei hasharet*, ("angels of service"), however, are prefigured in Psalms *(p. 68)*

DORFF (THEOLOGY)

[1] *"Peace to you, angels of service"* An allusion to the Talmud's statement that two ministering angels, one good and one evil, accompany worshipers home from Friday night services. If the home is prepared for Shabbat—candles lit, the table set, and the beds freshly made—the good angel says, "May it be so for another Shabbat," and the bad angel is forced to say, "Amen; so may it be." If the home is not prepared for Shabbat, the bad angel says, "May it be so for another Shabbat," and the good angel must say, "Amen; so may it be" (Shab. 119b).

[1] *"Angels"* Many Jews find talk of angels strange. They already have trouble conceptualizing "God- *(p. 69)*

FRANKEL (A WOMAN'S VOICE)

Shalom Aleikhem ("Peace to You") For adults, especially those who love ceremony, song, and schmoozing (pronounced SHMOO-zing, a Yiddish term for "chatting"), Friday night dinner is a joy and a delight. The pre-meal rituals whet the appetite and feed the soul. But for children, especially those who cannot sit still and who are tired and hungry, the long wait before the first mouthful of *challah* is excruciating. Perhaps that is why the Rabbis offered the following *(p. 70)*

C. SHALOM ALEIKHEM ("PEACE TO YOU")

[1] Peace to you, angels of service, angels on high, from the king over the kings of kings, the Holy One blessed be He.

[2] Come in peace, angels of peace, angels on high, from the king over the kings of kings, the Holy One blessed be He.

GRAY (TALMUD)

[1] *"Angels of service"* According to the Talmud (Shab. 119b), two angels of service, one good and one bad, accompany a person home from synagogue every Friday night. If lights are kindled and the table set, the good angel proclaims, "May it be God's will that it be this way next Shabbat," while the bad angel grudgingly responds, "Amen." If lights are not kindled and the table not set, the bad angel says, "May it be God's will that it be this way next Shabbat," while the good angel is forced to respond, "Amen." *(p. 71)*

KUSHNER & POLEN (CHASIDISM)

Shalom Aleikhem ("Peace to You") *Shalom Aleikhem* first appeared in *Tikkunei Shabbat* (Prague, 1641). Although it has been adopted with great enthusiasm by Jewish communities throughout the world, it remains the subject of continued controversy and even opposition.

The story of *Shalom Aleikhem* begins with the well-known passage in the Talmud, Shabbat 119b:

> Two ministering angels accompany a person on his or her way home *(p. 71)*

שָׁלוֹם עֲלֵיכֶם, מַלְאֲכֵי הַשָּׁרֵת, מַלְאֲכֵי עֶלְיוֹן, מִמֶּלֶךְ¹
מַלְכֵי הַמְּלָכִים הַקָּדוֹשׁ בָּרוּךְ הוּא.

בּוֹאֲכֶם לְשָׁלוֹם, מַלְאֲכֵי הַשָּׁלוֹם, מַלְאֲכֵי עֶלְיוֹן, מִמֶּלֶךְ²
מַלְכֵי הַמְּלָכִים, הַקָּדוֹשׁ בָּרוּךְ הוּא.

LANDES (HALAKHAH)

Shalom Aleikhem ("Peace To You") A major introductory theme of the Shabbat meal is "blessing." We are not to dawdle but, instead, to rush home from synagogue in order to "overhear" the angels blessing us with the hope that next week, too, we will merit a beautiful Shabbat table, lights, and rest (Shab. 114b). As we enter our home, the custom is to call out loudly and joyously, *Shabbat shalom um'vorach* (pronounced shah-BAHT shah-LOHM oo-m'-voh-RAKH), "A Sabbath of peace and blessing [to *(p. 72)*

L. HOFFMAN (HISTORY)

Shalom Aleikhem ("Peace to You") As we have it, this song is very recent, dating only from the beginning of the eighteenth century (*Otsar Hat'fillot,* p. 615), but almost universally said to be related to the older talmudic legend (Shab. 119b) to the effect that a good and bad angel visit our Shabbat table to make sure we have made adequate preparations. But why would we welcome the bad angel, not just the good one?

Jacob Lauterbach (scholar, professor at Hebrew Union College, 1873– *(p. 72)*

J. HOFFMAN (TRANSLATION)

¹*"Peace to you"* Although this literal translation cries out for a more idiomatic rendition, such as, perhaps, "We welcome you," we feel we must use the word "peace," because the stylistic point of the poem is that each of its four stanzas contains the key conceptual word *shalom,* "peace." "Peace! Angels of service" is barely intelligible, and so we resort to the awkward "Peace to you… ."

¹*"Of service"* Hebrew, *sharet,* from the root *sh.r.t,* "to serve." More idiomatic might be "ministering angels," as in Birnbaum, but parallel structure can be retained if we use "angels of service," a direct *(p. 73)*

³ Bless me with peace, angels of peace, angels on high, from the king over the kings of kings, the Holy One blessed be He.

⁴ Go in peace, angels of peace, angels on high, from the king over the kings of kings, the Holy One blessed be He.

³בָּרְכוּנִי לְשָׁלוֹם, מַלְאֲכֵי הַשָּׁלוֹם, מַלְאֲכֵי עֶלְיוֹן, מִמֶּלֶךְ מַלְכֵי הַמְּלָכִים הַקָּדוֹשׁ בָּרוּךְ הוּא.

⁴צֵאתְכֶם לְשָׁלוֹם, מַלְאֲכֵי הַשָּׁלוֹם, מַלְאֲכֵי עֶלְיוֹן, מִמֶּלֶךְ מַלְכֵי הַמְּלָכִים הַקָּדוֹשׁ בָּרוּךְ הוּא.

BRETTLER (BIBLE)

103:21 ("Bless Adonai, all his hosts, his servants [*m'shar'tav*] who do his will") and 104:4 ("He makes the winds his messengers" [*malakhav*—"his angels"], fiery flames his servants [*m'shar'tav*]").

The Bible never calls God "king over the kings of kings," though this ancient title was used of Mesopotamian kings and in two biblical Aramaic texts (Dan. 2:37; Ezra 7:12) to refer to powerful non-Israelite monarchs. Similarly, although the Bible frequently attributes holiness to God (e.g., Ps. 22:4), it never refers to God as "the Holy One" *(hakadosh)*. The names of God increased significantly in the post-biblical period, when reluctance to use the tetragrammaton (YHVH) prompted the invention of surrogates. This reluctance had already begun in late biblical days and is especially obvious in the Dead Sea Scrolls, where biblical texts are paraphrased to avoid citing the tetragrammaton.

² *"Come in peace"* The three words "come," "bless," and "go" belong together semantically, as in Deuteronomy 28:6, "Blessed *(barukh)* shall you be in your comings *(b'vo'ekha)* and blessed *(barukh)* shall you be in your goings *(b'tsetekha)*."

---

talk" as referring to a deity whom we neither see nor hear; adding angels makes Jewish theology even less believable. Worse, talk of angels probably sounds "Christian"—Catholics, in particular, speak of angels and depict them prominently in their iconography.

Actually, the existence of angels is a Jewish notion; Christians got it from us. The Hebrew Bible itself knows of a "messenger [or angel] of God" *(malakh adonai),* who speaks to Abraham (Gen. 16:7–11; 22:11, 15), Hagar (Gen. 21:17), Jacob (Gen. 28:12; 31:11; 32:11), Moses (Exod. 3:2), and others, including even Balaam (Num. 22:31–35) and his donkey (Num. 22:23, 25, 27). But God uses angels as more than a messenger service: an angel leads Israel from Egypt to the Land of Israel (Exod. 14:19; 23:20, 23; 33:2; Num. 20:16) and defeats the Assyrians (2 Kings 19:35; Isa. 37:36; 2 Chron. 32:21). Isaiah (chap. 6) and Ezekiel (chap. 1 and 3:12–13) describe some angels as winged creatures holding up God's throne. Job's piety is tested by a particular angel named Satan (chaps. 1 and 2), and the Rabbis thereafter (e.g., B.B. 16a; San. 89b) identify Satan (or Sama'el) as the angel who leads people astray. The last book of the Hebrew Bible to be written, Daniel (8:16; 9:21), features an angel named Gabriel, who appears 31 times in the Babylonian Talmud and 186 times in midrashic literature. The "three men" who announce Isaac's eventual birth (Gen. 18:2) are transformed by the Rabbis into three angels (Yoma 37a): "…Michael was in the middle, Gabriel on the right, and Refael on the left." They have distinct tasks described by their names: Michael ("Who is like God") announces that Sarah will give birth; Refael ("God heals") heals Abraham after his circumcision; and Gabriel ("God is my strength") destroys Sodom (B.M. 86b). Neither Michael nor Refael appears in the Bible, but Michael is mentioned 238 times and Refael 35 times in midrashic literature. Another popular angel, rabbinically, was Uriel ("God is my light"), who is associated with the light of Torah (Num. Rab. 2:10; Midrash T'hillim 17:3; 68:10).

What, then, shall we make of angels? Rabbinic tradition holds that they are subservient to God and can do nothing on their own. Still, medieval Jews (who estimated just part of the angelic population as ranging from a few hundred thousand to 496,000 myriads) actively invoked angelic help or sought to deceive Satan. Although technically an idolatrous "Amorite custom" forbidden in Leviticus 18:3, invoking angels was nevertheless permitted (*Sefer Hasidim,* thirteenth century) and became popular enough that rabbis were sometimes forced to accept such practices as amulets. But they labeled belief in such semi-divine powers as *emunah t'feilah,* "false belief" that undermines faith in God's direct role in our lives. By contrast, standard Catholic belief to this day posits angels and human saints actively interceding with God on behalf of those who pray to them to do so.

Jewish philosophy has interpreted angels in many ways. Philo of Alexandria (first century) saw them as incorporeal and immortal souls, "never craving things of the earth"; bodiless, they hover in the air and ascend to heaven, where they serve as instruments of divine providence when God does not want to act directly. They are also avenues toward knowledge about God, whom we cannot know directly, but whose characteristics become evident by knowing what God does through angels. Maimonides understood angels as personifications of God's powers and attributes, paralleling Aristotle's "separate intelligences" through which God governs the universe. Kabbalists saw angels as emanations of the divine light, inferior to human beings because they lack free will, but still ethereal powers that do God's work in the world.

I understand angels as personifications of life's experiences, so I do not worry about justifying their existence as real beings. At the same time, I am appreciative of the sheer poetry of angel-talk. As embodied creatures, we understand concrete things more than abstractions. Given Jewish belief in an unembodied God beyond all representation, angel-talk provides a graphic and emotionally potent way to conceptualize God at work in the world. None of this suggests that, because healing comes from Refael, for example, we should relinquish our own responsibility to heal through research and medical care. But if we do not make the angels idols, or pray to them as if they can replace God, then talk of angels is a helpful personification of the workings of God in our lives.

———◆———

FRANKEL (A WOMAN'S VOICE)

talmudic story, which my husband and I would tell our own children each Shabbat when they were young, before singing *Shalom Aleikhem,* a song about angels visiting Jewish homes on this night:

> Two angels accompany a person home from synagogue on Friday night, a good angel and an evil angel. If the person comes home to find the candles lit and the table set and the house in order, the good angel declares: "May the coming Shabbat be just like this one." And the evil angel has no choice but to respond, "Amen." But if he does not find the candles lit and the table set and the house in order, the evil angel declares, "May it be like this next Shabbat." And the good angel has no choice but to respond, "Amen" (Shab. 119b).

Whether out of pride or dread, our children were always glad that our Sabbath table looked so festive and the food smelled so appetizing, even if the delay challenged their patience to wait for the *Motsi* (pronounced MOH-tzee, the blessing over bread that begins meals). For them, the angels featured in *Shalom Aleikhem* were harbingers of redemption in a very tangible way.

———◆———

GRAY (TALMUD)

[3] *"Bless me with peace"* Notwithstanding the precedent of a talmudic legend (see prior comment, "Angels of service"), asking angels to "bless us" poses a theological problem. How can we ask angels for a blessing when we should pray to God alone? We are, presumably, not actually praying to the angels. Rather, just as guests wish their hosts well after enjoying their hospitality, so, by saying "Bless me with peace," we invite our angelic guests to do the same for us.

[4] *"Go in peace"* Two commentaries to the *Shulchan Arukh* (O. Ch. 262), *Machatzit Hashekel* (Samuel Halevi Kolin, 1770–1806) and *Sha'arei T'shuvah* (Chaim Mordecai Margaliot, eighteenth–nineteenth centuries), note rabbinic opposition to this stanza. Is it appropriate to ask angels to leave? *Sha'arei T'shuvah* recalls a certain rabbi being so disturbed by the idea that he refused to recite it. So both commentators reinterpret the stanza to mean only that whenever the angels choose to leave, their departure should take place in peace. Alternatively, like the earlier line, *bo'akhem l'shalom* ("Come in peace"), we are simply addressing the angels in a spirit consistent with Deuteronomy 28:6: "Blessed are you in your coming in and blessed are you in your going out."

◆

KUSHNER & POLEN (CHASIDISM)

> from the synagogue on *Erev Shabbat*. One angel is good and one evil. When the person arrives home and finds the Sabbath lamp lit, the table set, and the bed covered with a spread, the good angel exclaims, "So may it be for another Shabbos too," and the evil angel has no choice but to answer, "Amen." But, if the house has not been prepared for Shabbat, then the evil angel exclaims, "So may it be for another Shabbat as well," and the good angel is forced to respond, "Amen."

Several commentators raise questions, however, about the accuracy of the legend. Rabbi Yehuda Aryeh Leib of Ger (d. 1905), author of *S'fat Emet,* points out that there simply are no *bad* ministering angels. Rabbi Jacob Emden (1697–1776) was similarly uncomfortable with any requests made of angels. Puzzled by the last stanza—"*Tseitkhem l'shalom* (Go in peace...)"—he asks why we should send angels away. Wouldn't it make more sense to let them stay with us and rejoice in the Sabbath meal? Perhaps, Emden suggests, we want them to leave before something improper takes place, which might make them leave in anger. Rabbi Hayyim of Volozhin (1749–1821) had even stronger reservations. He writes that it is forbidden to make *any* requests of angels, for they have no independent power whatsoever. When a person is worthy, then angels have no choice but to offer blessing, just as if a person is unworthy angels have no choice but to curse. For this reason, the Volozhiner never recited the verse *Barkhuni l'shalom,* "Bless me with peace." And the Hatam Sofer did not sing *Shalom Aleikhem* at all, explaining that we are no longer on the spiritual level to have angels accompany us!

On the other hand, the *Shem Mishmu'el* of Rabbi Shmuel of Sochtchov notes that all week long a person is conflicted: the body pulling in one direction, the soul in another. But on Shabbat, the power of holiness is so strong that body and soul at last make peace with one another and, for this reason, the angels bless us. This seems to imply that the angels represent dimensions of our own psyches, which, on Shabbat, finally attain a harmonious balance. Finally, *Siddur Yeshu'at Yaakov* (Lublin, 1880) advises us that if there is a quarrel in the house and we refrain from reciting the last stanza, *Tseitkhem l'shalom,* "Go in peace," the quarrel will calm down (*N'tiv Binah* and *Be'er Hachasidut, Z'mirot Shabbat*).

LANDES (HALAKHAH)

you]."

Shalom Aleikhem need not be sung at the table. Indeed, it may be sung as a transition to the table, from an antechamber, hallway, living room, or parlor, where guests and family assemble. Some sing it three times, in accord with the principle that "a threefold cord does not easily break."

L. HOFFMAN (HISTORY)

1942) says that originally the greeting was not intended for these angels at all. Rather, it was offered to other angels who were said to accompany the extra soul, riding on myrtle branches (like a magic carpet?) and remaining throughout Shabbat (see "With our masters' and teachers' approval," p. 111, and "Varied spices" p. 167). By the early modern period, that belief was no longer common, so Jews had to find other angels who might be greeted: hence, the transfer of object to the good and bad angels mentioned in the Talmud.

[3] *"Bless me"* The Vilna Gaon (1720–1797) objected to a verse that requests blessing from angels instead of from God directly. The phrase *mimelekh...hakadosh barukh hu* ("from the king over the kings of kings, the Holy One blessed be He") may have been included specifically to overcome that objection. If we petition them, it is only insofar as they are representatives of God.

[4] *"Go in peace"* Jacob Emden (1697–1776) suggested lopping off this final verse because instead of sending the angels away, we ought to plead with them to remain with us even when Shabbat ends. He didn't like the poem altogether and suggests he would have gotten rid of it entirely, had he been able to do so.

[4] *"In peace* [l'shalom]*"* Literally *"to* peace." The author may have preferred using *l'shalom* ("to peace") because he was aware of the following lesson from Berakhot 64a:

Rabbi Avin Halevi said, "If you leave a friend, you should not say, 'Go *in* peace [*b'shalom*],' but 'Go *to* peace [*l'shalom*],' because Jethro [Moses' father-in-law] said to Moses (Exod. 4:18), 'Go *to* peace [*l'shalom*],' and he went on to success. But David said to Absalom (2 Sam. 15:9), 'Go *in* peace [*b'shalom*],' and he [Absalom] ended up being hanged." Prepositions are hard to translate because they are used so idiomatically and turn up meaning different things depending on the context, but *b'* usually means "in" or sometimes "with," while *l'* means "to." A second lesson by Rabbi Avin, immediately after the first, is this: on taking leave of the deceased, you should not say, "Go *to* peace [*l'shalom*]," but "Go *in* peace [*b'shalom*]," because [regarding Abraham's ultimate death] it is said (Gen. 15:15), "You will go to your ancestors in peace [*b'shalom*]."

Faced with two alternatives, *l'shalom* ("to" peace) and *b'shalom* ("in" peace), the Talmud recommends the former *(l'shalom)* for leaving a friend. The latter *(b'shalom)* implies that the person we are leaving will either die shortly or is already dead. So our author purposely has us say to the angels, *"Lekh l'shalom* (Go to peace)," and then replicates the same word *l'shalom* throughout the stanzas. The parallel English, "to peace," is senseless, so we render it differently (see Joel Hoffman, "With peace," below).

J. HOFFMAN (TRANSLATION)

parallel to "angels of peace," immediately below, and "angels on high" thereafter. The word "service" here functions roughly as it does in the phrase "How may I be of service?"

[1] *"On high"* "Of high" would better preserve the parallel structure, but it is poor English. Other translations differ from ours by assuming that the Hebrew *elyon* refers not to the angels, who are themselves "on high," but to God, who is "the [most] high"; thus, some translations render this phrase, "angels of the Most High."

[1] *"King over the kings of kings"* See Volume 6, *Tachanun and Concluding Prayers,* p. 147.

[1] *"The Holy One blessed be He"* As is often the case, we have to decide whether the Hebrew here is a statement about what is ("blessed is He") or what ought to be ("blessed be He"). We opt for the latter. The Hebrew could be either. An interesting alternative is "Holy One of blessing," the translation found in *Vetaher Libeinu,* the prayer book from Congregation Beth El of Sudbury, Massachusetts, which has a nice poetic ring.

[3] *"With peace* [l'shalom]" By using "with" here, we translate the most likely meaning of the Hebrew, but in so doing, we fail to capture the fact that the second, third, and fourth stanzas of this poem all share the same second word, *l'shalom* ("in peace"). "Come in peace," and "Go in peace" make perfect sense, and so does "Bless me in peace," but we think the proper connotation is "Bless me *with* peace," so that is how we render it, even though the English thereby departs from the parallelism in the Hebrew.

D. *ESHET CHAYIL* ("A WORTHY WOMAN")

¹אֵשֶׁת חַיִל מִי יִמְצָא וְרָחֹק מִפְּנִינִים מִכְרָהּ.

²בָּטַח בָּהּ לֵב בַּעְלָהּ וְשָׁלָל לֹא יֶחְסָר.

³גְּמָלַתְהוּ טוֹב וְלֹא רָע כֹּל יְמֵי חַיֶּיהָ.

⁴דָּרְשָׁה צֶמֶר וּפִשְׁתִּים וַתַּעַשׂ בְּחֵפֶץ כַּפֶּיהָ.

⁵הָיְתָה כָּאֳנִיּוֹת סוֹחֵר מִמֶּרְחָק תָּבִיא לַחְמָהּ.

⁶וַתָּקָם בְּעוֹד לַיְלָה וַתִּתֵּן טֶרֶף לְבֵיתָהּ וְחֹק לְנַעֲרֹתֶיהָ.

⁷זָמְמָה שָׂדֶה וַתִּקָּחֵהוּ מִפְּרִי כַפֶּיהָ נָטְעָה כָּרֶם.

⁸חָגְרָה בְעוֹז מָתְנֶיהָ וַתְּאַמֵּץ זְרוֹעֹתֶיהָ.

⁹טָעֲמָה כִּי טוֹב סַחְרָהּ לֹא יִכְבֶּה בַלַּיְלָה נֵרָהּ.

¹⁰יָדֶיהָ שִׁלְּחָה בַכִּישׁוֹר וְכַפֶּיהָ תָּמְכוּ פָלֶךְ.

¹¹כַּפָּהּ פָּרְשָׂה לֶעָנִי וְיָדֶיהָ שִׁלְּחָה לָאֶבְיוֹן.

¹²לֹא תִירָא לְבֵיתָהּ מִשָּׁלֶג כִּי כָל בֵּיתָהּ לָבֻשׁ שָׁנִים.

¹³מַרְבַדִּים עָשְׂתָה לָּהּ שֵׁשׁ וְאַרְגָּמָן לְבוּשָׁהּ.

¹⁴נוֹדָע בַּשְּׁעָרִים בַּעְלָהּ בְּשִׁבְתּוֹ עִם זִקְנֵי אָרֶץ.

How hard to find a worthy woman, one whose worth surpasses rubies.

2 Her husband trusts her, and he lacks nothing.

3 She rewards him with good and not bad all the days of her life.

4 She seeks clothing material to work with her willing hands.

5 Like a merchant ship, she brings her bread from afar.

6 She rises before night ends to give food to her house, and their due to her help.

7 She considers a field and acquires it, from the fruit of her hands planting a vineyard.

8 She braces herself and strengthens her arms.

9 She finds that her merchandise is good, and her lamp remains lit at night.

10 She sends her fingers to the spinning wheel, and her hands hold the spindle.

11 She stretches out her hand to the poor, her every finger helping the needy.

12 She need not worry about snow in her household, because her entire household is clothed in crimson.

13 She makes herself warm clothing, wearing linen and scarlet.

14 Her husband is known at the gates as he sits with the elders of the land.

15 She makes linen to sell and gives ties to the merchant.

16 Clothed in strength and honor, she smiles at the future.

15 סָדִין עָשְׂתָה וַתִּמְכֹּר וַחֲגוֹר נָתְנָה לַכְּנַעֲנִי.

16 עֹז וְהָדָר לְבוּשָׁהּ וַתִּשְׂחַק לְיוֹם אַחֲרוֹן.

17 פִּיהָ פָּתְחָה בְחָכְמָה וְתוֹרַת חֶסֶד עַל לְשׁוֹנָהּ.

18 צוֹפִיָּה הֲלִיכוֹת בֵּיתָהּ וְלֶחֶם עַצְלוּת לֹא תֹאכֵל.

19 קָמוּ בָנֶיהָ וַיְאַשְּׁרוּהָ בַּעְלָהּ וַיְהַלְלָהּ.

20 רַבּוֹת בָּנוֹת עָשׂוּ חָיִל וְאַתְּ עָלִית עַל כֻּלָּנָה.

21 שֶׁקֶר הַחֵן וְהֶבֶל הַיֹּפִי אִשָּׁה יִרְאַת יְיָ הִיא תִתְהַלָּל.

22 תְּנוּ לָהּ מִפְּרִי יָדֶיהָ וִיהַלְלוּהָ בַשְּׁעָרִים מַעֲשֶׂיהָ.

⁶ She rises before night ends to give food to her house, and their due to her help.

⁷ She considers a field and acquires it, from the fruit of her hands planting a vineyard.

⁸ She braces herself and strengthens her arms.

⁹ She finds that her merchandise is good, and her lamp remains lit at night.

¹⁰ She sends her fingers to the spinning wheel, and her hands hold the spindle.

¹¹ She stretches out her hand to the poor, *(p. 79)*

¹ *"A worthy woman"* The biblical noun *chayil* has various senses, including the military, the upper class, wealth, property, or power. The traditional translation, "woman of valor," captures the military sense of *chayil,* as "valiant"; but "powerful" or "capable" fit the context equally. It is uncertain *(p. 81)* work of the woman's hands and the gates, where her husband sat as an elder.

———◆———

DORFF (THEOLOGY)

Eshet Chayil ("A Worthy Woman") This acrostic poem from the Book *(p. 83)*

from before sunrise to after sunset. She provides food for her entire household, she sews and weaves clothing and even tapestries (some of which she sells), and she runs a vineyard. She indeed "never eats the bread of idleness."

This picture mirrors reality for modern American women, but is it a good reality? True, Jewish tradition values work. The Torah (Exod. 23:12) commands, "Six days shall you do your work" just as much as it commands "and on the seventh day you shall cease from labor"; and the Rabbis *(p. 84)*

¹⁷ She opens her mouth with wisdom, with kind teaching on her tongue.

¹⁸ She oversees the comings and goings of her household, never eating the bread of idleness.

¹⁹ Her children rise to make her happy, her husband to praise her:

²⁰ "Many women are worthy, but you rise above them all."

²¹ Grace is deceptive and beauty vain, but a woman who fears Adonai is to be praised.

poem to his wife around the Shabbat table, where children and guests can witness the respect and love he has for her.

———◆———

ELLENSON (MODERN LITURGIES)

Eshet Chayil ("A Worthy Woman") Marcia Falk summarizes the objections that many liberal Jews have to this recitation of Proverbs 31:10–31, which the husband customarily recites on Friday night as a tribute to the *(p. 84)*

Falk rejects the traditional passage from Proverbs altogether, so provides no parallel passage for husbands. Instead, she seeks a statement of reciprocal intimacy to express the spirit of gratitude and love that holds sway between two partners who have formed a household; she also expressly provides wording for same-sex households, not just for the traditional heterosexual marriage. Falk draws her inspiration for such expression from the biblical Song of Songs and labels her blessing, "Blessing the Beloved." The first partner states, "How fine you are, my

love, how fine you are," while the second partner responds, "How fine you are, my love, what joy is ours." Together, both partners then say, "Of all pleasure, how sweet is the taste of love."

—◆—

FRANKEL (A Woman's Voice)

Eshet Chayil ("A Worthy Woman") For some Jewish women, this table song, excerpted from chapter 31 of Proverbs and traditionally sung by a husband to his wife before he   *(p. 85)*

GRAY (TALMUD)

Eshet Chayil ("A Worthy Woman") The significance of reciting *Eshet Chayil* can be understood on three levels: (1) reading the plain meaning of the text; (2) identifying the *Eshet Chayil* as Torah; and (3) seeing *Eshet Chayil* as Shabbat.

The plain meaning of the text expresses a husband's effusive recognition of his wife's hard work for her family. This recognition advances the traditional theme associated with lighting Shabbat candles and blessing one's children: the creation of a peaceful and loving Shabbat atmosphere at home.

But *Eshet Chayil* can also be seen as Torah. Proverbs 8 personifies wisdom as a woman, and verse 8:11 ("wisdom is better than rubies") corresponds stunningly to 31:10 ("whose worth [the worth of the *eshet chayil*] surpasses rubies" [v. 1])—making wisdom equal to the *eshet chayil*. But wisdom is Torah. (Gen. Rab. 1:1 uses Proverbs 8 [vss. 22, 30] to describe Torah as God's blueprint for creation.) We thus get the equation, *Eshet chayil* of Proverbs 31:10–31 = wisdom of Proverbs 8 = Torah of the Midrash. *Eshet chayil* is thus the Torah, which brings peace and prosperity to her "husband," Israel.

Finally, *eshet chayil* may be Shabbat, the wife of her "husband," Israel. Genesis Rabbah 11:8   *(p. 86)*

¹אֵשֶׁת חַיִל מִי יִמְצָא וְרָחֹק מִפְּנִינִים מִכְרָהּ.

²בָּטַח בָּהּ לֵב בַּעְלָהּ וְשָׁלָל לֹא יֶחְסָר.

³גְּמָלַתְהוּ טוֹב וְלֹא רָע כֹּל יְמֵי חַיֶּיהָ.

⁴דָּרְשָׁה צֶמֶר וּפִשְׁתִּים וַתַּעַשׂ בְּחֵפֶץ כַּפֶּיהָ.

22 Let her have the fruit of her hands, that her works praise her in the gates.

⁵הָיְתָה כָּאֳנִיּוֹת סוֹחֵר מִמֶּרְחָק תָּבִיא לַחְמָהּ.

⁶וַתָּקָם בְּעוֹד לַיְלָה וַתִּתֵּן טֶרֶף לְבֵיתָהּ וְחֹק לְנַעֲרֹתֶיהָ.

⁷זָמְמָה שָׂדֶה וַתִּקָּחֵהוּ מִפְּרִי כַפֶּיהָ נָטְעָה כָּרֶם.

⁸חָגְרָה בְעוֹז מָתְנֶיהָ וַתְּאַמֵּץ זְרוֹעֹתֶיהָ.

⁹טָעֲמָה כִּי טוֹב סַחְרָהּ לֹא יִכְבֶּה בַלַּיְלָה נֵרָהּ.

¹⁰יָדֶיהָ שִׁלְּחָה בַכִּישׁוֹר וְכַפֶּיהָ תָּמְכוּ פָלֶךְ.

¹¹כַּפָּהּ פָּרְשָׂה לֶעָנִי וְיָדֶיהָ שִׁלְּחָה לָאֶבְיוֹן.

¹²לֹא תִירָא לְבֵיתָהּ מִשָּׁלֶג כִּי כָל בֵּיתָהּ לָבֻשׁ שָׁנִים.

¹³מַרְבַדִּים עָשְׂתָה לָּהּ שֵׁשׁ וְאַרְגָּמָן לְבוּשָׁהּ.

¹⁴נוֹדָע בַּשְּׁעָרִים בַּעְלָהּ בְּשִׁבְתּוֹ עִם זִקְנֵי אָרֶץ.

¹⁵סָדִין עָשְׂתָה וַתִּמְכֹּר וַחֲגוֹר נָתְנָה לַכְּנַעֲנִי.

¹⁶עֹז וְהָדָר לְבוּשָׁהּ וַתִּשְׂחַק לְיוֹם אַחֲרוֹן.

¹⁷פִּיהָ פָּתְחָה בְחָכְמָה וְתוֹרַת חֶסֶד עַל לְשׁוֹנָהּ.

D. *ESHET CHAYIL* ("A WORTHY WOMAN")

[1] How hard to find a worthy woman, one whose worth surpasses rubies.

[2] Her husband trusts her, and he lacks nothing.

[3] She rewards him with good and not bad all the days of her life.

[4] She seeks clothing material to work with her willing hands.

[5] Like a merchant ship, she brings her bread from afar.

[18] צוֹפִיָּה הֲלִיכוֹת בֵּיתָהּ וְלֶחֶם עַצְלוּת לֹא תֹאכֵל.

[19] קָמוּ בָנֶיהָ וַיְאַשְּׁרוּהָ בַּעְלָהּ וַיְהַלְלָהּ.

[20] רַבּוֹת בָּנוֹת עָשׂוּ חָיִל וְאַתְּ עָלִית עַל כֻּלָּנָה.

[21] שֶׁקֶר הַחֵן וְהֶבֶל הַיֹּפִי אִשָּׁה יִרְאַת יְיָ הִיא תִתְהַלָּל.

[22] תְּנוּ לָהּ מִפְּרִי יָדֶיהָ וִיהַלְלוּהָ בַשְּׁעָרִים מַעֲשֶׂיהָ.

BRETTLER (BIBLE)

her every finger helping the needy.

[12] She need not worry about snow in her household, because her entire household is clothed in crimson.

[13] She makes herself warm clothing, wearing linen and scarlet.

[14] Her husband is known at the gates as he sits with the elders of the land.

[15] She makes linen to sell and gives ties to the merchant.

[16] Clothed in strength and honor, she smiles at the future.

[17] She opens her mouth with wisdom, with kind teaching on her tongue.

[18] She oversees the comings and goings of her household, never eating the bread of idleness.

[19] Her children rise to make her happy, her husband to praise her:

[20] "Many women are worthy, but you rise above them all."

[21] Grace is deceptive and beauty vain, but a woman who fears Adonai is to be

praised.

[22] Let her have the fruit of her hands, that her works praise her in the gates.

BRETTLER (BIBLE)

Eshet Chayil ("A Worthy Woman") This acrostic poem (on acrostics, see Volume 3, *P'sukei D'zimrah*, p. 116) concludes the Book of Proverbs as a conscious attempt to provide a positive attitude toward women in the face of negative views that are typical of the book—or even of this chapter (31:3), "Do not give your strength to women, / Your vigor, to those who destroy kings." Alternatively, the subject of the poem may be no actual woman at all; rather, it celebrates *chokhmah*, "wisdom" personified, in which case the poem is a paean to Dame Wisdom.

DORFF (THEOLOGY)

whether such a woman is described as being just difficult or actually impossible to find. The latter interpretation would suggest that the chapter is lauding the feminine personification of "wisdom," rather than an actual wife.

[2] *"Trusts her"* After the opening exclamation, the poem focuses on the husband, who appears twice more—near the poem's center and at its conclusion—suggesting that as powerful as this woman is, her prestige is largely derived from her husband.

[4] *"Clothing material"* She works at all stages of clothing production, beginning with securing its two main staples (wool and flax); she engages in long-range trading transactions for food, which she distributes to family and servants. She is even involved in labor-intensive viniculture. This range of activities was atypical of the average Israelite woman. These verses are framed by "hands" *(kapeha),* which is repeated along with "fingers" *(yadeha)* and "arms" *(z'ro'oteha)* seven times in this section, emphasizing her "hands-on" management style.

[8] *"Braces herself"* Possibly referring to a smock of some sort worn for protection during work. It adds to the poem's emphasis on the woman's practical competence, ignoring her sexuality. (See below, "Grace is deceptive," v. 21.)

[9] *"Her lamp remains lit"* If literal, she is like the ideal man who studies Torah day and night (Ps. 1:2), though Proverbs (e.g., 24:20) employs "light" and "lamps" also as metaphors for success.

[10] *"She sends her fingers"* Almost at the center of the poem, the words *yad* and *kaf* are repeated in reverse (chiastic) order, joining the two verses together. Archaeological excavations suggest that the *falekh* is most likely a spindle-whorl, a circular weight of clay or other material with a hole in the middle that would pull down on the wool as it was spun. The pair of tightly joined verses emphasizes that she uses her hands for good purposes only: to support her family, and to support the poor. Care for the poor is a major theme of biblical literature (see, e.g., Prov. 14:31; 22:22), as well as wisdom literature in general throughout the ancient Near East.

[12] *"Snow"* Snow is relatively infrequent in Israel, but the *eshet chayil* keeps her household prepared for it by clothing them in *shanim,* usually translated as "crimson." But how could crimson help in a snowstorm? Biblical vocalization is late, however, and sometimes in error. Here, we should probably follow the Septuagint, the early Greek biblical translation, which read these same consonants as *shenayim,* "double," in the sense of two layers of clothing.

[13] *"Warm clothing"* Wearing clothes of linen and scarlet confirms that she belongs to the upper classes, as is evident from her property holdings and trading ventures.

[14] *"Known at the gates"* The intention is to depict her husband not as idle, but as important, sitting among the elders as they made judicial decisions.

[15] *"Merchant"* Kena'ani here means "trader," or "merchant," not Canaanite (as in Zech. 14:21), a reference to Canaan's location on major land and sea trade routes.

[16] *"Clothed in strength"* Her clothing connotes strength rather than anything enticing or sexual (see below, "Grace is deceptive," v. 21); her strength allows her to "smile at the future."

[17] *"She opens her mouth"* The text moves from her hands to her mouth, usually a center of sensuality (see, e.g., Prov. 5:2; Song of Songs 4:11), but here, it is desexualized to connote "wisdom."

[19] *"Her children rise"* The poem's conclusion reiterates its initial motifs, the woman's husband and her own character as "worthy."

[21] *"Grace is deceptive"* The seductive temptress depicted in Proverbs (chaps. 1–9, esp. chap. 7) is the antithesis of this ideal woman, who is characterized by *yirat Adonai,* "fear of Adonai"; especially in wisdom literature, "fear of Adonai" denotes ideal behavior motivated by such "fear" rather than the "fear" itself. Thus, her care for the poor is a manifestation of "fearing God." If, however, this poem praises wisdom personified as the ideal woman (see above, *Eshet Chayil* ["A Worthy Woman"]), this phrase may mean "It is a woman [whose name is] Fear of Adonai—she should be praised;" that is, Dame Wisdom ("Fear of Adonai") is the ideal wife. The Greek Septuagint translation may suggest an original reading: "an intelligent woman" rather than "a woman who fears Adonai."

[22] *"Let her have"* The poem concludes by recapitulating its two main themes: the

of Proverbs is used by husbands to honor their wives as industrious (the literal meaning of *chayil*); they take care of household duties while also engaging in business, such as buying a field and tending a vineyard. To do it all, such a wife rises before sunrise and works into the night—a workaholic "supermom" beyond belief. Its portrait of women who raise a family but also establish careers has become everyday reality for many modern women. The poem was far ahead of its time. Still, the poem is problematic in that it does not praise single women, women without children, or women who do not work outside the home. Is it, therefore, a good model for us?

Marriage and children are desirable in Jewish tradition, which would look askance at modern decisions to postpone marriage and a family to the point of suffering from infertility. The primary cause of infertility is, in fact, age. Biologically, the best age for women and men to procreate is twenty-two. Infertility begins to set in at twenty-seven; it then rises exponentially after thirty-five, with birth defects becoming more frequent; and after forty it is possible, but rare, to bear a healthy child. Infertility is a problem for men, not just women. Sperm count and motility go down with age, sperm becomes misshapen, and impotence occurs.

Jews, who attend college and graduate school in unusually high percentages, often postpone marriage until their late twenties and have children in their thirties. Most American Jews, then, have only one or two children, so that American Jews as a group are not even reproducing themselves.

We need to sympathize with couples experiencing infertility, which creates marital tension, tremendous frustration, and a painful rethinking of "who I am as a man or woman and who we are as a couple if we cannot have children." Couples who cannot reproduce through sexual intercourse should know that Judaism welcomes, but does not require, their use of medical technology to do so. (See Elliot Dorff, *Matters of Life and Death: A Jewish Approach to Modern Medical Ethics* [Philadelphia: Jewish Publication Society, 1998], chap. 3 and 4.)

At the same time, we should encourage teenagers to apply to colleges with a substantial Jewish population and make it clear that the college years are not too early to look for a mate, and even to marry, so as to begin a family while in graduate school, before infertility begins to set in. We also need to help singles meet each other after the college years. Finally, we need to encourage couples to have three or four children, not only for the blessings they bring, but so that Jewish life can continue.

In emphasizing marriage and family, then, this poem very much articulates a Jewish ideal, not only for women but also for men.

It is the poem's second theme that creates problems. The woman depicted works

FRANKEL (A WOMAN'S VOICE)

find work valuable not only for what it produces, but also for what it contributes to a person's well-being. Thus, Rabban Gamaliel (M. Avot 1:2) forbids the exclusive study of Torah without work as well, "for study of Torah unaccompanied by work is ultimately in vain and leads to sin." Similarly, a wealthy woman with plenty of servants must do some work herself, "for idleness leads to lewdness" (M. Ket. 5:5).

But in the end, Jewish tradition values family over work. When, for example, the men of the tribes of Reuben, Gad, and Manasseh volunteer as shock troops for the conquest of the land west of the Jordan River on condition that they may build "sheepfolds for our flocks and towns for our children" on the eastern bank that they have already conquered, Moses agrees; but tellingly, he reverses the order of their request. The Rabbis conclude that first comes family and only then work (Num. 32:16; 24; Num. Rab. 22:9). By contrast, the American middle-class work ethic has made work a virtual idol, to the point that "net worth" is equated with monetary assets alone. Insofar as our poem supports the model of working 24/7, one wonders whether this poem is a proper model today.

In its favor, the poem does praise other character traits that Judaism does and should prize. The *eshet chayil* gives to the poor. "She smiles at the future." Her husband trusts her and takes pride in her, telling her that in his eyes she rises above all other women. Her children also bless her. This high regard arises not because she is physically attractive, but because she is God-fearing in the way she leads her life. These are the verses that should correctly occupy the consciousness of a man who says or sings this

GRAY (TALMUD)

wife and mother of the house, when she observes, "While the intent behind this recitation may be loving, many Jewish women today find it patronizing." No doubt motivated by just such sentiments, even those liturgies that include the passage do so with significant changes, pruning the content to reflect the modern notions of gender equality. The British Reform *Forms of Prayer*, for instance, omits verses such as, "She rises while it is yet night, and gives food to her household." Another way of dealing with the desire for egalitarian gender roles is to balance a husband's praise of his wife with a wife's blessing for her husband. American Reform selects an excerpt from Psalm 112. Its 1977 translation in *Gates of the House* and the 1994 revision in *On the Doorposts of Your House* are identical, except that in the 1994 edition, the masculine "Lord" becomes "The Eternal One."

> Blessed is the man loyal to God, who greatly delights in the Eternal One's commandments!
> His descendants will be honored in the land; the generation of the upright will be blessed.
> His household prospers, and his righteousness endures forever.

> Light dawns in the darkness for the upright; for the man who is gracious, merciful and just.
> He is not afraid of evil tidings; his mind is firm, trusting in the Eternal One.
> His heart is steady; he is not afraid.
> He has been generous, has given freely to the poor; his righteousness endures forever; his life is exalted in honor

The same psalm (but translated differently) occurs in the Conservative *Sim Shalom* (1998). Both versions are selective, observing modern ethical sensitivity by omitting, for example, verse 8b, "In the end he will see the fall of his foes," and verse 10, "The wicked man shall see [what happens to the righteous] and be vexed; / He shall gnash his teeth; / his courage shall fail. / The desire of the wicked shall come to nothing."

KUSHNER & POLEN (CHASIDISM)

recites *Kiddush,* poses numerous problems: Why should a husband praise his wife, and not the other way around, or why shouldn't they praise each other? What is the woman being praised for, and what is being left unsaid? Is this song meant to deceive the woman into thinking that her religious status equals her husband's, when in fact she is barred from the more important roles in worship and observance? Are the women's roles that are enumerated in this song—seamstress, farmer, realtor, philanthropist, cook, counselor, major-domo—still desirable today? Is this song a description of a "worthy woman"—or of a drudge?

Certainly in its own time, this poem was meant to convey high praise. The fact that it is an acrostic, each succeeding verse beginning with the next letter of the Hebrew alphabet, suggests that it is formulaic, summing up a woman's virtues from "A to Z." If the tasks described refer primarily to the household and marketplace, that is due more to the economic realities of its time than to misogyny: if anything, this chapter reveals that Israelite women were engaged much more actively in public life than we might have assumed.

Other issues surround this song: it praises only the wife, not her partner; it reflects an ancient reality, not our own; it extols workaholism as a virtue, not a neurosis; it fails to consider that partners might share tasks in a marriage; it obviously excludes the possibility of same sex partnerships. It is disingenuous, of course, to fault the Bible for not speaking out on our current reality, but still, some have chosen to omit this part of the Friday night ritual altogether. In other households, everyone at the table sings the song, captivated so much by its melody that the words don't seem to matter. Elsewhere still, in an effort to address these modern concerns, some families have added or substituted an additional psalm or a selection from Song of Songs.

◆

J. HOFFMAN (TRANSLATION)

reports, "Shabbat said to the Holy Blessed One: 'Master of the worlds! Everything has a partner except me?' The Holy Blessed One said to her: 'The Congregation of Israel is your partner.'" *Eshet chayil* as Shabbat bestows blessing on its partner Israel (see Beitzah 16a; Shab. 119a). With the understanding of *eshet chayil* as Torah, we can understand why (v. 6) "she rises before night ends" and why "her lamp remains lit at night" (v. 9). It is said (Josh. 1:8), "Recite it [the Torah] day and night."

[16] *"She smiles at the future"* Yom acharon, translated here as "future," means, literally, "the last day," that is, Shabbat. Thus *eshet chayil,* as Shabbat, smiles over all her hard work for her family. But how can Shabbat work hard? The Talmud (Beitzah 16a) says that a person's annual income is decided from on high between Rosh Hashanah and Yom Kippur. But our salary fluctuates in direct proportion to the amount of money we spend preparing for Shabbat. So by honoring Shabbat, we ensure that Shabbat will work indirectly for us.

———◆———

KUSHNER & POLEN (CHASIDISM)

Eshet Chayil ("A Worthy Woman") Proverbs 31, known as *Eshet Chayil,* is customarily sung at the Sabbath table in praise of the woman of the house by her husband. Rabbi Naftali Tzvi of Ropschitz, however, used to invert the plain meaning of Proverbs 31:20, "She stretches out her hand to the poor..." (v. 11) by citing Leviticus Rabbah 34; Ruth Rabbah 5:9: "More than what the householder does for the poor person, the poor person does for the householder." In simplest terms, when we have company for dinner, we are on our best behavior. In this way, even the poorest guest brings good and blessing to the table of the host. And, for this reason, when a husband chants, "She stretches out her hand to the poor," rather than meaning that she does so in generous hospitality, it means she does so in receipt of the gifts created by simply having any guest at the table.

Professor Elliot Ginsburg of the University of Michigan notes that, for the kabbalist, the observance of Shabbat affects the inner life of God. Shabbat becomes the occasion of a mystical union *within* the divine. The male dimension, known as *Kudsha B'rikh Hu,* "the Holy One," (corresponding to the *s'firah* of *Tiferet*) unites with the female dimension, known as *Sh'khinah,* "the Presence," or *K'nesset Yisra'el,* "the community of Israel," (corresponding to the *s'firah* of *Malkhut*). And the chanting of *Eshet Chayil* thus becomes a love song to the *Sh'khinah.*

We read in *Zohar* II, 135a–b, a passage known as the *Raza d'Shabbos* ("The Secret of the Sabbath"), or simply by its first Aramaic word, *K'gavna.* It succinctly captures centuries of the Jewish mystical intuition regarding the romance of Shabbat and the role of each Jew in that supernal love. The following is a paraphrase:

> Just as they are united on high in the One, so also She is united here below in the secret of the One. Above and below, one corresponding to the other. Even the Holy

One who is One is unable to ascend his throne until She likewise has been transformed through the secret: One with Him. And behold, this then is the secret of the only God whose name is One.

And just this is the secret of Shabbat: She is Shabbat concealed within the secret of their One, bringing the secret of the One upon her. And this is the prayer for the entrance of Shabbat: She is the throne of the presence of the Holy One joined now in the secret of the One. Prepared at last for the supernal king to dwell upon her.

When Shabbat enters, She is unique, separate from the "other side." And since all judgment is alien to her, She remains unique in that holy light. She is crowned with so many crowns in the presence of the holy king that all the forces of anger and arrogance of judgment flee; now there is no other ruler throughout all the worlds.

Her face so radiant with that supernal light and crowned here below by a holy people even as all of them are, in turn, blessed with new names. Now commences the prayer to bless her with joy and faces of light: *"Bar'khu et Adonai ham'vorakh...."* Yes, God, Godself, let the window of blessing open onto all creation....

—◆—

L. HOFFMAN (HISTORY)

Eshet Chayil ("A Worthy Woman") Much of the liturgy for Friday night, for both home and synagogue, assumes a knowledge of some Kabbalah. True, the prayers can all be understood on a literal level, but as we saw in the introduction (see pp. 1–22), they were often included because of their esoteric dimension. *Eshet Chayil* may be the best example.

On the face of it, it is simply a passage from Proverbs, but liturgically, it functions in a much deeper manner. The woman here praised is only secondarily the speaker's wife; primarily, she represents the female aspect of God (see pp. 147–154).

—◆—

J. HOFFMAN (TRANSLATION)

[1] *"How hard to find"* Literally, "Who can find?" The phrase probably meant "a worthy woman is hard to find," but that simple rendition does not do justice to the poetic introduction of lyric Hebrew, and so we resort to something a little more poetic, but not so odd in English as Birnbaum, "A good wife, who can find?" The phrase may parallel Proverbs 20:6, literally, "A faithful man, who can find?" which we would translate, "How hard to find a faithful man." We also have a potentially much bigger problem. The traditional understanding of this poem is that it praises the woman, but significant parts of it seem rather to mock women in general and, by extension perhaps, the particular woman to whom the poem is read. This line could equally be translated, "A good wife is so hard to find," with the presumption that the speaker has *not* found a good wife and probably will not (similar to the lament about bad staff, "Good help is so hard to find"). We have chosen to assume that the poem reflects positive connotations, and translated accordingly, but

throughout the poem we have noted some surprising word choices that may buttress a negative interpretation of the content.

[1] *"A worthy woman"* Each of the opening two Hebrew words (which appear in the second half of the line in our translation) is difficult to translate. The first word, *eshet,* means both "woman" and "wife." The second word, *chayil,* refers to various positive attributes a person might have, from military prowess to worthiness of character. It is difficult to know the exact nuance the author intended here. Ruth (in Ruth 3:11) is likewise called an *eshet chayil,* there translated in JPS as "fine woman." Other possibilities here include "capable" or even "strong."

Modern Hebrew has preserved "strong" as the meaning of *chayil,* relating it to the similar Hebrew word *chayal,* "soldier." Based on these meanings, when the television series "Wonder Woman" was brought to Israel, the translators chose *Eshet Chayil* as the Hebrew title.

[1] *"Surpasses"* Literally, "is far from." The Hebrew construction is odd and, but for context, could mean "her worth is far from rubies." This is the second time in this line that we see a phrase whose common modern interpretation is positive but whose actual tone may have been mocking. Rather than starting off, "How hard to find a worthy woman, one whose worth surpasses rubies," the poem may begin, "A good wife is so hard to find. This one's worth is a far cry from rubies."

[1] *"Rubies"* We do not know exactly what *p'ninim* were. Rubies is one possibility; coral is more likely, but because "better than coral" sounds so odd in English, we stick with "rubies." (The English expression "good as gold" sounds too trite to our ears.) The point is that *p'ninim* were rare objects of beauty. Twice elsewhere (Job 28:18 and Proverbs 8:11) it is "wisdom" that surpasses the value of *p'ninim,* which may indicate that "better than *p'ninim*" was an idiom in the Bible, perhaps an idiom specifically related to wisdom.

[2] *"Her husband"* Literally, "her husband's heart." See Volume 1, *The Sh'ma and Its Blessings,* pp. 100–102, where we discuss the biblical impact of the word *lev,* literally, "heart."

[2] *"Nothing"* Literally, "spoils" as in "war spoils." Once again, we find a surprisingly negative word where only positive ones ought to appear. The surprising inclusion of this image may be repeated below, when she is likened to a merchant ship.

[4] *"Clothing material"* Literally, "wool and flax," but because many readers don't know what "flax" is, this common biblical idiom seems best paraphrased. ("Flax" is a plant used to make clothes, and "wool" is an animal product used for the same purpose.) The idiom "wool and flax" appears a few times in the Bible, once (Lev. 13:47) apparently representing "any sort of clothing" and once (Deut. 22:11) in an exhortation not to mix wool and flax.

[4] *"Willing hands"* Literally, "to work willingly with her hands." But because translation ought to capture the sense of a phrase, not necessarily its syntax, we freely interchange adverbs ("willingly") and adjectives ("willing").

[5] *"Her bread"* The Hebrew, *lechem,* is a generic word for "food" and also the more specific "bread," exactly the way "bread" functions in "break bread with friends." (A similar process in Arabic took the cognate word *lachmu* ["food"] and turned it into "meat.") In this instance, we would prefer "food," but because we have another word used for "food" below, we translate *lechem* as "bread" here.

[6] *"Before night ends"* Literally, "while it is still night."

[6] *"Give food"* The word for "food" here, *teref,* usually carries connotations of "prey," as in Psalm 124:6, which gives thanks to Adonai for not "letting us become *teref* in their teeth." Similarly, in Job 4:11, *teref* is clearly what a lion eats. Once again, we see a potentially mocking tone. Perhaps the woman "brings home food…but gives prey to her household."

[6] *"Help"* Literally, "maids," but the ancient notion of a "maid" differs considerably from the modern one, encompassing "attendant," "servant," and "helper."

[7] *"Considers"* As with "food," above, a word with surprising connotations appears here. *Zamam,* while meaning "consider," usually has connotations of taking evil action.

[7] *"Acquires"* Others, "buys" or "takes."

[7] *"Fruit of her hands"* The phrase "fruit of her hands" is a bit odd, but still, we think, better than Birnbaum's "earnings" or JPS's "her own labors," both of which miss both the play on words between "fruit…plants" and the repeated reference to "her hands" immediately above. Probably the idea is that rather than planting a vineyard from the fruit of the vine, she metaphorically plants a vineyard from the fruit of her hands.

[8] *"Braces herself"* Literally, "ties her *motnayim,*" where *motnayim* is either "loins" or a garment worn around the loins. Either way, "tying *motnayim*" formed a biblical idiom, best not translated literally. However, if *motnayim* refers to a part of the body, it parallels "arms" immediately following in a way we do not capture here.

[9] *"Finds"* Literally, "tastes." This line thus continues the imagery from above of "food" and the "fruit of her hands."

[9] *"Merchandise"* From the same root as "merchant" in "merchant ship," above (v. 5). But in adhering to so literal an interpretation of the words, we may have missed the overall meaning. Birnbaum suggests "…her trade is profitable," similar to JPS's "her business thrives." But the third-century-B.C.E. translation of the Bible into Greek has a different understanding of the text: "She finds that it is good to work." Either way, the connection between this half of the line and the second is not entirely clear.

[9] *"Lamp"* Hebrew, *ner*: oil lamp. See "Candle," pp. 43, 55.

[9] *"Remains lit"* Literally, "does not go out." We prefer "remains lit" for euphony.

[10] *"Fingers"* Literally, "hands" (*yad* in Hebrew), but we will need "hands" in the second half of this line to translate *kaf*, another Hebrew word for "hand."

[10] *"Spinning wheel"* Others, "distaff." A "distaff"—from the Old English "dis" (meaning "flax") and "staff"—is a staff around which flax was wound as part of the spinning process. The notion that *kishor*, the Hebrew word here, means "distaff" is based primarily on its seemingly parallel use with "spindle." (Unfortunately, our translation here may erroneously leave the reader with the impression that the woman about whom this poem was written was a colonial American.)

[11] *"Her every finger helping the needy"* Literally, "sending her hand to the needy," where the word for "hand" here is the same as the one we translate above as "finger." We thus have two lines: the first refers to "finger," then "hand"; the second to "hand" and then "finger." (This inverted parallel structure—"finger, hand" then "hand, finger"—is a common biblical stylistic device called chiasmus, from the Latinized version of the Greek *chiasma*, or "crossing," as in the Greek letter *chi*, X.) We retain the chiastic style here, even though the obvious and literal translation, "she sends her finger to the needy," is clearly wrong. Her fingers, like her hands, stay attached to her

¹וַיְהִי עֶרֶב וַיְהִי בֹקֶר:

ל וֹם הַשִּׁשִּׁי. ²וַיְכֻלּוּ הַשָּׁמַיִם וְהָאָרֶץ וְכָל צְבָאָם. ³וַיְכַל אֱלֹהִים בַּיּוֹם הַשְּׁבִיעִי מְלַאכְתּוֹ אֲשֶׁר עָשָׂה, וַיִּשְׁבֹּת בַּיּוֹם הַשְּׁבִיעִי מִכָּל מְלַאכְתּוֹ אֲשֶׁר עָשָׂה. ⁴וַיְבָרֶךְ אֱלֹהִים אֶת יוֹם הַשְּׁבִיעִי וַיְקַדֵּשׁ אֹתוֹ, כִּי בוֹ שָׁבַת מִכָּל מְלַאכְתּוֹ אֲשֶׁר בָּרָא אֱלֹהִים לַעֲשׂוֹת.

⁵סָבְרֵי מָרָנָן וְרַבּוֹתַי.

⁶בָּרוּךְ אַתָּה, יְיָ אֱלֹהֵינוּ, מֶלֶךְ הָעוֹלָם, בּוֹרֵא פְּרִי הַגָּפֶן.

⁷בָּרוּךְ אַתָּה, יְיָ אֱלֹהֵינוּ, מֶלֶךְ הָעוֹלָם, אֲשֶׁר קִדְּשָׁנוּ בְּמִצְוֹתָיו וְרָצָה בָנוּ, וְשַׁבַּת קָדְשׁוֹ בְּאַהֲבָה וּבְרָצוֹן הִנְחִילָנוּ, זִכָּרוֹן לְמַעֲשֵׂה בְרֵאשִׁית. ⁸כִּי הוּא יוֹם תְּחִלָּה לְמִקְרָאֵי קֹדֶשׁ, זֵכֶר לִיצִיאַת מִצְרָיִם. ⁹כִּי בָנוּ בָחַרְתָּ וְאוֹתָנוּ קִדַּשְׁתָּ מִכָּל הָעַמִּים, וְשַׁבַּת קָדְשְׁךָ בְּאַהֲבָה וּבְרָצוֹן הִנְחַלְתָּנוּ. ¹⁰בָּרוּךְ אַתָּה, יְיָ, מְקַדֵּשׁ הַשַּׁבָּת.

snow) clothes, but rather royal (crimson red) ones.

[13] *"Warm clothing"* We do not know the exact meaning of the Hebrew *marvadim,* which occurs only here and in Proverbs 7:16. The root may mean "layer," and so *marvadim* may be layered clothes, that is, warm clothes. From Proverbs 7:16 we see that a bed is made with *marvadim,* perhaps a blanket or quilt-like comforter, that is, a blanket with layers. The same root seems to appear in Genesis

(p. 95)

[1] There was evening and there was morning:

A sixth day. [2] Heaven and earth and everything associated with them were completed. [3] On the seventh day, God completed the work He had done. On the seventh day, He rested from all the work He had done. [4] God blessed the seventh day and sanctified it, for on it He

(p. 96)

BRETTLER (BIBLE)

[1] *"There was evening and there was morning"* A preamble to the *Kiddush* from (1) Genesis 1:31, the last half of the last verse describing the creation of day six, followed by (2) the description of day seven (Gen. 2:1–3), the primeval Shabbat of creation. Day one

(p. 99)

[7] *"Lovingly and adoringly"* The positive aspects of Shabbat, counterbalancing the biblical view that highlights Shabbat as a time for strict observance and Shabbat violation as a capital crime (e.g., Exod. 31:14–15).

[7] *"Granting us…as our inheritance"* A strange verb here, because it usually expresses the legacy of the Land of Israel. Perhaps its use in this context expresses the idea that, ultimately, Shabbat (as sacred time) replaces the Land of Israel (as sacred space). In any event, "granting us…as

(p. 100)

body.

[12] *"Need not"* Or "does not." But "she does not worry about snow" seems so less poetic than "she need not."

[12] *"Snow"* "Snow" is out of context here. The Greek translation reads, "Her husband is not worried about those at home when he *tarries,* because everyone in her household is clothed." But the Greek roots for "tarry" *(xroni)* and for snow *(xioni)* are so close that we must assume that the use of "tarry" is the result of error in

and associated with the Exodus (Deut. 5:15). The *Kiddush* reconciles all three by mentioning them together.

[9] *"You have chosen us"* Israel's chosenness and holiness are connected in Deuteronomy 7:6 and 14:2: "For you are a people consecrated [lit., 'made holy'] to Adonai your God…God chose you…"

[10] *"Sanctifies the Shabbat"* Here, God sanctifies Shabbat, as in Genesis 2:3, "God blessed the seventh day and sanctified it." However, the idea *(p. 100)*

hundred years to reconcile notions of Jewish particularity and the ideal of the Jews as the "chosen people" with theological and philosophical commitments and beliefs of a more expansive and universal nature. Abraham Geiger and the authors of the 1895 and 1940 editions of the *Union Prayer Book,* therefore, omitted this phrase from their prayer books, as they felt it reflected, to use Geiger's phrase, "a noxious particularism."

The founder of Reconstructionism, Mordecai Kaplan, was *(p. 104)*

¹וַיְהִי עֶרֶב וַיְהִי בֹקֶר:

יוֹם הַשִּׁשִּׁי. ²וַיְכֻלּוּ הַשָּׁמַיִם וְהָאָרֶץ וְכָל צְבָאָם. ³וַיְכַל אֱלֹהִים בַּיּוֹם הַשְּׁבִיעִי מְלַאכְתּוֹ אֲשֶׁר עָשָׂה, וַיִּשְׁבֹּת בַּיּוֹם הַשְּׁבִיעִי מִכָּל מְלַאכְתּוֹ אֲשֶׁר עָשָׂה. ⁴וַיְבָרֶךְ אֱלֹהִים אֶת יוֹם הַשְּׁבִיעִי וַיְקַדֵּשׁ אֹתוֹ, כִּי בוֹ שָׁבַת מִכָּל מְלַאכְתּוֹ אֲשֶׁר בָּרָא אֱלֹהִים לַעֲשׂוֹת.

creation included even the creation of death—hardly a theme with which to begin Shabbat.

¹*"A sixth day"* Rashi observes the unique inclusion of the definite article *heh* ("the") here, in contrast to the account of the first five days of creation, which lacks it. The numerical value of *heh* is five, a reference to the Five Books of Torah. On the sixth day, therefore, God promised that if the Jewish People accepts the Five Books of Torah, the world will endure (Shab. 88a). Alternatively, Rashi interprets *(p. 105)*

1. *Kiddush* should be recited with the mind focused on fulfilling the *mitzvah* to "remember the Shabbat day, by sanctifying it [*l'kadsho*]."

2. Because this is the most important *Kiddush* (there is a shorter one for Saturday noon), if it was omitted, for any reason, on Friday night, it should be recited as early as possible up to the very end of Shabbat.

3. Once Shabbat has begun, one should neither eat nor drink, except (if need be) water, before *Kiddush* (Pes. 105a and Maimonides, "Shabbat" 29:4).

(p. 110)

verses 1–4. They were added to the liturgy in post-talmudic times (after 550 C.E.), but it is hard to know exactly when.

Take verses 2–4 (Gen. 2:1–3) first. Writing from Egypt, Maimonides (1135–1204) says ("Laws of Shabbat" 29:7), "It is common custom" to say "[Heaven and earth...] were completed." He surely means Genesis 2:1–3, which must have been added to the Shabbat *Kiddush* because it describes the creation of Shabbat. Eleazer of Worms (*Sefer Roke'ach,* "Laws of Shabbat" 49), who lived about the same time (1160–1238), includes those verses also, and he traces the custom to a midrashic collection called *Vay'khulu.* The original version of *Vay'khulu* is missing, however, and is known to us *(p. 114)* transmitting the Greek. (It cannot be the result of scribal error in Hebrew, because only in Greek are the two words similar.)

[12] *"Crimson"* Literally, "crimsons," and possibly fine crimson clothes. But neither "crimsons" nor "fine crimson clothes" would do anything to protect against the snow. Another possibility, reinforced by the word *marvadim* ("clothing") in the next line, is that the word is not "crimson(s)," but rather "twice." (The letters would be the same in Hebrew, with only the vowels differing.) Some sort of double garment would indeed protect against the snow. But snow was so rare in biblical times that it wouldn't have been a major concern for anyone's household, whether or not headed by a worthy woman. Perhaps the point is that "she's prepared even for such rare occurrences as snow." We also consider a third possible understanding of this line. "Snow" is commonly used in the biblical idiom "white as snow." Perhaps the point here is that the members of her house will not wear plain (white as

⁵סָבְרִי מָרָנָן וְרַבּוֹתַי.

⁶בָּרוּךְ אַתָּה, יְיָ אֱלֹהֵינוּ, מֶלֶךְ הָעוֹלָם, בּוֹרֵא פְּרִי הַגָּֽפֶן.

⁷בָּרוּךְ אַתָּה, יְיָ אֱלֹהֵינוּ, מֶלֶךְ הָעוֹלָם, אֲשֶׁר קִדְּשָֽׁנוּ בְּמִצְוֹתָיו וְרָצָה בָֽנוּ, וְשַׁבַּת קָדְשׁוֹ בְּאַהֲבָה וּבְרָצוֹן הִנְחִילָֽנוּ, זִכָּרוֹן לְמַעֲשֵׂה בְרֵאשִׁית. ⁸כִּי הוּא יוֹם תְּחִלָּה לְמִקְרָאֵי קֹֽדֶשׁ, זֵֽכֶר לִיצִיאַת מִצְרָֽיִם. ⁹כִּי בָֽנוּ בָחַֽרְתָּ וְאוֹתָֽנוּ קִדַּֽשְׁתָּ מִכָּל הָעַמִּים, וְשַׁבַּת קָדְשְׁךָ בְּאַהֲבָה וּבְרָצוֹן הִנְחַלְתָּֽנוּ. ¹⁰בָּרוּךְ אַתָּה, יְיָ, מְקַדֵּשׁ הַשַּׁבָּת.

41:42, where, in a different form, it might mean "chain." A chain and some fabrics might be woven, suggesting another understanding for *marvadim*.

¹³ *"Linen and scarlet"* "Scarlet linen" would make much more sense, but that's not what the Hebrew has.

¹⁴ *"Gates"* City gates, where people would gather for commerce, judicial proceedings, and socializing.

¹⁵ *"Linen"* Another word for linen, *sadin*, is used here. As with so many other technical terms, we do not know exactly what *sadin* is. It may be a kind of cloth or a kind of clothing.

¹⁵ *"To sell"* Or "and sells it."

¹⁵ *"Ties"* Or "girdles." From the same root as "braces herself" (v. 8). We have no better English word, but the obvious connotations of "tie," such as "necktie," are obviously wrong.

¹⁵ *"Merchant"* Literally, "Canaanite." It is common to see a nationality used for something associated with it, and the Canaanites were associated with being merchants. We see a similar phenomenon in English with the breakfast food called "a Danish," which comes from "Danish pastry."

¹⁶ *"Smiles at the future"* One understanding of enigmatic Hebrew.

¹⁷ *"Kind teaching"* Literally, a *torah* of kindness; *torah* usually means "teaching" in the Bible.

¹⁸ *"Comings and goings"* Literally, "goings," translated by some as "activities."

²⁰ *"Worthy"* This is the same word, *chayil,* that we saw in verse 1.

²¹ *"Woman who fears Adonai is to be praised"* Or, more accurately but less poetically, "it is a woman who fears Adonai that is to be praised."

²² *"Gates"* Perhaps a reference to her husband (v. 14), who was put in the gates.

◆ ◆ ◆

E. *KIDDUSH* ("SANCTIFICATION")

DORFF (THEOLOGY)

rested from all the work God had created to do.

[5] With our masters' and teachers' approval:

[6] Blessed are You, Adonai our God, ruler of the world, creator of the fruit of the vine.

[7] Blessed are You, Adonai our God, ruler of the world, who sanctified us with his commandments and adored us, lovingly and adoringly granting us his holy Shabbat as our inheritance, in memory of acts of creation. [8] For it is the first day of holy festivals, a memorial of the Exodus from Egypt. [9] For You have chosen us and sanctified us above all nations, lovingly and adoringly granting us your holy Shabbat as our inheritance. [10] Blessed are You, Adonai, who sanctifies the Shabbat.

[At this point, it is traditional to wash one's hands, then say the Motsi, *the blessing over bread that*

introduces the meal. Following the meal, Birkat Hamazon *("Grace after Meals") is recited, along with*

additions appropriate to Shabbat.]

E. *KIDDUSH* ("SANCTIFICATION")

[1] There was evening and there was morning:

A sixth day. [2] Heaven and earth and everything associated with them were completed. [3] On the seventh day, God completed the work He had done. On the seventh day, He rested from all the work He had done. [4] God blessed the seventh day and sanctified it, for on it He rested from all the work God had created to do.

[5] With our masters' and teachers' approval:

[6] Blessed are You, Adonai our God, ruler of the world, creator of the fruit of the vine.

[7] Blessed are You, Adonai our God, ruler of the world, who sanctified us with his commandments and adored us, lovingly and adoringly granting us his holy Shabbat as our inheritance, in memory of acts of creation. [8] For it is the first day of holy festivals, a memorial of the Exodus from Egypt. [9] For You have chosen us and sanctified us above all nations, lovingly and adoringly granting us your holy Shabbat as our inheritance. [10] Blessed are You, Adonai, who sanctifies the Shabbat.

[At this point, it is traditional to wash one's hands, then say the Motsi, *the blessing over bread that introduces the meal. Following the meal, Birkat Hamazon ("Grace after Meals") is recited, along with additions appropriate to Shabbat.]*

ELLENSON (MODERN LITURGIES)

of the biblical narrative begins, "In the beginning of God's creation of heaven and earth...." Day seven begins, "The heaven and earth were finished," a perfect recapitulation of the way the story began.

2–3 *"Completed...completed...the work [m'lakhto]"* The use of *m'lakhto* indicates that creation is viewed as a *m'lakhah,* the kind of work prohibited on Shabbat (e.g., Exod. 20:10; 31:14–15; 35:2). Moreover, although verse 1 is in the passive voice ("The heaven and earth were finished"), verse 2 returns to the active form, telling us, "God finished on the seventh day"—implying that God continued to work into the early part of Shabbat. It is striking that the Samaritan Pentateuch, the Septuagint (ancient Greek translation) and the Peshitta (ancient Syriac translation) suggest a text that reads: "God finished on the *sixth* day," implying that God rested on the seventh because He was tired. The anonymous sixth-century prophet whom we call Second Isaiah polemicized against this view (Isa. 40:28): "Do you not know? Have you not heard? Adonai is God from of old, creator of the earth from end to end, He never grows faint or weary."

As for *vay'kaddesh,* God had "blessed" *(vay'varekh)* other elements on the fifth and sixth days of creation (Gen. 1:22, 28), but only the Shabbat is "sanctified" as its pinnacle. It is henceforth intrinsically holy as a commemoration of God's work as creator. That is why sanctions for Shabbat violations are so serious—the Jew who does "work" on Shabbat is implicitly denying the role of God in the "work of creation."

3 *"Seventh [sh'vi'i]"* This verse introduces alliterative word play that continues in the next verse also: *sh'vi'i* ("seventh"), *asah* ("did"), and *shavat* ("rested"). (The pronunciation of the Hebrew consonants *shin* [as in *sh'vi'i* and *shavat*] and *sin* [as in *asah*] were closer in antiquity than they are now.)

6 *"Blessed...fruit of the vine"* The standard formula for rabbinic blessings, based, in part, on late biblical texts (Ps. 119:12 and 1 Chron. 29:10). "Fruit of the vine" is post-biblical but derived from similar biblical precedent: "fruit of the tree" (e.g., Gen. 3:3) and "fruit of the earth" (e.g., Gen. 4:3), which are used in rabbinic blessings for fruit and vegetables, respectively.

Wine rather than water was the standard biblical beverage; it is mentioned close to two hundred times, and nine Hebrew words are used for wine or types of wine.

7 *"With his commandments"* The Bible never mentions the idea that God's commandments, generally, sanctify Israel. But, especially in the Holiness Collection, specific commandments (Lev. 19:2; 20:26) are coupled with the injunction that Israel should be holy. Israel's holiness is also connected explicitly to its observance of Shabbat (Exod. 31:13), "You must keep my Sabbaths [Hebrew *shabbatot* is plural]; this is a sign between Me and you throughout the ages, that you may know that I, Adonai, have consecrated you." Ezekiel adds (20:12), "Moreover, I gave them my Sabbaths to serve as a sign between Me and them, that they might know that it is I, Adonai, who sanctify them." In this case, the mention of "his commandments" anticipates the Shabbat in particular, which is the sign of God's "adoring" Israel, because the Shabbat, in existence since creation, was first revealed to Israel.

FRANKEL (A WOMAN'S VOICE)

our inheritance" here introduces a verbal frame that is concluded twenty-four words later with "granting us...as our inheritance" (v. 9).

[7] *"His holy Sabbath"* The holiness of Shabbat is regularly affirmed in the Bible (e.g., Gen. 2:3; Exod. 16:23; 20:8, 11; 31:13–15). The wording here comes from Nehemiah 9:14, "your holy Shabbat."

[7-8] *"In memory...a memorial"* Biblical texts describe Shabbat variously as connected to creation (Exod. 20:11), linked to the beginning of a festival calendar (Lev. 23:1–3),

GRAY (TALMUD)

that Israel, not God, must sanctify Shabbat is more frequent in the Bible (e.g., Jer. 17:22; Ezek. 20:20; Neh. 13:22). This a subtle but important difference: is Shabbat intrinsically holy from creation, or is it holy only when properly observed by Jews? God's sanctification of the Shabbat recollects God's sanctification of Israel (see above, "With his commandments"), thus uniting God, Israel, and Shabbat as a crucial theological threesome.

———◆———

DORFF (THEOLOGY)

[1] *"A sixth day"* This paragraph (Gen. 1:31–2:3) is omitted when *Kiddush* is chanted in the synagogue because the people there have already recited it as part of the evening *Amidah*. Because women and young children traditionally did not attend synagogue before Shabbat dinner, however, it entered home liturgy as a reminder of the *mitzvah* of sanctifying Shabbat.

This is the familiar account of creation, wherein God works six days to bring the universe into being and then rests on the seventh. Jews sometimes wonder, given what we now know scientifically, whether we really believe that the world was created that way. Their question is not new. For centuries Jews have interpreted the Genesis account to accord with the science of their time. Philo (first century, Alexandria) compared Genesis to Plato's account of creation *(Timaeus),* the scientific view of his time, but he made Plato fit Genesis. For example, like Plato, Philo maintains that an eternal God brought the world into existence, but in response to Plato's claim that God created the world out of pre-existent matter, Philo asserts that God created the pre-existent matter out of nothing. More than a thousand years later, Maimonides (twelfth century) interpreted Genesis to accord with Aristotle (*Metaphysics,* Book 12), the preferred science of that time. Reason, he argued, cannot tell us whether matter was created or was already pre-existent, but when reason fails, revelation settles the question (*Guide for the Perplexed,* part 2, chaps. 15, 21–25). Similarly, some modern Jews see Genesis affirming the big bang theory. It may also accord with evolution, because Genesis 1 does indeed describe a developmental process from plant to animal life and ultimately to human beings.

Other Jews observe that, understandably, the Bible reflects the science of its author's time, so it need not imply that biblical science should be ours as well. They don't look to the Bible for science, but for lessons on how to live. (This is similar to the philosophic is/ought distinction taught by David Hume [1711–1776] and Immanuel Kant [1724–1804]: science tells you what is; religion tells you what ought to be.) Every religion affirms our membership in its own group and what membership means in terms of ethical behavior. That is why the Latin root of the "lig" in the word "religion" means "a tie or bond": religions present broad pictures of how we are connected to our family, our local community, the larger human community, the environment, and the transcendent; each religion differentiates right from wrong, telling us what to eschew and what we should strive to become.

In this latter view, it makes no difference whether God actually created the world as described in Genesis. The point of the story is not science but morality, not what "is" but what "ought to be." As Rabbi Louis Jacobs put it, the Torah's "purpose is to teach men the way to go to heaven, not the way the heavens go" (*We Have Reason to Believe* [London: Vallentine, Mitchell, 1957], p. 83).

Rabbi Mordecai M. Kaplan thought God's creative role in the creation tale teaches "that creativity, or the continuous emergence of aspects of life not prepared for or determined by the past, constitutes the most divine phase of reality" (Mordecai M. Kaplan, *The Meaning of God in Modern Jewish Religion* [New York: Jewish Reconstructionist Press, 1937], pp. 59ff.). Accordingly, we should work hard to realize the potential of our world. But simultaneously, it reminds us not to turn work into an idol; rather, we desist from it one day in seven. We can then step back from our work, as artists do from their canvas, to see our life in context and make corrective changes in the week to come. Shabbat frees us from the compulsion to work so that we can devote ourselves to family, community, and God.

[7] *"Lovingly and adoringly"* We experience Shabbat not as a burden occasioned by

Shabbat regulations, but as God's loving gift in which the very rules of Shabbat are what enable us to create it. Rabbi Abraham Joshua Heschel *(The Sabbath)* describes Shabbat as a palace in time; its regulations are the moat that protects it from encroachment by weekday concerns. It is a gift filled with God's love and good will.

7–8 *"A memory…a memorial"* The two versions of the Decalogue (Exod. 20:11; Deut. 5:15) disagree on the rationale for Shabbat. According to one, it goes back to God's resting at the end of creation. For the other, it is a reminder of our slavery in Egypt and the Exodus that freed us. The *Kiddush* includes both of them. God desisted from work on creation's seventh day. As slaves liberated from Egyptian bondage, we should rest also, rather than enslave ourselves anew.

7 *"Granting us his holy Shabbat"* Shabbat is not required of, nor given to, non-Jews. This theme appears also in the *Kiddush* before Shabbat lunch (see *Kiddusha Rabbah,* pp. 155–164).

8 *"The first day of holy festivals"* But Shabbat is not first among the holy festivals in the order of the Torah. True, Genesis 2 says God rested on the seventh day, but our obligation to do so comes only with Exodus 16:4–5, 22–27, when we hear that the Israelites will have a double portion of manna on Friday (to cover Saturday as well), because the seventh day "is a Sabbath for the Lord" on which no manna will fall, and that is only for the generation of the desert. Not until the Decalogue (Exod. 20:8–11) are Jews of all generations commanded to observe Shabbat. By contrast, Passover is commanded for all time as a recollection of the Exodus eight chapters back: Exodus 12:14–20. Shabbat is also not preeminent among all holy days in its degree of holiness; that honor goes to Yom Kippur, the Day of Atonement, which the Torah calls "the Sabbath of Sabbaths" (Lev. 23:32).

How, then, is Shabbat "the first day of holy festivals" that recalls "the Exodus from Egypt"? Perhaps the liturgical writer was thinking of God's creation of the world, even though no commandment for us to rest follows from it. But still, that account is hardly a recollection of the Exodus from Egypt. Or perhaps Shabbat is first among holy days because the list of holidays in Leviticus 23 mentions it first; or because of all the holy days, only Shabbat occurs weekly; or because, theologically speaking, Shabbat affirms God's ownership of the world (including ourselves) and the necessity for us to submit to the divine owner's command that we desist from work—a relationship between us and God that undergirds the other holy days also.

10 *"Who sanctifies the Shabbat"* God sanctifies Shabbat but we recite *Kiddush,* thus playing a role in that sanctification ourselves. Our action follows from the Torah's commands to "remember" and to "observe" the Sabbath day "to make it holy" (Exod. 20:8 and Deut. 5:12). Again (see pp. 42, 44) we see a partnership between God and ourselves, whereby both parties play crucial roles. God sanctifies Shabbat, but so do we.

ELLENSON (MODERN LITURGIES)

Kiddush ("Sanctification") As a central element in the synagogue service, not just the home ceremony for Shabbat eve, the Friday evening *Kiddush* is a staple in virtually all nineteenth-century Reform prayer books. It is found in both the 1819 and the 1841 editions of the *Hamburg Temple Prayer Books* as well as in the 1854 and 1870 prayer books of Abraham Geiger. Isaac Mayer Wise also included the traditional *Kiddush* in his *Minhag America.* David Einhorn, therefore, stands alone among early Reform liturgists when he decided to omit the text for Friday Night *Kiddush* from his *Olath Tamid* (though he probably assumed people would say it at home anyway).

The *Union Prayer Book* has vacillated in its approach to *Kiddush,* though it should be remembered that at issue is not *Kiddush* at home, but whether to include *Kiddush* as a component of the Shabbat eve service, a decision that may have depended on the timing and nature of the service in question. The 1895 edition of the *UPB* included the *Kiddush* text, but the synagogue service for Friday night was still being held at the traditional time—at nightfall—and the *Kiddush* had been a standard part of that traditional service for centuries, explained (usually) as a *Kiddush* to inaugurate Shabbat for visitors being billeted at the synagogue overnight. In 1895, of course, overnight wayfarers had ceased, but there was no ideological reason to stop using the traditional *Kiddush* to introduce Shabbat in the synagogue.

By 1921, however, the traditional Friday service at sundown had largely been replaced with a late Friday service, after dinner at home, in which case synagogue candle lighting would have had to take place well after nightfall, and by people who probably had made *Kiddush* at home already. So the 1921 edition of the *UPB* followed the example established by Einhorn and purged the text for *Kiddush* from its pages. But the 1940 edition of the *UPB* restored the *Kiddush* text, even for the late service, possibly because it was no longer certain that most people were making *Kiddush* at home. Eventually, that practice became standard even as home ritual increased, so all subsequent *UPB* editions have included *Kiddush,* without regard to what transpires earlier in Reform Jewish homes.

In keeping with its theological commitment to transfer "the activity of sanctification from the realm of the divine into human hands," *The Book of Blessings* offers a completely new text for the Friday night as well as the Saturday afternoon *Kiddush.* The new text that is used on both occasions reads, "Let us bless the source of life that ripens fruit on the vine as we hallow the Sabbath day in remembrance of creation, for the Sabbath is the first among holy days, recalling the Exodus and the covenant."

[9] *"You have chosen us"* As we have seen throughout the previous volumes in this series, the authors of liberal prayer books have struggled throughout the past two

KUSHNER & POLEN (CHASIDISM)

particularly outspoken in his opposition to the doctrine of chosenness. In his 1945 Reconstructionist prayer book, in lieu of "You have chosen us," he substituted the phrase "For you have drawn us near to your service," a corrective, as he put it, to "the chauvinism and triumphalism" that the traditional phraseology "has often sheltered." The most recent manifestation of Reconstructionist liturgy, *Kol Haneshamah,* opts for the phrase "For you have called to us" as its own attempt to deal with what is construed as the problematic element in this prayer. In so doing, this version, in the words of the commentary found in *Kol Haneshamah,* "imagines a God who calls all humanity and makes holy those who, like Israel, heed the call and engage in God's service."

——◆——

FRANKEL (A WOMAN'S VOICE)

Kiddush ("Sanctification") Although Jews borrowed the idea of using wine in their sacred rituals from their pagan neighbors, they radically altered its symbolic meaning by hallowing its use with a blessing. *Kiddush,* which literally means "separate," "sanctified," or "consecrated," serves as a protective shield around the intoxicant it sanctions, focusing us more on its potential for holiness than on its sweetness or potency. *Kiddush* turns the wine into an agent of memory rather than of forgetfulness, recalling to mind the two creation stories that have shaped us: *ma'aseh b'reishit* (pronounced mah-ah-SEH b'-ray-SHEET), "the acts of creation," and *y'tsi'at mitsrayim* (pronounced y'-tsee-AHT meetz-RAH-yeem), "the Exodus from Egypt." Significantly, we do not memorialize in our blessing over the wine another creation story, the covenant after the Flood, which Noah celebrated by planting a vineyard and getting drunk. Noah's *Kiddush* is not what the Sabbath and Judaism are supposed to be about.

——◆——

GRAY (TALMUD)

[1] *"There was evening and there was morning: a sixth day"* We extract just these final words from Genesis 1:31 instead of reading the verse in its entirety: "And God saw all that He had made, and found it very good. There was evening and there was morning: a sixth day." The Chatam Sofer (Moses Sofer, 1762–1839) held that the original point was to juxtapose *Yom Hashishi* (the last two Hebrew words of Genesis 1:31) with *Vay'khulu Hashamayim* (the two opening words of the next verse, Genesis 2:1) because their combined initials form the ineffable name of God (YHVH). Because, however, these last two words alone (*yom hashishi* = "…a sixth day") are devoid of meaning, the words preceding them (*vay'hi erev vay'hi voker* = "There was evening and there was morning…") were included as well. Nonetheless, we avoid reciting the entire verse aloud because the Midrash (Gen. Rab. 9:4) sees in this verse the implication that the completion of

LANDES (HALAKHAH)

the *heh* of "the" sixth day as a reference to the sixth day of the month of Sivan, the day Israel accepted the Torah at Sinai.

[2] "*Were completed* [vay'khulu]" Maimonides ("Shabbat" 29:7) calls the recitation of Genesis 1:31 and 2:1–3 a "widespread custom." The *Maggid Mishneh* (Vidal Yom Tov of Tolosa, fourteenth century) locates its origin in the Talmud (Shab. 119b), which mandates Genesis 2:1–3 even for a person praying alone, who thereby becomes "like a partner with the Holy Blessed One in the work of creation." This lesson is derived by revocalizing the passive voice *vay'khulu* ("were completed") to the active voice *vay'khalu* ("they completed"). The plural "they" must mean God and us when we recite Genesis 2:1–3. Our act of uttering these words of praise makes us a partner because, legally and materially, words can be effective acts, as taught by Psalm 33:6: "By Adonai's word the heavens were made" (Shab. 119b).

Shabbat 119b also pictures the two angels who accompany a person home from synagogue placing their hands on the head of anyone who recites Genesis 2:1–3 and reciting the angelic declaration to the prophet Isaiah (Isa. 6:7): "Your sins are turned away, and your iniquity is forgiven."

[3] "*God completed the work He had done*" It sounds as if on the seventh day all God's work was already done. Torah commentator *Or Hachayim* (Chayim ibn Attar, eighteenth century, Morocco) explains that when Shabbat arrived, the newly created world was still in a weak and volatile state; so God set it on firmer footing by creating the "soul" of the world. Exodus 31:17, therefore, says, *"shavat vayinafash"* (God "ceased from work and rested," or, literally, "souled," because the root of *vayinafash* is *nefesh,* meaning "soul"). So while the world received its physical properties during the first six days, its soul or spiritual dimension arrived on the seventh.

But if so, how do we explain the creation of human beings "in the image of God" (Gen. 1:27) on the sixth day? Doesn't that imply the creation of a spiritual dimension earlier—especially because the Talmud (San. 91b) understands that a person's soul arrives even before birth? We may answer with a resounding yes. Human beings were indeed provided with a soul earlier, but the universe was not ready to receive them in their full spiritual dimension, nor be a fit environment for human activity, until it too had a soul. That is why humans are created in Genesis 1:27 but do not encounter the divine until well into chapter 2. Only after the world got its own soul on Shabbat could human history properly begin.

[3–4] "[*Which*] *He had done…*[*which*] *He had done…*[*which*] *God had created to do* [asher]" *Hagahot Maimuniyot* (R. Meir of Rothenburg, thirteenth–fourteenth centuries) cites a midrash according to which a person must recite Genesis 2:1–3 three times every Shabbat: in the Friday night *Amidah;* in the prayer immediately afterward (called *Magen Avot,* pronounced mah-GAYN ah-VOHT; see forthcoming Volume 8, *Shabbat in the Synagogue*); and at home before *Kiddush.* This threefold obligation is derived from the three mentions of *asher* ("which") in these Torah verses.

[4] *"God blessed the seventh day and sanctified it"* Genesis Rabbah 11:2 explains that God "blessed" Shabbat with manna (an extra portion fell on Fridays) and "sanctified" it with manna (in that none fell on Shabbat itself). God's determination not to send manna on Shabbat, moreover, shows God to be Sabbath observant. Genesis 2:1–3 apparently commands Shabbat not just for us but for God as well.

[4] *"And sanctified it"* God's own sanctification of the seventh day is background for Israel's obligation (Exod. 20:8) to "remember the Sabbath day to sanctify it." Shabbat requires both divine and human sanctification. This divine-human relationship underlies the talmudic dictum that reciting this preamble to the *Kiddush* (Gen. 1:31; 2:1–3) makes us partners with God in the work of creation (Shab. 119b).

[5] *"With our masters' and teachers' approval"* This short address goes unmentioned in both Talmuds and in Maimonides' version of the *Kiddush* ("Shabbat" 29:2). Later, David Abudarham (fourteenth century, Spain) offers several explanations for its inclusion, one of which he marks as "correct." Berakhot 43a rules that if wine is served to a table of diners during the meal, each diner should make the appropriate blessing him or herself, because people in the midst of chewing and swallowing might choke if they had to answer "Amen" to someone else's blessing. Here, however, no one is yet eating, so one person can make the blessing for everyone else, who can safely respond, "Amen." This opening invitation to join in the blessing is taken to mean, "Teachers and masters, do you intend to listen to my blessing with the intention of fulfilling your obligation through my recitation?" When they answer affirmatively (Sefardim even respond, *"L'chayim!"*), the reciter proceeds with the blessing over the wine.

[6] *"Creator of the fruit of the vine"* The standard blessing for wine, possibly dating to the third century (M. Ber. 6:1). It is said prior to the *Kiddush* in accordance with the teaching of Bet Hillel (M. Ber. 8:1; Ber. 51b), who reasoned (1) without wine, there would be no *Kiddush* (this particular view is ultimately not normative, as *Kiddush* may be recited over bread); and (2) the blessing over wine (recited whenever wine is drunk) is more common than *Kiddush* (which is recited only once a week). The Talmud rules (Ber. 27a, 51b), "[When faced with a choice between first doing] a frequent thing or an infrequent thing, the frequent thing takes precedence [*tadir v'she'eino tadir, tadir kodem*]." The Talmud rejects Bet Shammai's competing view: that *Kiddush* should be recited before the blessing over the wine.

[6] *"Fruit of the vine"* The Talmud expressly links the sanctification of Shabbat with wine by teaching that *zakhor*, "Remember [the Sabbath day to sanctify it]" (Exod. 20:8) means to "remember" it with wine (Pes. 106a). The Tosafot (eleventh–thirteenth centuries) and Abudarham (fourteenth century) find the link between "remembering" and wine in Hosea 14:8 ("Remember Lebanon like wine") and Song of Songs 1:4 ("Your love is more memorable than wine").

Wine is particularly suited for the Shabbat and holiday *Kiddush* because it is singled out in both the Bible and the Talmud as gladdening the hearts of human beings (Judg. 9:13; Ps. 104:15; Ber. 35a).

[7] *"Blessed…who sanctified us…"* (the Kiddush) The Talmud (Ber. 33a) ascribes the institution of "blessings, prayers, sanctifications [*kiddushot*] and separations [*havdalot*]" to the legendary Men of the Great Assembly, probably an attempt to give their own institution of *Kiddush* a noble and ancient pedigree.

[7] *"In memory of acts of creation"* An allusion to the first of Torah's two rationales for the observance of Shabbat—remembering creation (Exod. 20:11): "In six days Adonai made heaven and earth and sea, and all that is in them, and He rested on the seventh day; therefore Adonai blessed the Sabbath day and hallowed it."

[8] *"For it [Shabbat] is the first day of holy festivals"* Holiday dates vary because they are counted from the first day of the lunar month, and lunar months (the time it takes for the moon to go around the earth) are somewhere between twenty-nine and thirty days, making the new month either the thirtieth or the thirty-first day after the old lunar month began. Nowadays we use a mathematical computation, but originally the New Moon was determined by eyewitness testimony before the Sanhedrin (the court), so that festival dates were set, literally, by Israel (Exod. 12:1; M. R.H. 1:3–9; 2; 3:1; R.H. 18a–26a; Beitzah 4b–5a). By contrast, Shabbat, which falls every seventh day regardless of the lunar calendar, is determined solely by God (compare Rambam, *Kiddush Ha-Hodesh* 1:5).

Rashi thus questions Shabbat and holidays both being classified as God's "holy festivals" (Lev. 23: 2–4). Aren't they different in type? He answers with a midrash regarding the juxtaposition of Shabbat and holidays in Leviticus 23. They go together because desecrating or honoring festivals is tantamount to desecrating or honoring Shabbat. Alternatively, we may understand Shabbat as the first period of time that God sanctified. Although still not a festival, strictly speaking, it is the first instance of sacred time, a concept later transferred to the proclamation of the Festivals.

[8] *"Memorial of the Exodus from Egypt"* An allusion to Torah's second rationale for observing Shabbat—remembering the Exodus (Deut. 5:15): "Remember that you were a slave in the land of Egypt and Adonai your God freed you from there with a mighty hand and an outstretched arm; therefore Adonai your God has commanded you to observe the Sabbath day."

[9] *"You have chosen us"* The Shabbat *Kiddush* first acknowledges Israel's sanctification ("who sanctified us with his commandments" [v. 7]) and then its chosenness ("and adored us" [v. 7]). That order, says Abudarham (fourteenth century, Spain), follows the historical record as given in the Talmud (San. 56b): Shabbat was one of three commandments given to Israel at Marah (Exod. 15:25); the others were the purification rite of the red heifer (Num. 19:2–22) and, in general, rules regarding courts of justice. Only later, at Sinai (Exod. 19:5), was Israel chosen as God's "treasure." But Israel received commandments about the Festivals after its election (Lev. 23:4), so the holiday

Kiddush reverses the order, citing Israel's election before mentioning its sanctification through commandments.

—◆—

KUSHNER & POLEN (CHASIDISM)

[2] *"Heaven and earth...were completed"* When chanted at home, the *Kiddush* is preceded by the first three verses of Genesis 2. They are known by their first word as the *vay'khulu* ("[heaven and earth...] were completed..."). Jewish tradition explains why these three verses are included where they are (that is, at the end of Genesis 1, which details the first six days of creation). The Sabbath, goes Jewish logic, is not another story but an integral part of the creation.

There is an additional custom of prefacing the *vay'khulu* (Gen. 2:1–3) with the final six words of the preceding chapter, *vay'hi erev vay'hi voker, yom hashishi*, "and there was evening and there was morning, the sixth day." Although such an addition certainly joins the days of creation with the Sabbath, it also serves a more mystical purpose. The first two words of Genesis 2, *vay'khulu hashamayim*, "and the heavens were finished..." begin, respectively, with the Hebrew letters *vav* and *heh*. By appending the last two words of Genesis 1, *yom hashishi*, "the sixth day," we add two words whose first letters are, respectively, *yod* and *heh*. Now we have *yod* and *heh* followed by *vav* and *heh*, the tetragrammaton, the awesome, four-letter *shem ham'forash*, the ineffable name of God. By joining the work of creation with Sabbath rest, we also reunify the letters of the divine name—hopefully making it and ourselves whole once again.

We also have a tradition from Talmud, Shabbat 119b, that deliberately misreads the word *vay'khulu*. Instead of pronouncing the biblical text (which, of course, is not vocalized and thus permits such variations) *vay'khulu*, "and they [the heavens and the earth] were completed," in the *passive* voice, we can also read it as *vay'khalu*, "and they [God and humanity] completed." In this way, just as we have been partners in creation, so do we now become partners in saying *vay'khalu*, "Whew! We're done with our world-work!"

There is a tradition that, while chanting *Kiddush*, one should focus his or her gaze on the Sabbath candles. According to the Talmud (Ber. 43b; Shab. 113a), when we run around doing our work during the week, every step takes 1/500th of the light of the eyes or, perhaps, of our mental acuity. But, by gazing at the candles during the recitation of *Kiddush*, our vision, our alertness, our vital energy are renewed and restored.

"Handwashing...meals" The Chasidim are fond of citing the verse in Exodus 24:11 describing God's encounter with Moses, Aaron, and the seventy elders: "And they saw God, and they ate and drank," as an indication of the liturgical potential of eating. Not only does the matter (of food) literally become energy, but the Jew who consumes it in holiness effectively frees the holy sparks contained within it. Eating thus becomes a sacred act.

According to Chasidic tradition, the Sabbath table thus becomes more than the mere locus of a meal; it is transformed into an altar evoking the sacrificial altar in the

Temple of old. And each Jew therefore becomes a priest performing a sacred ritual. It is not unlike a tea ceremony. Before the Jew are a series of ritual objects, each requiring its own sequence of gestures, melodies, and (for Jews, of course) words. Thus the *challah* is salted in accordance with the verse in Leviticus 2:13, "You shall season your every offering of meal with salt…." Ezekiel 41:22 speaks of being shown "an altar of wood, three cubits high," which his guide identified as "the table that is before Adonai."

Berakhot 55a notes that the verse opens with "altar" and finishes with "table." Rabbi Yochanan and Rabbi Eleazar both explain that as long as the Temple stood, the altar atoned for Israel, but now our table atones for us" (cf. Chag. 27a).

◆

LANDES (HALAKHAH)

Kiddush ("Sanctification") This *Kiddush* for Friday night is said not only at home but also in synagogue, for the benefit of travelers spending Shabbat as guests in town (Pes. 101a). By the geonic period, guests staying overnight in the synagogue were uncommon, so Hai Gaon forbade the synagogue recital of *Kiddush,* based on the principle *ein kiddush ela bim'kom s'udah,* "there can be no *Kiddush* without an accompanying meal." Earlier, however, Natronai Gaon had permitted the practice not only for out-of-town guests, but also for local inhabitants who might not be able to afford wine and who would have to make their home *Kiddush* without it (it can be recited, if need be, over bread). The Rashba (Solomon ben Abraham Aderet, 1235–1310, Barcelona, Responsa 37, 323) likened the twofold recitation of *Kiddush* to our repetition of the *Amidah,* instituted for the benefit of illiterate people who might not be able to say a private version. Although illiteracy has largely ended, we retain the reader's repetition; similarly, we say *Kiddush* in synagogue regardless of whether guests are actually present.

Supporting the decision is the fact that the requirement to recite *Kiddush* as Shabbat commences is *mid'ora'ita,* "from the Torah" itself, while the requirement of an accompanying meal is only *mid'rabbanan* "by rabbinic enactment," and thus secondary. A synagogue *Kiddush* is therefore permitted (though not mandated).

In the Land of Israel, and especially in Jerusalem, the synagogue *Kiddush* is omitted. Most Ashkenazi communities in the diaspora say it and drink wine with it, although some give the wine to underage children—a practice frowned upon by the Rashba, for if wine is permitted, an adult should drink it, and if it is forbidden, a child should not drink it, because doing so constitutes a negative education.

Today, *minhag hamakom* (pronounced min-HAHG hah-mah-KOHM or, commonly, MIN-hahg hah-mah-KOHM), "the usual custom of the community," is decisive. If there is no usual custom, logic would dictate that where there are no guests, *Kiddush* should be omitted. But if it is likely that some people who come to services may not know how to make *Kiddush* at home, saying it in synagogue may be continued.

Whatever we decide for the synagogue, the home *Kiddush* is primary. It alone properly fulfills the obligation to "remember Shabbat by sanctifying it." So even someone who has said *Kiddush* at synagogue is expected to say it again at home, at the very least for the household. The principle we saw above ("there can be no *Kiddush* without an accompanying meal") was created with this *Kiddush* in mind (Rashbam, R. Samuel ben Meir, 1080–c. 1158, France, Pes. 101a).

Accordingly, from *Kiddush* one moves directly into the meal. Undue delay vitiates the full meaning of the *Kiddush* as announcing Shabbat at the beginning of the Shabbat meal. The following rules for *Kiddush* apply:

L. HOFFMAN (HISTORY)

4. There are three customs regarding posture during *Kiddush:*

   a. Stand during the introductory verses of Genesis (from "Heaven and earth" to "created to do," *Vay'khulu...la'asot*), for this testifies to God's creation of the world (Shab. 11a), and testimony is delivered standing. Then sit, starting with *Barukh...borei p'ri hagafen* ("Blessed"..."fruit of the vine"), as all blessings of enjoyment are preferably recited sitting (Gra).

   b. Sit during the entire *Kiddush,* for it is one unit (R'ma, O. Ch. 271).

   c. Following the Ari, stand during the entire *Kiddush,* for Shabbat is likened mystically to a bride, whose blessings under the *chuppah* (wedding canopy) are said standing *(Siddur Hash'lah).*

5. Given these alternatives, one should follow one's own family *minhag* ("custom"), but the following should be done:

   a. Everyone should drink from the cup while sitting, for drinking establishes intent to "establish a meal" (*kove'a s'udah,* pronounced koh-VAY-ah s'-oo'DAH). The idea here is that the Shabbat meal is not a cocktail party, where one "nibbles and sips." It is a formal sit-down meal.

   b. The one making *Kiddush* (*ham'kadesh,* pronounced hah-m'-kah-DESH but, commonly, hah-m'-KAH-desh) should drink *k'malei lugmav* (almost a cheekful of wine). If this is impossible, someone else should quickly drink from the cup, making up that amount.

6. Everyone around the table should assume the stance of the one making *Kiddush.* Stand when he or she does, and sit when he or she sits.

7. Generally, one person makes *Kiddush* for everyone present, because "in the multitudes is praise for God" (the talmudic understanding of Prov. 14:28). If others want to join in or say *Kiddush* separately, they need their own full cup of wine.

8. Men and women are equally commanded to make *Kiddush.* Normally, one spouse lights candles and the other makes *Kiddush,* on a regular basis. When there is only one leading family member, he or she can certainly do both. As an "adult" activity, *Kiddush* should not be made by underage children, although, for

educational purposes, children may make their own *Kiddush,* in full or in part.

Our halakhic description for the entire table liturgy assumes a family and/or friendship circle that celebrates Shabbat. Because many have no access to such circles, those who do must fulfill the *mitzvah* of "welcoming guests" (*hachnasat orchim,* pronounced hahkh-nah-SAHT ohr-KHEEM)—not just social friends, but those who are alone, for whatever reason. It is crucial for communities and synagogues to create *hachnasat orchim* committees to provide Shabbat homes for singles, widows, the elderly, and others.

[1] *"A sixth day"* This is the end of an entire verse that reads, "Adonai saw all that He had made and it was very good [*tov m'od*]. And there was evening and there was morning: a sixth day." According to tradition, the original custom was to recite the entire verse.

The first part—up to and including "it was very good"—was dropped, because the Midrash identifies "very good" with death—a notion that our finitude itself is a blessing to be accepted from the infinite One who bestowed it upon us, but it is an association that ill befits the joy of *Kiddush.*

Still, the two Hebrew words for "a sixth day" *(yom hashishi)* were retained, because their initials (Y,H) along with those of *vay'khulu hashamayim,* the two words following (V,H), spell out the four-letter name of God. Later, the custom grew to introduce all this with the half-sentence *Vay'hi erev vay'hi voker* ("And there was evening and there was morning") said softly. The change provided the full sentence to which *yom hashishi* belongs and demonstrates that it is not part of the following verse, *Vay'khulu* (Chatam Sofer, Moses Sofer [Schreiber], 1762–1839, Pressburg, Hungary, O. Ch. 10).

[2] *"Heaven and earth…were completed* [Vay'khulu]" This recitation of Genesis 2:1–3 is recognized by Maimonides as "a custom spread throughout all of Israel" ("Shabbat" 29:7), based on the talmudic statement of Rav Hamnuna: "Whoever prays on Shabbat eve and says *vay'khulu* is accounted by Scripture as having become a partner to the Holy One in the act of creation" (Shab. 119b). Some will have said it already in the evening *Amidah* at synagogue, but saying it now allows others also to become divine partners.

[5] *"With our masters' and teachers' approval"* A phrase included to get the full attention of all present. It cannot be an actual request for permission, however, because making *Kiddush* is an obligation upon all present and requires no permission (*Shibolei Haleket,* Zedekiah ben Avraham Hafofei, thirteenth century, Italy, quoting Hai Gaon. See also *Bet Yosef,* Joseph Caro [1488–1575], Safed, O. Ch. 167).

Prisoners about to be executed were once given strong wine laced with saffron, a very intoxicating mixture. The custom arose, therefore, to follow "With our masters' and teachers' approval" with a joyous *"L'Chayim"* (generally pronounced l'-KHAH-yim, "To life"), as if to say, "This cup is for life, not death, for blessing, not a curse" (*Kolbo,* unknown, end of thirteenth century, beginning of fourteenth century,

Ashkenaz).

[6] *"Creator of the fruit of the vine"* According to Bet Shammai, the only real reason to drink wine is that we are about to make *Kiddush,* which logically presupposes the presence of wine (and its blessing). The blessing would therefore be said after *Kiddush.* But we follow Bet Hillel, who maintained that in actual fact, at this very moment, the presence of wine provides the opportunity to make *Kiddush.* Therefore, the blessing on wine comes first.

The halakhic rules regarding *Kiddush* are as follows:

1. One should make *Kiddush* over wine (Pes. 106a), but if there is no wine, or if one has a greater desire for bread, one ritually washes one's hands, says the *Motsi* (blessing over bread), recites the whole *Kiddush,* slices the bread, and eats from it.

2. The wine we use for *Kiddush* should meet the high standard once required for the Temple wine libations *(nissukh hayayin).* It should be pure, without additions that make it sweeter or drier (B.B. 97a); if necessary, wine with additives is allowed, as long as it still smells and tastes pleasant (PT Pes. 10:1).

3. Red wine is superior to white; some authorities (such as Ramban) actually forbid white wine. But if the available white wine is better, it should be used in place of the more inferior red (*Shulchan Arukh,* O. Ch. 272:4; *Mishnah B'rurah,* n. 10).

4. The wine must be kosher, preferably from Eretz Yisrael.

5. Because the *Kiddush* cup must be worthy of having a blessing made over it *(kos shera'u'i liv'rakhah),* it should not be disposable, unless no others are available; it should sit on a plate; and it should be fully clean inside and out (Ber. 51b; Maimonides, "Blessings" 7:15; *Shulchan Arukh,* O. Ch. 183). The cup should contain at least ninety fluid grams (a *r'vi'it,* pronounced r'-vee-EET) and be poured to the top but not overflowing.

6. The wine cup is lifted at least one hand-width high, following Psalm 116:13, "I raise the cup of deliverance and invoke the name of Adonai." It is raised with the right hand (traditionally considered more important) only, not two hands, lest it look like a burden. Some raise it with a single hand, but hold it from below, so that one's fingers encircle it from below like a petal.

7. Halakhically, wine with an alcoholic content is preferred. But nonalcoholic grape juice has long been permitted for children, the old, and the ill. Today, with the acknowledgment of alcoholism as a serious disease, there is no question that grape juice would be permitted. Further, grape juice should be present as a matter of course when guests come, so that no one will have to ask for it and feel uneasy about attention being drawn to his or her choice. If it seems likely that such embarrassment might ensue, the person making *Kiddush* should use grape juice.

8. If other bottles of wine are opened during the Shabbat meal, and if that wine is different and arguably better, then the benediction *Hatov v'hameitiv* ("Blessed is God…who is good and does good") may be expressed to recognize thanks for our

ever-increasing blessings from God. But under no circumstance can Shabbat dinner become an occasion of inebriation.

[8] *"A memorial of the Exodus from Egypt"* From Pesachim 117b: "We are obliged to remember the Exodus from Egypt during the *Kiddush* for it is written in Deuteronomy 16:3, 'Remember the day of your departure from the land of Egypt' and in Exodus 20:8, 'Remember the Sabbath day and sanctify it.'" Exodus and creation intertwine in our observance of Shabbat.

Nachmanides worried that we may come to doubt God's act of creation. If so, we are to "remember what your eyes saw at the Exodus" which is "evidence" of God's work at creation, for Shabbat testifies to "an eternal God, who, being all-powerful, created everything according to his will" (Nachmanides, Moshe ben Nachman, 1194–1270, Gerona, Spain, on Deut. 5:15).

[9] *"You have chosen us"* Unlike *Kiddush* for holidays, the Shabbat version omits the phrase "who has chosen us" *(asher bachar banu),* because the *mitzvah* of Shabbat was given at Mara (San. 56b, on Exod. 16:29), and only later, at Sinai, were we chosen as God's people (Abudarham). But on Shabbat (though not on holidays) we say *b'ahavah uv'ratson* ("lovingly and adoringly")—using the word *ratson,* which means not only "adoringly" but also "willingly"—to imply free will, for, according to the Talmud (Shab. 88a), we accepted Torah at Sinai under compulsion: "They stood at the foot of [literally, "underneath"] the mountain" (Exod. 19:17). This teaches us that God suspended the mountain over them as a tub, saying: "If you accept my Torah, good! If not, then this shall be your burial place!" At Mara, however, we accepted Shabbat freely (*Ramban L'am* [ed. Mordecai Leib Sacks, mid-twentieth century, Jerusalem] to Maimonides, "Shabbat" 29:2).

[10] *"Who sanctifies the Shabbat"* Upon finishing *Kiddush,* everyone says "Amen," while sitting. When the *m'kadesh* (the person reciting *Kiddush*) has commenced sipping, all others may do so too. Alternatively, people wait until wine is poured into their own glass from the *Kiddush* cup, either by the *m'kadesh* or by passing the cup around.

The holiday *Kiddush* ends with "who sanctifies Israel and the times of year." Here, on Shabbat, we say only, "who sanctifies the Shabbat," not what would be a parallel form to the holidays, "who sanctifies Israel and the Shabbat." That is because "Shabbat preceded Israel" (*Massechet Sofrim* 13).

On Shabbat, we use two loaves of bread called *challot* (pronounced khah-LOHT; sing. *challah,* pronounced khah-LAH or, commonly, KHAH-lah). Before eating bread at any time, we say a blessing called *Hamotsi* (commonly pronounced ha-MOH-tsee). Also, the *challot* of Shabbat symbolize the manna that fell from heaven when the Israelites were wandering through the desert. On Shabbat, *Hamotsi* follows *Kiddush,* and during *Kiddush,* it is customary to keep the *challot* covered, because when the manna fell, it was covered with protective dew (Exod. 16:14–15, 31; Num. 11:9; *Or Zarua* 22, by R. Isaac ben Moses Riaz, end of twelfth and first half of thirteenth century, Vienna; *Shibolei Haleket,* by Zedekiah ben Avraham Harofei, thirteenth century, Italy).

Additionally, the bread is covered so that it does not "see its shame" in that it is omitted for *Kiddush* (*Tur,* O. Ch. 271).

"Handwashing followed by the Motsi" For all three Shabbat meals, two loaves of bread are required, as a recollection of *lechem mishneh* (pronounced LEH-khem MISH-neh), the "double bread" (the double portion of manna) that fell on Fridays to last through Shabbat (Exod. 16:22; Shab. 117b; *Mekhilta B'shalach* says expressly *lechem kaful,* "double [portion of] bread").

The Talmud (Shab. 117b) records a debate as to how the *challot* should be eaten. Rabbi Abba said a blessing over both loaves, no matter how much he might eat, to recall the "double portion." Rav Kahana said a blessing over two loaves, holding them both in his hand, but sliced only one, so as not to appear ravenous. Rabbi Zeira said a blessing over a large chunk, big enough to last a whole meal, to show how much he relished eating a Shabbat meal.

Hai Gaon permits any of these customs. The Maharshal (Solomon Luria, 1510–1573, Poland) ate from one loaf on Friday night and two the next day, to indicate the greater honor due the holiness of the day. The *Tur* and the *Shulchan Arukh* (O. Ch. 274) advocate slicing only one loaf (like Rav Kahana), but eating as much of it as desired (like Rabbi Zeira). In a celebrated incident, the Gra (the Vilna Gaon, Elijah of Vilna, 1720–1797) sliced all the loaves placed before him (twelve in all) even though they were there only symbolically (as in the custom of the Ari, who used one loaf for each tribe of Israel), saying that he had said a blessing over all of them and therefore needed to cut bread from them all.

———◆———

L. HOFFMAN (HISTORY)

[1-4] *"There was evening…. A sixth day. Heaven and earth…were completed… had created to do"* Genesis 1:31 ("There was evening…a sixth day") and the very next biblical verses, Genesis 2:1–3 ("Heaven and earth..had created to do") are numbered liturgically here as

J. HOFFMAN (TRANSLATION)

only in fragments cited by people such as Eleazer himself, so there is no way to check his reference. But *Vay'khulu* was compiled only in the eleventh century, about one hundred years before Maimonides and Eleazer lived, so it is possible, and even likely, that Eleazer read the midrash and saw the custom there.

Eleazer further claims that according to *Vay'khulu,* these three verses had been mandated earlier by Rava, a famous fourth-century authority in the Babylonian Talmud. But our version of the Talmud never represents Rava as saying anything about it. It is therefore unlikely that the verses were added that early.

Because (1) the earliest people certain to have said these verses, Maimonides (in Egypt) and Eleazer (in Germany), both lived in the twelfth century; and because (2) the midrash said to have been the source of the custom came into being only a hundred years before; and, finally, because (3) Maimonides calls it only a "popular *custom*" (not a necessary part of the prayers), it is likely that the verses were still a relatively new innovation, added only in the eleventh and twelfth centuries, and were attributed falsely to the earlier talmudic master, Rava.

Now turn to Genesis 1:31 ("There was evening…a sixth day"), which immediately precedes Genesis 2:1–3 in the Bible. It concludes the Bible's description of God's creating day six. Although Maimonides and Eleazer say that they recited Genesis 2:1–3, they say nothing about the prior verse, Genesis 1:31, which must, therefore, have been added to the litrugy later still. Moses Isserles (1530–1572) and Mordecai Jaffe (1535–1612) are the first major codifiers to mention it, probably because it was still fairly recent, an outgrowth of sixteenth-century Lurianic Kabbalah. The point of the addition was to begin Shabbat with the acrostic of God's four-letter name, formed by the first letters of the last two words of Genesis 1: 31 *(yod* and *heh)* and the first two words of the next verse, Genesis 2:1 *(vav* and *heh),* as follows:

Yom Hashishi (YH) + *Vay'khulu Hashamayim* (VH) = YHVH

The acrostic would have been of interest to anyone, but it suited kabbalistic theory in particular, because the point of Shabbat, according to the Kabbalah, was to unify the masculine and feminine sides of God in a royal marriage (see the introduction, pp. 21–22), a feat symbolized by the unification of God's name. The existence of that name in an acrostic precisely at the point where the Torah describes Shabbat coming into being seemed an extraordinary affirmation of this kabbalistic perspective. By making *Kiddush,* one might, as it were, voice aloud the combined name just as the divine union was actually coming into being.

A further issue now arose. While some people said all of Genesis 1:31, some people whispered the first part and said aloud only the last two words that were necessary to make the acrostic. Kabbalists tried to ascertain the right custom by consulting their favorite mystical text, the *Zohar.*

The kabbalistic system depended on finding some numerical way in which prayer passages corresponded to God's name. The *Zohar* had already inherited the custom of adding Genesis 2:1–3 to the *Kiddush* and had added up the number of Hebrew words in those two passages: Genesis 2:1–3 had 35 words and the *Kiddush* had 45, producing a total of 80—which had no significance whatsoever! A midrash, however, had noted that while Israel became the chosen People only at Sinai, it received the Torah some time earlier. It followed, then, that the Hebrew phrase in the *Kiddush* corresponding to Israel's being chosen ("For you have chosen us and sanctified us above all nations") should be eliminated as irrelevant to Shabbat. The phrase had seven Hebrew words; taking them away from the *Kiddush* left only 38, not 45. Adding the remaining 38 words of the *Kiddush* to the 35 words of Genesis 2:1–3 now totaled 73—still a meaningless number. But people figured out that if they added just two more words—

in this case, the two necessary words of Genesis 1:31 they got 75, and that was only

three words more than 72, which was an important number for kabbalists. They had devised a way of spelling out the letters in God's four-letter name to get a permutation of that name containing 72 letters. Still, 72 is three short of 75.

But three of the *Kiddush* words, *ki hu yom* ("For it is the first day"), seemed extraneous: one could just as easily skip them. Some people, therefore, omitted from the *Kiddush* the three words that seemed unnecessary to arrive at the required total of 72 (75 – 3 = 72).

To be sure, most of these permutations of the text ultimately failed to achieve widespread acceptance, but it did become common to say only the last two Hebrew words of Genesis 1:31 out loud and to say the other words of the verse silently.

[5] *"With our masters' and teachers' approval"* From the Aramaic root *s.v.r,* one meaning of which is "to look upon with favor," hence, here, it must mean "with permission," or "with approval," parallel to the common liturgical preamble elsewhere that begins *bir'shut* ("with the permission of"). But many medievals disagreed.

Rashi's teacher, Isaac ben Judah of Mainz, explains that in Halakhah, *savrei* can also mean "understand." He imagines, therefore, that in the *Kiddush* it refers back to an *understanding* prompted by the power of wine to cause drunkenness. "Wine," he says, "has brought about an eternal curse, ever since Noah became drunk and a curse fell on Canaan [his son]. That is

[1] וֹם זֶה לְיִשְׂרָאֵל אוֹרָה וְשִׂמְחָה שַׁבָּת
מְנוּחָה:

[2] צִוִּיתָ פִּקוּדִים, בְּמַעֲמַד הַר סִינַי,
שַׁבָּת וּמוֹעֲדִים, לִשְׁמֹר בְּכָל שָׁנַי,
לַעֲרֹךְ לְפָנַי, מַשְׂאֵת וַאֲרוּחָה,
שַׁבָּת מְנוּחָה:
יוֹם זֶה...

[3] חֶמְדַּת הַלְּבָבוֹת, לְאֻמָּה שְׁבוּרָה,
לִנְפָשׁוֹת נִכְאָבוֹת, נְשָׁמָה יְתֵרָה,
לְנֶפֶשׁ מְצֵרָה, תָּסִיר אֲנָחָה,
שַׁבָּת מְנוּחָה:
יוֹם זֶה...

[4] קִדַּשְׁתָּ בֵּרַכְתָּ, אוֹתוֹ מִכָּל יָמִים,
בְּשֵׁשֶׁת כִּלִּיתָ מְלֶאכֶת עוֹלָמִים,
בּוֹ מָצְאוּ עֲגוּמִים, הַשְׁקֵט וּבִטְחָה,
שַׁבָּת מְנוּחָה:
יוֹם זֶה...

[5] לֶאֱסוֹר מְלָאכָה, צִוִּיתָנוּ נוֹרָא,
אֶזְכֶּה הוֹד מְלוּכָה, אִם שַׁבָּת אֶשְׁמֹרָה,
אַקְרִיב שַׁי לַמּוֹרָא, מִנְחָה מֶרְקָחָה,
שַׁבָּת מְנוּחָה:
יוֹם זֶה...

why we say *savru* [a variant of *savrei*]. It is as if we say [to those gathered at the table], '*Understand* that my intention is to drink from that which causes a curse. Let it be in your minds, then, that as I drink, I be not injured.' That is why it is customary for people to respond, *Chayim* ['life'], 'May this act of drinking bring you life [*chayim*] not injury'" (*Ma'aseh Hageonim*, Freiman, 63).

A related belief may be the medieval notion that good angels visit our homes on Shabbat. These angels come, it was believed, because people celebrated Shabbat with the sweet smell of myrtle leaves, on which angels, apparently, liked to ride (see below, "Varied spices"). Isaac Luria (the sixteenth-century kabbalist) would put two bunches of myrtle on his Shabbat table. Before *Kiddush,* he would take them in hand and walk around the table to his right. Then he would recite the blessing over them, smell them, and walk around the table again, to his left, this time saying, "'Remember' and 'Keep' were said in one utterance." (The idea of the two *mitzvot* being said together comes from the Talmud's attempt to understand why one set of the Ten Commandments [Exod. 20:8] tells Israel to "remember" Shabbat, while the second set [Deut. 5:12] mandates "keeping" it. A talmudic story pictures a man carrying two sprigs of myrtle on Friday night and explaining to the Rabbis who ask him about it that they correspond to the two commandments.)

Later that century, the Palestinian mystical adept Isaiah Horowitz said

חַדֵּשׁ מִקְדָּשֵׁנוּ זָכְרָה נֶחֱרֶבֶת,[6]

טוּבְךָ מוֹשִׁיעֵנוּ, תְּנָה לַנֶּעֱצֶבֶת,

בְּשַׁבָּת יוֹשֶׁבֶת, בְּזֶמֶר וּשְׁבָחָה,

שַׁבַּת מְנוּחָה:

יוֹם זֶה...

[7] *"Who sanctified us"* Blessings come in two varieties: one-liners (such as the blessing over wine, above, v. 6) and mini-essays on theology that are longer but which end in a statement that summarizes the blessing's theme. This, the *Kiddush* ("Sanctification"), or more properly *K'dushat Hayom* ("Sanctification of the Day"), is the latter, a blessing-essay on Shabbat as sacred time. It is carefully construed so as to weave together two related themes: (1) the sanctity of Israel (Israel's chosenness), which entails Israel's keeping (2) the sanctity of time.

The dual theme is set immediately: God sanctified us with commandments (commandments *(p. 121)*

been through are just as real as always. I can say, "Like all *spaces on the face of the planet,* so too all *times in the flow of history* leave their mark on the human race." Both time and space affect us; they both prompt memories. But all spaces exist simultaneously on a single plane, whereas time is part of a flow that passes and is gone forever.

The Rabbis thought of time the way we think of space. For them, it was possible literally to revisit the past or, better, to summon the past to reappear before us again, as if we were in it all over again. "Memory," then, in the sense of *zekher,* denotes real revisiting of time. *Zekher* is like a signpost in time, pointing our way as we revisit it, the way a directional sign *(p. 121)*

[8] *"The first day of holy festivals"* The Sabbath is called "the first" here, probably because of the order in which sacred times are stipulated in Leviticus 23:1–44 and Exodus 23:12–17. These are the two places in Torah where Shabbat and the Festivals are commanded together. In both cases, Shabbat is mentioned "first."

———◆———

J. HOFFMAN (TRANSLATION)

[1] *"The sixth day"* Or "a sixth *(p. 122)*

that people kept two bunches of myrtle on the Shabbat table, although they seem to have abandoned the magic circles around the table that Luria had specified. Even in the nineteenth century, Safed residents used myrtle. It was given to them at synagogue services, whence they brought it home, put it on the table, and then said the blessing over it while smelling it—just as for *Havdalah.*

For most of us, the use of myrtle has long disappeared. But we have retained the custom of bringing something sweet-smelling to the Shabbat

retains these additional meanings. The Hebrew word for "male," *zakhar,* comes from the same root *z.kh.r,* reflecting the pointing of the male organ. (The word for "female," *n'kevah,* comes from the root *n.k.v* ["to pierce"].)

[8] *"First day"* Literally, "day of beginning." This may reflect the notion of "most important" (similar to "first family" in America, which refers to the president's family) or perhaps just "day on which things begin."

[8] *"Memorial"* Hebrew, *(p. 123)*

6 Renew our Temple. Remember the ruined
   city.
Grant your goodness, our savior, to the sad
   city
That rests on Shabbat in song and praise
A Shabbat of rest.
This is Israel's…

יֹום זֶה לְיִשְׂרָאֵל אוֹרָה וְשִׂמְחָה שַׁבַּת מְנוּחָה: ¹

צִוִּיתָ פִּקוּדִים, בְּמַעֲמַד הַר סִינַי, ²
שַׁבָּת וּמוֹעֲדִים, לִשְׁמֹר בְּכָל שָׁנַי,
לַעֲרֹךְ לְפָנַי, מַשְׂאֵת וַאֲרוּחָה,
שַׁבַּת מְנוּחָה:
יֹום זֶה...

I. YOM ZEH L'YISRA'EL
("THIS IS ISRAEL'S DAY")

¹ This is Israel's day of light
and joy, a Shabbat of rest.

² You announced
commandments on Mount Sinai:
Shabbat and Festivals for me to keep
all my years
Food and meals to set before me
A Shabbat of rest.
This is Israel's…

3 Heart's delight, to a broken nation,
To souls in pain, grant an extra soul.
To a soul at work, remove our sorrow.
A Shabbat of rest.
This is Israel's…

4 You sanctified it, blessed it, above all days.
On the sixth day You finished your work on
   the world.
On it the sorrowful find quiet and respite.
A Shabbat of rest.
This is Israel's…

5 Awesome One, your command forbids
   work.
I'll merit royal splendor when I

(p. 124)

(p. 124)

table: a bouquet of flowers, with all the sweetness of myrtle but none of the mysticism. (See "Varied spices," p. 167, for more detail on the use of myrtle.)

6 "Creator of the fruit of the vine" The "blessing over wine" *(birkat yayin),* one of many food blessings from antiquity. It is attested to in the Mishnah (c. 200 C.E.). Wine was ubiquitous by the first century C.E., the drink of choice at meals.

Three prescribed cups were the rule: one before eating, one after eating, and at least one (usually more) during dinner. But there is evidence aplenty that too much drinking was common. The Mishnah's instructions for the Passover Seder limit the amount of wine, lest people nod off from having imbibed too much. The apostle Paul berates the church in Corinth for ruining the Lord's Supper by drinking to excess. And the problem was not new. A dialogue by Plato (428–347 B.C.E.) features a pre-dinner discussion on the danger to health posed by becoming drunk at dinner.

The blessing over wine should not be confused with the *Kiddush* proper, which is only the following lengthy blessing that goes from "Blessed are You...who sanctified us" to "Blessed are You...who sanctifies the Shabbat."

³ חֶמְדַּת הַלְּבָבוֹת, לְאֻמָּה שְׁבוּרָה,
לִנְפָשׁוֹת נִכְאָבוֹת, נְשָׁמָה יְתֵרָה,
לְנֶפֶשׁ מְצֵרָה, תָּסִיר אֲנָחָה,
שַׁבָּת מְנוּחָה:
יוֹם זֶה...

⁴ קִדַּשְׁתָּ בֵּרַכְתָּ, אוֹתוֹ מִכָּל יָמִים,
בְּשֵׁשֶׁת כִּלִּיתָ מְלֶאכֶת עוֹלָמִים,
בּוֹ מָצְאוּ עֲגוּמִים, הַשְׁקֵט וּבִטְחָה,
שַׁבָּת מְנוּחָה:
יוֹם זֶה...

⁵ לְאִסּוּר מְלָאכָה, צִוִּיתָנוּ נוֹרָא,
אֶזְכֶּה הוֹד מְלוּכָה, אִם שַׁבָּת אֶשְׁמֹרָה,
אַקְרִיב שַׁי לַמּוֹרָא, מִנְחָה מֶרְקָחָה,
שַׁבָּת מְנוּחָה:
יוֹם זֶה...

⁶ חַדֵּשׁ מִקְדָּשֵׁנוּ זָכְרָה נֶחֱרֶבֶת,
טוּבְךָ מוֹשִׁיעֵנוּ, תְּנָה לַנֶּעֱצֶבֶת,
בְּשַׁבָּת יוֹשֶׁבֶת, בְּזֶמֶר וּשְׁבָחָה,
שַׁבָּת מְנוּחָה:
יוֹם זֶה...

BRETTLER (BIBLE)

are the entailment of chosenness) and set a time (Shabbat) that we are to declare as sanctified. All of this is done in love. Verse 9 repeats the theme: God chose us, sanctified us, and bequeathed to us the holy time of Shabbat—again, all in love.

The final verse (the concluding summary statement, or *chatimah*) seems here to mention only the second idea, the sanctity of Shabbat. On festivals, however, when the sacred time in question recurs seasonally as Passover, Shavuot, and Sukkot, the conclusion is "Blessed are You, Adonai, who sanctifies Israel and the seasons." Here both themes—the sanctity of Israel and of time—are interwoven. Later Jewish thought explains the different conclusions halakhically, but originally they were probably alternative forms of blessing, one of which was more thorough than the other.

7–9 "Adored us [v'ratsah vanu]…*lovingly and adoringly* [b'ahavah uv'ratson]*" Ratsah* and *ratson* are references to God's will, but they are used here as synonyms for God's love. These terms are found (though not here) especially with regard to sacrifices, while *ahavah,* the alternative word denoting love, tends to be found regarding prayer. Frequently, as here, they occur together, the idea being that God's will is an expression of divine love.

7–8 "Memory…memorial" Liturgically, these two expressions are used interchangeably to mean "in memory of" or in "recollection of," but it is hard for us today to appreciate what the Rabbis of antiquity meant by "memory."

Unlike the Rabbis, we think of time as a succession of scenes flowing past our eyes like a movie that we are in. We "remember" the scenes that we have already acted out. What we remember is the unrecoverable past. By contrast, we think of space as recoverable—we can revisit it, physically, literally, whereas time that is past exists only in memory, so it is not "real" in the sense that spaces we once visited are. Time, we say, acts on us: "Time passes us by"; it is not we who "pass by time." So we are at time's mercy. Once it passes, it is gone forever. With space, it is just the opposite. We never say, "Space passed us by." But we do believe that "we pass through space." With time ("Time passed us by"), we are the object, and time is the subject, so we have no control over it. But with space ("We pass through space"), we are the subject, and space is the object, so we can return to it if we wish. Time exists only in subjective "memory," but spaces we have

DORFF (THEOLOGY)

at a crossroads sends us to a destination in space where we have stood before.

At our Passover Seder, we quote Hillel, who ate *matzah, maror,* and the *pesach* (the paschal lamb offering) "in memory of [*zekher l'*] the Temple." But Hillel lived before the Temple was destroyed. How could he have done something "in memory of" what still existed? He could do so precisely because the Rabbis thought of time and space as similar. The Temple might have still stood in time, but it was distant in space and had to be summoned up.

Both time and space, then, could be summoned from afar to re-present themselves to us as perfectly real, but only with pointers that showed the way to them. Liturgy, in general, served as such pointers. By enacting the liturgy, things past and far away became present and real.

Jesus spoke as a Jew when he told his disciples at the Last Supper, "Do this in memory of me." He meant that they should reenact a liturgy that would make him present. Christian theology uses the Greek word *anamnesis* to indicate the ancient meaning of "remembrance" as a pointer that summons to consciousness things past and far away as if they still were here and now. *Zekher* and *zikaron* are parallel forms of the original concept from which *anamnesis* is derived.

FRANKEL (A WOMAN'S VOICE)

day." The Hebrew is actually ungrammatical. In Hebrew, both adjectives and nouns can take the word "the," but when they do, they have to match. So the grammatical way to say "the sixth day" is "the day the sixth," or *hayom hashishi*. By contrast, "a sixth day" is "day sixth," or *yom shishi*. This text, from Genesis, combines both forms. Rashi notices the extra *heh* and offers midrashic explanations for it, including a suggestion that the *heh*, whose numerical value in Hebrew is "5," is an oblique mystical reference to the Five Books of Torah. By contrast, Ibn Ezra, the medieval commentator most interested in grammar, notes several parallel cases in Torah. With regard to the creation narrative, it turns up also as *yom hashvi'i* ("the seventh day") in Genesis 2:3.

[2] *"Associated with them"* Others, the literal "their host," but the connotations of the English "host" (host and hostess, for example) are so wrong that we prefer not to use this word. One possibility is that "their host" is the planets and other celestial bodies.

[3] *"Rested"* The Hebrew word for "rested" *(shavat)* is from the same root as "Sabbath" *(Shabbat)*, creating a word play, similar to "he rested on the day of rest" or "he sabbathed on the Sabbath," that we cannot capture in English.

[4] *"Had created to do"* That is, God created work to do ("the work God had created to do"), and having done it, on the seventh day God rested from it. This somewhat awkward phrase is probably the result of the author trying to include both the verb *bara* ("create") and the verb *asah* ("do").

[5] *"With our masters' and teachers' approval"* Composed in Aramaic, not Hebrew. Probably it was at first an informal invitation, along the lines of "Shall we...."

[7] *"Adored us"* The word *ratsah*, often translated as "pleased with us" (Birnbaum, e.g.) or "found favor," probably refers to a specific type of love. (See Volume 3, *P'sukei D'zimrah: Morning Psalms*, pp. 138–139, where we discuss words used by different

languages for different kinds of love.) "Adored" isn't exactly the right nuance here, but we need another word for "love" to complement *ahavah* ("love") next.

[7] *"Lovingly"* Unlike the word for "adoringly" (see prior comment), the word for "lovingly" here comes from the usual root for "love," *a.h.v.*

[7] *"In memory"* Hebrew, *zikaron,* related to the word *zekher* ("memorial," v. 8). Both words come from the root *z.kh.r,* which meant not only "to remember," but also "to point, to point out, highlight, mention, or call to mind." The related Arabic root, *z.k.r,*

GRAY (TALMUD)

zekher, related to *zikaron,* as discussed above.

[9] *"Above"* Literally, "from."

[9] *"All"* Frequently, as here, "all" is used for "all others."

♦ ♦ ♦

F. *Z'MIROT* (TABLE SONGS)

I. *YOM ZEH L'YISRA'EL* ("THIS IS ISRAEL'S DAY")

[1] This is Israel's day of light and joy, a Shabbat of rest.

[2] You announced commandments on Mount Sinai:
Shabbat and Festivals for me to keep all my years
Food and meals to set before me
A Shabbat of rest.
This is Israel's…

LANDES (HALAKHAH)

keep Shabbat.
I'll offer gifts to the awesome One, fragrant sacrifices.
A Shabbat of rest.
This is Israel's…

J. HOFFMAN (TRANSLATION)

[3] Heart's delight, to a broken nation,
To souls in pain, grant an extra soul.
To a soul at work, remove our sorrow.
A Shabbat of rest.
This is Israel's…

[4] You sanctified it, blessed it, above all days.
On the sixth day You finished your work on the world.
On it the sorrowful find quiet and respite.
A Shabbat of rest.
This is Israel's…

[5] Awesome One, your command forbids work.
I'll merit royal splendor when I keep Shabbat.
I'll offer gifts to the awesome One, fragrant sacrifices.
A Shabbat of rest.
This is Israel's...

[6] Renew our Temple. Remember the ruined city.
Grant your goodness, our savior, to the sad city
That rests on Shabbat in song and praise
A Shabbat of rest.
This is Israel's...

BRETTLER (BIBLE)

[1] *"This is Israel's day"* Following Isaiah 58:13, "If you call Shabbat 'delight,'" this refrain sets the poem's tone by regarding Shabbat positively, as opposed to the more typical Torah viewpoint that emphasizes its prohibitions and the severe punishment that follows from not keeping them.

[1] *"Light and joy"* From Esther 8:16, regarding military victory over oppressors. In the medieval period, such victories were unimaginable (note how stanza 3 labels Israel "a broken nation," so the phrase came to be seen as alluding to the joy of the weekly Shabbat, which offsets Israel's powerlessness).

[2] *"Announced commandments"* Shabbat and festival practices were ordained on Sinai (Exod. 23:10–19; 34:18–26; Leviticus 23).

[2] *"To set before me"* Food plays no special role in the observance of the biblical Shabbat, other than the double portion of manna that fell on Friday in anticipation of Shabbat (Exodus 16). Otherwise, there are no special foods for Shabbat, although there are special laws about how to prepare food then.

[3] *"Heart's delight"* What might be called the spiritual aspect of Shabbat is largely absent from the Bible, although Psalm 92, which suggests that Shabbat is a particularly opportune time to praise God, may reflect the beginning of such a notion.

[4] *"You sanctified it, blessed it"* A citation of Genesis 2:3, "God blessed the seventh day and declared it holy,"

1 דְּרוֹר יִקְרָא לְבֵן עִם בַּת,
וְיִנְצָרְכֶם כְּמוֹ בָבַת.
נְעִים שִׁמְכֶם וְלֹא יֻשְׁבַּת,
שְׁבוּ וְנוּחוּ בְּיוֹם שַׁבָּת:

2 דְּרוֹשׁ נָוִי וְאוּלְמִי,
וְאוֹת יֶשַׁע עֲשֵׂה עִמִּי.
נְטַע שׂוֹרֵק בְּתוֹךְ כַּרְמִי
שְׁעֵה שַׁוְעַת בְּנֵי עַמִּי:

3 דְּרוֹךְ פּוּרָה בְּתוֹךְ בָּצְרָה,
וְגַם בָּבֶל אֲשֶׁר גָּבְרָה.
נְתוֹץ צָרַי בְּאַף וְעֶבְרָה,
שְׁמַע קוֹלִי בְּיוֹם אֶקְרָא:

4 אֱלֹהִים תֵּן בַּמִּדְבָּר הַר,
הֲדַס שִׁטָּה בְּרוֹשׁ תִּדְהָר.
וְלַמַּזְהִיר וְלַנִּזְהָר,
שְׁלוֹמִים תֵּן כְּמֵי נָהָר:

5 הֲדוֹךְ קָמַי אֵל קַנָּא,
בְּמוֹג לֵבָב וּבַמְּגִינָה.
וְנַרְחִיב פֶּה וּנְמַלְאֶנָּה,
לְשׁוֹנֵנוּ לְךָ רִנָּה:

6 דְּעֵה חָכְמָה לְנַפְשֶׁךָ,
וְהִיא כֶתֶר לְרֹאשֶׁךָ.
נְצוֹר מִצְוַת קְדוֹשֶׁךָ,
שְׁמוֹר שַׁבַּת קָדְשֶׁךָ:

² *"You announced commandments"* Although the refrain associates Shabbat with light, joy, and rest, this first verse insists that Jews observe the Sabbath not in order to have these benefits, but to fulfill the commandment of God. Light, joy, and rest are the result of observing Shabbat, not the purpose of doing so—just the opposite of current apologetics to the effect that we should keep Shabbat because it is good for us.

³ *"Souls in pain"* This verse, in particular, indicates the oppression that the author and his contemporaries were experiencing. Under such circumstances, the "extra soul" that the Talmud promises on Shabbat (Beitzah 16a; Ta'an. 27b) was even more *(p. 130)*

praise such as this one, their wives ignore the ban against work, *isur m'lakhah* (v. 5), as they knock themselves out to ready the house for the Sabbath rest of others.

Fortunately, in our own day, this scenario is no longer the universal Jewish norm. Increasingly, men share the burdens of Shabbat preparation together with their partners; increasingly, women join in the chorus of praise at the end of the Sabbath meal, no longer too exhausted to find the strength to sing. Although this is a far cry from messianic redemption, it is a step in that direction. And so when we sing *chadesh mikdasheinu,* "renew our Temple" (v. 6), we *(p. 132)*

of Shabbat as he did his weekday grocery shopping. When he saw a particularly nice cut of meat, he would set it aside and say, "This is for Shabbat!" If he found a nicer cut later in the week, he would eat the first one and set the nicer cut aside, saying, "This is for Shabbat!"

³ *"Extra soul* [n'shamah y'teirah]*"* Every Friday evening, we are each given an extra soul (Ta'an. 27b; Beitzah 16a), which departs on Saturday night after Shabbat ends. This lesson is derived from a creative *(p. 132)*

and Exodus 20:11, "Therefore Adonai blessed the Shabbat day and hallowed it"—but reversing the order of the verbs.

⁴ *"Quiet and respite"* An adaptation of Isaiah 30:15, where the context is unconnected to Shabbat. God simply promises, "Your victory shall come about through quiet and respite." Newly connecting this verse to Shabbat emphasizes the poem's main theme: how Shabbat compensates for political powerlessness.

⁵ *"Forbids work"* This stanza likely develops from

review of Jewish history: Sinai, persecution, the rebuilding of the Temple, and ultimate redemption. Singing this *zemer* on Shabbat thus calls to mind the famous talmudic dictum: "Were Israel to observe two Shabbatot properly, they would immediately be redeemed" (Shab. 118b)—and its even more generous formulation in the Yerushalmi, which requires only one Shabbat of proper observance to merit redemption (PT Ta'an. 1:1, 64a). The *mitzvah* of Shabbat has the power to effect redemption because *(p. 133)* wine at that (*Shulchan Arukh*, O. Ch. 250:2). Nonetheless, the "students of the Ri" (the commentary of Rabbi Yonah ben Abraham of Geronah [1200–1263, Spain], on the RiF to Berachot, as edited by his students) identify the inclusion of meat and wine as a *r'shut*, just a preferred option for fulfilling the *mitzvah*, but not a *chovah*, a requirement (see also *Magen Avraham* [Abraham Gumbiner, 1637–1683, Poland] O. Ch., 572:5). Thus, vegetarians and those who must limit or eliminate alcohol can fulfill the *mitzvah* of *oneg Shabbat* perfectly well by substituting vegan gourmet dishes and organic grape juice.

(p. 133)

——◆——

¹דְּרוֹר יִקְרָא לְבֵן עִם בַּת,

וְיִנְצָרְכֶם כְּמוֹ בָבַת.

נְעִים שִׁמְכֶם וְלֹא יֻשְׁבַּת,

שְׁבוּ וְנוּחוּ בְּיוֹם שַׁבָּת:

²דְּרוֹשׁ נָוִי וְאוּלָמִי,

וְאוֹת יֶשַׁע עֲשֵׂה עִמִּי.

¹ *"This is Israel's day of light and joy"* More literally, "this day is for Israel light and joy."

² *"Announced commandments"* More literally, "commanded regulations." Once again, we try to translate the import of the whole phrase, rather than each word one at a time. "Commanded announcements" would mimic the Hebrew words more closely, but our translation better conveys the Hebrew phrase.

² *"On Mount Sinai"* Literally, "on the Mount Sinai stand," that is, "while standing at Mount Sinai." The phrase is common in Rabbinic Hebrew.

³ *"Delight"* The Hebrew for (p. 134)

Jeremiah 17:19–27, which connects Shabbat observance to the maintenance of the Davidic monarchy and the sacrificial system. Our celebration of Shabbat not only compensates for lost political power, but also leads to a renewal of that power, with a messianic king and a restored Temple.

⁶*"Renew our Temple"* Likely an oblique reference to the hope for a return from exile and a national restoration, as anticipated at the end of Lamentations, especially "Renew (chadesh) our days as of old!" (5:21).

⁶*"Your goodness"* Following Jeremiah 31:12 and Psalm 65:5, God's "goodness" (tuv) may indicate the restoration of Jerusalem and the Temple.

———◆———

DORFF (THEOLOGY)

¹*"Day of light and joy"* An opening emphasis on the joy of Shabbat, shortly to be contrasted with the problems Jews face throughout the week.

נְטַע שׁוֹרֵק בְּתוֹךְ כַּרְמִי

שְׁעֵה שַׁוְעַת בְּנֵי עַמִּי:

³דְּרוֹךְ פּוּרָה בְּתוֹךְ בָּצְרָה,

וְגַם בָּבֶל אֲשֶׁר גָּבְרָה.

נְתוֹץ צָרַי בְּאַף וְעֶבְרָה,

שְׁמַע קוֹלִי בְּיוֹם אֶקְרָא:

⁴אֱלֹהִים תֵּן בַּמִּדְבָּר הַר,

הֲדַס שִׁטָּה בְּרוֹשׁ תִּדְהָר.

וְלַמַּזְהִיר וְלַנִּזְהָר,

שְׁלוֹמִים תֵּן כְּמֵי נָהָר:

⁵הֲדוֹךְ קָמַי אֵל קַנָּא,

בְּמוֹג לֵבָב וּבַמְּגִינָה.

וְנַרְחִיב פֶּה וּנְמַלְאֶנָּה,

לִשׁוֹנֵנוּ לְךָ רִנָּה:

⁶דְּעֵה חָכְמָה לְנַפְשֶׁךָ,

וְהִיא כֶתֶר לְרֹאשֶׁךָ.

נְצוֹר מִצְוַת קְדוֹשֶׁךָ,

שְׁמוֹר שַׁבָּת קָדְשֶׁךָ:

BRETTLER (BIBLE)

meaningful than it is for Jews today, who enjoy freedom. Still, even we may be weighed down with sadness, and if so, we too may appreciate Shabbat as an unusually great gift.

⁵*"I'll offer gifts"* Shabbat is not only God's gift to us, but also our gift back to God!

⁶*"Renew our Temple"* When the Temple stood, an additional communal sacrifice

(*Musaf*) was offered on Shabbat. With its destruction, we have only the *Musaf Amidah* to offer in its stead. Our poem hopes for the restoration of Shabbat as described in the Torah, including the rebuilding of the Temple.

But a revival of sacrifice may not be the author's main point. More than just a place of worship, the Temple had been the center of Jewish religious, national, and civic life. The supreme court sat there, and if the New Testament accurately depicts Jesus expelling money changers, meaning bankers (Matt. 21:12ff.; Mark 11:15ff.; Luke 19:45ff.; John 2:13ff.), it was also the economic center of the country—the Wall Street of ancient Israel. Above all, then, the poem is an expression of messianic anticipation of Israel's return to self-governance in our land.

FRANKEL (A WOMAN'S VOICE)

Yom Zeh L'yisra'el ("Israel's Day") The medieval Jew who composed this song holds two religious realities in tension within its verses: the gladness of Shabbat and the sorrow of exile. Three of the five stanzas remind us that we are an *umah sh'vurah,* a "broken nation" (v. 3); *agumim,* "sorrowful" (v. 4); *ne'etsevet,* "sad" when remembering *necherevet,* "the ruined city" (v. 6). As an antidote to this legacy of painful memory, the poet points to the gifts provided by Shabbat: *n'shamah y'teirah,* "an extra soul" (v. 3); *hashket u'vitchah,* "quiet and respite" (v. 4); *hod m'lukhah,* "royal splendor" (v. 5); and ultimate redemption in the form of Jerusalem and the Temple restored. What bridges and reconciles these two realities is our observance of Sabbath rituals at home, through banquets, song, praise, and abstention from labor. Through a kind of alchemical process, the gloom of Jewish history is transmuted on this sacred day into *orah v'simchah* and *Shabbat m'nuchah,* "light and joy," and "a Shabbat of rest" (v. 1). Or, looked at another way, if we uphold our part of the covenantal bargain by imitating God's example, resting every seventh day as God did at creation, then God will grant us a special boon of *tov,* divine "goodness" (v. 6), a true souvenir of original grace. What a sweet vision this is!

But how precisely does this weekly idyll come about? Is there perhaps a serpent in this Edenic garden? For if we stand up from the Sabbath table and walk only a few paces into the kitchen, we will find women, with few exceptions, laboring behind the scenes to make this magic happen. It is they, the *baleh bustehs* (pronounced bah-L' BUS-t's, a virtually untranslatable Yiddish phrase meaning "good homemakers"), the *n'shei chayil* ("worthy women," plural of *eshet chayil*—see prayer, p. 74) who are busy preparing the *mas'eit va'aruchah,* "food and meals" (v. 1) celebrated in this song. While their husbands and children obey the command to abandon *anachah,* their "sorrow" (v. 3), on this day of rest, the women groan with exertion as they pummel the *challah* dough, stir the soup pot, flavor the chicken, and roll the strudel. As the men regale their creator with songs of

DORFF (THEOLOGY)

can remind ourselves that the Rabbis referred to our Sabbath and festival table as a *mikdash m'at,* "a miniature sanctuary," a surrogate altar until the Temple is rebuilt. As we all share in the grief of exile and the hope of redemption, we can also all share in the renewal provided each week known as *Shabbat m'nuchah.* So were we all commanded, the song reminds us, *b'ma'amad sinai,* "as we all stood together at Sinai" (v. 2).

——◆——

GRAY (TALMUD)

[2] *"Food and meals"* The Talmud (Pes. 68b) cites Isaiah 58:13, "Call Shabbat a delight," to demonstrate that Shabbat is not only for spiritual pursuits, but for bodily pleasures as well. So on Shabbat, the Talmud (Shab. 117b) requires three meals (instead of the weekday norm of two): Friday evening, Shabbat morning after services, and Shabbat afternoon around *Minchah* (Maimonides, "Shabbat" 30:9, *Shulchan Arukh,* O. Ch. 291). (For details, see introductory essay by Michael Chernick, *"S'udah Sh'lishit:* A Rite of Modest Majesty," pp. 30–36.)

In addition, Shabbat calls for the best food one can afford (*Tur,* O. Ch. 242). The Talmud (Beitzah 16a) tells the charming story of Shammai the Elder, who was mindful

FRANKEL (A WOMAN'S VOICE)

reading of Exodus 31:17, "[God] ceased from work [*shavat*] and [*va*] was refreshed [*yinafash*]." Resh Lakish read these words as "[Once the Jew] has ceased from work [*shavat,* that is, "already finished observing Shabbat"], then [instead of "and"] the [extra] soul [*nefesh,* from *yinafash*] is lost!"

[5] *"Forbids work* [m'lakhah]" The Torah regularly stresses the Shabbat prohibition of work (see, e.g., Exod. 20:8–11). Similarly, among the prophets, Second Isaiah (sixth century B.C.E.) admonished people against pursuing worldly goals on Shabbat (Isa. 58:13), just as Jeremiah had done nearly a century before (Jer. 17:22–24).

In rabbinic times, the Mishnah (Shab. 7:2–4) elaborated thirty-nine principal categories of labor known as *avot* ("father categories"), each with subcategories called *toladot* ("offspring categories"), a scheme allegedly based on the kinds of work that went into building the desert tabernacle (Shab. 49b). As a technical term for labor, *m'lakhah* includes genuine work, such as planting and harvesting, but also such things as carrying an item from a private to a public domain and vice versa. Predictably, the Talmud devotes much attention to analyzing these various *avot* and *toladot,* but so too does post-talmudic Halakhah because of the need to rethink the old categories in an ever-changing world.

[6] *"Renew our Temple"* Now that we have come to the end of this *zemer,* let us examine it thematically. It begins with the commandment to honor and enjoy Shabbat, and then explores Shabbat as the mainstay of a persecuted and oppressed people. In the final stanza, the mood changes, turning to the Shabbat sacrificial service. Here, it anticipates the rebuilding of the Temple in the messianic era and all the other good things that God will bring to the downtrodden People Israel. All in all, we have a mini-

GRAY (TALMUD)

Shabbat is equal to all the other *mitzvot* of Torah (PT Ber. 1:8, 3c).

LANDES (HALAKHAH)

Z'mirot ("Table Songs") The halakhic origin of singing *z'mirot* is given in Megillah 12b: On Shabbat, "Israel should eat, drink, and speak Torah and words of praise." The *z'mirot* fulfill all these commands, for they are (1) words of praise, that contain (2) many words of Torah, and celebrate (3) eating and (4) drinking. *Z'mirot* seem connected to *oneg Shabbat* ("Shabbat joy"; see *Hadlakat Nerot,* p. 50) as the sensual/spiritual meeting place of Shabbat. Although we hope to be fortunate enough to have a surfeit of Shabbat food, the spirit of the songs should remind us that according to the Talmud, even a small amount of food can be eaten in a way that fulfills the requirement of *oneg* (Shab. 118b). True, the Talmud identifies *oneg* as meat and wine (Chul. 84a)—and robust

L. HOFFMAN (HISTORY)

L. HOFFMAN (HISTORY)

Yom Zeh L'yisra'el ("Israel's Day") With the help of the newly developed printing press, the kabbalistic theories of Isaac Luria from Safed (see pp. 18–22) traveled throughout the Jewish world, giving Luria international renown. His emphasis on Shabbat as the day most likely to produce a foretaste of the world-to-come (see p. 20), led him to compose several *z'mirot* as table songs to accompany Shabbat dinner. Traditional opinion counts *Yom Zeh L'yisra'el* among his contributions, even though, in all probability, it is by Isaac Handali, a fifteenth-century Crimean poet about whom we know almost nothing.

J. HOFFMAN (TRANSLATION)

J. HOFFMAN (TRANSLATION)

"delight" here is *chemdat,* from the root *ch.m.d,* "to desire." This phrase, an epithet for God, differs from *y'did nefesh* (see p. 137), which is also an epithet for God and is sometimes translated as "heart's delight."

[3] *"Pain"* Or "distress."

[3] *"Grant"* The Hebrew has no verb here, creating a poetic feel that we cannot capture in English.

[3] *"Extra soul"* The word for "soul" here is *n'shamah,* different than the word we just saw *(nefesh).* We would normally avoid using the same word in English for two different words in Hebrew, but in this case, we have no choice. The only reasonable alternative, "spirit," doesn't work in either case. It has a better chance in the translation of *n'shamah y'teirah,* as discussed extensively by other commentators in this volume; by commonly used convention, however, that technical term is always called an "extra soul" in English, so we cannot change it here.

[3] *"Sorrow* [anachah]" Literally, something like "sighing." The Hebrew word was chosen to rhyme with *m'nuchah,* at the end of the next line.

[4] *"Sixth day"* Literally, just "sixth."

[4] *"Work on the world"* The word for "world" in Hebrew also means "eternity," so this line also has connotations of God finishing "eternal work."

[5] *"Awesome One* [nora]" In typical *paytanic* (Hebrew poetic) style, the author uses an epithet ("awesome One," or *nora*) to refer to God. Liturgical poetry rarely calls anyone, including God, by a proper name. Instead, adjectives are preferred, as here: *nora* = awesome.

[5] *"Your command forbids work"* More literally, "You commanded us regarding forbidding work."

[5] *"When"* Or "if." The Hebrew is ambiguous, but the difference is important. One possibility is that the author gets rewarded in the form of royal splendor on Shabbat, that is, "when" he keeps Shabbat. The other possibility is that the author gets the reward throughout the week, but only "if" he keeps Shabbat. The former is more likely, but the Hebrew can mean both.

[5] *"Offer"* Literally, "sacrifice," a concept we introduce in translating *minchah* as

"sacrifice," rather than the particular sacrifice that it is (see next comment).

⁵ *"Sacrifices"* The sacrifice stipulated here is the *minchah,* a particular kind of biblical sacrifice, described in Leviticus 2. The author selects the *minchah* as his example because *minchah* sounds like *m'nuchah* ("rest") in the next line.

⁶ *"Remember the"* Or "remembered by."

⁶ *"Ruined city"* The Hebrew just reads, "remember the ruined" (which is grammatical in Hebrew), but because the adjective is feminine, the reference is almost certainly to "city," which is also feminine in Hebrew. This is the first of three oblique references to "city" that appear simply as adjectives.

Again, we see the *paytanic* (poetic) preference for adjectives to refer to proper nouns (see above, "Awesome One").

⁶ *"Rests* [yoshevet] *on Shabbat* [shabbat]" Literally, "sits" or "dwells" on Shabbat. The verb in Hebrew (*yoshevet*) sounds like the word *shabbat,* creating a word play we cannot capture in English.

❖❖❖

¹ יְדִיד נֶפֶשׁ, אַב הָרַחֲמָן, מְשׁוֹךְ עַבְדְּךָ אֶל רְצוֹנֶךָ
יָרוּץ עַבְדְּךָ כְּמוֹ אַיָּל, יִשְׁתַּחֲוֶה אֶל מוּל הֲדָרֶךָ
יֶעֱרַב לוֹ יְדִידוּתָךְ מִנֹּפֶת צוּף וְכָל-טָעַם.

² הָדוּר, נָאֶה, זִיו הָעוֹלָם, נַפְשִׁי חוֹלַת אַהֲבָתֶךָ
אָנָּא, אֵל נָא, רְפָא נָא לָהּ בְּהַרְאוֹת לָהּ נֹעַם זִיוֶךָ
אָז תִּתְחַזֵּק וְתִתְרַפֵּא, וְהָיְתָה לָךְ שִׁפְחַת עוֹלָם.

³ וָתִיק, יֶהֱמוּ רַחֲמֶיךָ, וְחוּס נָא עַל בֵּן אוֹהֲבָךְ
כִּי זֶה כַּמָּה נִכְסוֹף נִכְסַף לִרְאוֹת בְּתִפְאֶרֶת עֻזֶּךָ
אָנָּא, אֵלִי, מַחְמַד לִבִּי, חוּשָׁה נָּא, וְאַל תִּתְעַלָּם.

⁴ הִגָּלֶה נָא וּפְרוֹשׂ, חָבִיב, עָלַי אֶת-סֻכַּת שְׁלוֹמֶךָ
תָּאִיר אֶרֶץ מִכְּבוֹדָךְ, נָגִילָה וְנִשְׂמְחָה בָךְ
מַהֵר, אָהוּב, כִּי בָא מוֹעֵד, וְחָנֵּנִי כִּימֵי עוֹלָם.

II. D'ROR YIKRA ("LET HIM PROCLAIM FREEDOM")

[1] Let Him proclaim freedom to men and women
And guard you like the apple of his eye.
Your name is pleasant. It will not be destroyed.
Sit down and rest on Shabbat.

[2] Seek my pasture and hall
And grant a sign of salvation to my people.

[5] *"We'll open our mouth"* This couplet begins with a play on Psalm 81:11, "I, Adonai, am your God who brought you out of the land of Egypt; open your mouth wide and I will fill it."

[6] *"Know wisdom"* From Proverbs 4:9, concerning wisdom *(chokhmah),* the subject here as well: "She will adorn your head with a graceful wreath; crown you with a glorious diadem."

[6] *"Guard your Holy One's* (p. 141)

(p. 138)

[3] *"Hear my voice"* A common motif in Psalms, as in 20:10, "May the king answer us on the day that we call."

[4] *"A mountain in the desert"* Restoration imagery, born in Babylonian exile (Isa. 41:19: "I will plant cedars in the wilderness…" [*eten bamidbar erez*]).

[4] *"Like the water of a river"* More restoration imagery (see prior comment), from Isaiah 66:12, "For thus said Adonai: I will extend to her prosperity like a river [*k'nahar shalom*], the wealth of nations like a wadi [a seasonal stream of great intensity, filled by torrential (p. 140)

II. D'ROR YIKRA ("LET HIM PROCLAIM FREEDOM")

[1] Let Him proclaim freedom to men and women
And guard you like the apple of his eye.
Your name is pleasant. It will not be destroyed.
Sit down and rest on Shabbat.

[2] Seek my pasture and hall
And grant a sign of salvation to my people.
Plant a vine in my vineyard.

as an everlasting sign that you shall not perish.

❖

FRANKEL (A WOMAN'S VOICE)

D'ror Yikra ("Let Him Proclaim Freedom") The essence of this medieval poem derives from the landscape of the Middle East and its tragic Jewish history. Throughout the song, the composer, Dunash ben Labrat (perhaps), refers liberally to the natural and agricultural elements (p. 142)

God for personal salvation, praying that God will notice him and plant a vine within his vineyard.

Because Dunash switches freely between addressing God and addressing his audience, it is not always clear whether he is serving as our spokesman or as his own. Perhaps that is the rhythm of Jewish prayer: to blur distinctions between personal and national petition as we yoke our individual fortunes to that of our nation.

Most puzzling of all is the first line of the song: *D'ror yikra l'ven im bat,* "Let

jubilee year put things right. The *zemer*'s linking of this yearlong "super" Shabbat with our own weekly Shabbat implies that if we desist from creative activity, the world around us will be put right.

In Isaiah 61:1, the prophet imagines someone, possibly the messiah, anointed to proclaim freedom *(d'ror)* to captives. During the six days of the workweek, we too are held "captive" to our daily mundane lives, but on Shabbat, God proclaims a *d'ror* for us to be truly free and whole, in anticipation of the coming of the messiah.

◆

(p. 143)

¹לְדִיד נֶפֶשׁ, אַב הָרַחֲמָן, מְשׁוֹךְ עַבְדְּךָ אֶל רְצוֹנֶךָ

יָרוּץ עַבְדְּךָ כְּמוֹ אַיָּל, יִשְׁתַּחֲוֶה אֶל מוּל הֲדָרֶךָ

יֶעֱרַב לוֹ יְדִידוֹתֶךָ מִנֹּפֶת צוּף וְכָל־טָעַם.

²הָדוּר, נָאֶה, זִיו הָעוֹלָם, נַפְשִׁי חוֹלַת אַהֲבָתֶךָ

L. HOFFMAN

popular poem for Shabbat singing to *Machzor Vitry* in France and (later) elsewhere. The version reproduced here is one of two extant possibilities, not the version from *Vitry*, but a variant that occurs in most other places.

◆

J. HOFFMAN (TRANSLATION)

¹ *"Freedom"* Hebrew, *d'ror*, used in connection with the "jubilee" year, that is, the fiftieth year, during which slaves and workers are to be set free. (The English word "jubilee" comes from a translation error. In Hebrew, the year is called *yovel*, which means "horn," probably because a horn was to be sounded in the fiftieth year, marking everyone's freedom. But the (p. 143)

Him proclaim freedom to men and woman." As Americans, it is difficult to ignore the allusion here to Leviticus 25:10, a verse that is engraved on our own Liberty Bell: *U'k'ratem d'ror ba'aretz l'khol yoshveha*, "Proclaim liberty throughout the land to all its inhabitants." But exactly what sort of liberty is being proclaimed here? Some traditional commentators interpret the phrase as referring to the messianic redemption or freedom from the week's labors. But how significant (p. 142)

See my people's cry for help.

³ Tread upon the winepress in Bozrah,
And also the growing city of Babylonia.
Pluck my foes with raging fury.
Hear my voice when I cry out.

⁴ God, grant a mountain in the desert:
Myrtle, wheat, cypress, and elm.
And to the one who warns and the one
   who is warned
Grant peace like the water of a river.

⁵ Stamp out my enemies, my jealous God,
With melting of heart and with anguish.
We'll open our mouth wide and fill it,
Along with our tongue, with joy for You.

⁶ Know wisdom for your soul,
That she be a crown upon your head.
Guard your Holy One's commandment.
Keep your holy Shabbat.

אָנָּא, אֵל נָא, רְפָא נָא לָהּ בְּהֵרָאוֹת לָהּ
נְעַם זִיוָךְ

אָז תִּתְחַזֵּק וְתִתְרַפֵּא, וְהָיְתָה לָךְ שִׁפְחַת
עוֹלָם.

³ רְתִיק, יֶהֱמוּ רַחֲמֶיךָ, וְחוּס נָא עַל בֵּן
אוֹהֲבָךְ

כִּי זֶה כַּמָּה נִכְסוֹף נִכְסַף לִרְאוֹת
בְּתִפְאֶרֶת עֻזָּךְ

אָנָּא, אֵלִי, מַחְמַד לִבִּי, חוּשָׁה נָא, וְאַל
תִּתְעַלָּם.

⁴ גָּלֵה נָא וּפְרוֹשׂ, חָבִיב, עָלַי אֶת־
סֻכַּת שְׁלוֹמָךְ

תָּאִיר אֶרֶץ מִכְּבוֹדָךְ, נָגִילָה
וְנִשְׂמְחָה בָךְ

מַהֵר, אָהוּב, כִּי בָא מוֹעֵד, וְחָנֵּנִי
כִּימֵי עוֹלָם.

BRETTLER (BIBLE)

Plant a vine in my vineyard.
See my people's cry for help.

³ Tread upon the winepress in Bozrah,
And also the growing city of Babylonia.
Pluck my foes with raging fury.
Hear my voice when I cry out.

⁴ God, grant a mountain in the desert:
Myrtle, wheat, cypress, and elm.

And to the one who warns and the one who is warned

Grant peace like the water of a river.

[5] Stamp out my enemies, my jealous God,

With melting of heart and with anguish.

We'll open our mouth wide and fill it,

Along with our tongue, with joy for You.

[6] Know wisdom for your soul,

That she be a crown upon your head.

Guard your Holy One's commandment.

Keep your holy Shabbat.

BRETTLER (BIBLE)

[1] *"Let Him proclaim freedom* [d'ror]*"* "Freedom" [*d'ror*] is used in reference to the Jubilee year, the ultimate Shabbat (Lev. 25:10).

[1] *"To men and women"* According to the Decalogue (Exod. 20:10; Deut. 5:14), both sons and daughters must rest.

[1] *"Guard you like the apple of his eye"* Based on Psalm 17:8, "Guard me like the apple of your eye" *(bat ayin)*.

[1] *"Sit down and rest"* An oblique reference to the commandment before Moses climbs Sinai (Exod. 16:29), "Let everyone remain [*sh'vu*] in place."

[2] *"A sign of salvation"* The main theme is here introduced: Shabbat as anticipation of Israel's restored military might. As in *Havdalah* (see "God is my salvation," p.166), the idea develops initially through variants of the Hebrew root, *y.sh.ʻ*, used biblically concerning God's ultimate deliverance of Israel. Throughout, the poem contrasts Shabbat with God's violent defeat of Israel's enemies.

[2] *"Vine"* An oblique reference to Isaiah 5:2 and Jeremiah 2:21, where a farmer (God) plants a vine, from which only wild, inedible grapes grow. By contrast, the poet hopes for an ideal vineyard, representing redemption.

[3] *"Tread upon the winepress"* Based on Isaiah 63:1–3, where God bloodies Himself in battle against the nations. This is envisioned happening at Edom's capital Bozrah—a pun on the root *b.ts.r*, "to pick grapes."

[3] *"Raging fury"* Likely a reference to Isaiah 13:9, "Lo! The day of Adonai is coming with raging fury and wrath."

DORFF (THEOLOGY)

rain] in flood; and you shall drink of it. You shall be carried on shoulders and bounced upon knees."

[5] *"Jealous God"* In the Bible, God as jealous God stands ready to punish Israel (Exod. 20:5; 34:14; Deut. 4:24; 5:9; 6:15); here, punishment is aimed at other nations.

[5] *"Anguish"* "Anguish" *(m'ginah)* appears only once in the Bible (Lam. 3:63), imploring God for vengeance upon Israel's enemies: "Give them, Adonai, their deserts according to their deeds. Give them anguish [*m'ginah*] of heart; your curse be upon them! Oh, pursue them in wrath and destroy them...."

FRANKEL (A WOMAN'S VOICE)

commandments" Several biblical texts (e.g., Isa. 56:2; Jer. 17:19–27; Ezek. 20:16) describe Shabbat as the *mitzvah* par excellence. As the poem ends, it returns to the opening theme of Shabbat, giving it an air of authority by paraphrasing the Decalogue (Deut. 5:12), "Observe the Shabbat day and keep it holy."

———◆———

DORFF (THEOLOGY)

[1] *"Freedom"* The freedom of which the poem speaks is not freedom from work, but from oppression. Shabbat takes on new symbolism: rest from constantly having to defend ourselves from would-be destroyers.

[1] *"Apple of his eye"* An image drawn from Deuteronomy 32:10:

> He [God] found him [Jacob, as the symbol for Israel] in a desert region,
> In an empty howling waste.
> He engirded him, watched over him,
> Guarded him as the apple of his eye.

Our reprieve from oppressors will arise not through military action, but because God watches over us.

[3] *"Pluck my foes with raging fury"* The point of the poem (repeated in verse 5, lines 17–20)—that God will eventually crush our enemies—seems like a bellicose and bloody theme for Shabbat, but not if we recall how Jews have often lived in circumstances where their very lives were threatened. That is, unfortunately, still the case in many parts of the world, including Israel. So while most readers of this commentary have the luxury of associating Shabbat purely with freedom from work, the poem's concern remains the historical reality of the threat of attack. For Jews in that situation, Shabbat is not just rest, but peace.

[3] *"Babylonia"* The reference to Babylonia as Israel's enemy recalls the vision by Second Isaiah of Israel's return from Babylonian exile to its land (Isa. 55:12–13):

> Yea, you shall leave [the Babylonian exile] in joy and be led home secure.
> Before you, mount and hill shall shout aloud,
> and all the trees of the field shall clap their hands.
> Instead of the brier, a cypress shall rise;
> instead of the nettle, a myrtle shall rise.
> These shall stand as a testimony to Adonai,

GRAY (TALMUD)

common to the region—vineyard, winepress, desert, mountain, myrtle, acacia, cypress, box tree, river. But set against this scenic backdrop is Israel's ceaseless conflict with its neighbors, represented in this song as Bozrah (v. 3), that is, Babylon, together with *tzara'i, kama'i*, "foes, enemies" (vv. 3, 5).

In counterpoint to this large-scale national drama occupying half of the poet's attention is a smaller scale domestic plot: the individual Jew seeking God's blessing. In fact, if we were to delete lines 5, 6, and 9 (which urge God to take vengeance on Israel's enemies), we would find ourselves with a very different sort of song, an alternating dialogue between the poet and the Jewish people, and the poet and God. In the former, Dunash exhorts his fellow Jews to praise God, study Torah, and observe the Sabbath, in reward for which God will protect, honor, and redeem them. In the latter, he turns to

KUSHNER & POLEN (CHASIDISM)

that this tenth-century poet chose to extend this freedom to women together with men. The ideal Sabbath is envisioned here as a day of liberation for all whose *l'shoneinu l'kha rinah*, "tongues offer joyful song to God" (v. 5).

——◆——

GRAY (TALMUD)

[1] *"Let Him proclaim freedom* [d'ror]*"* The Hebrew word *d'ror* ("freedom") is found five times in the Bible (Lev. 25:10; Isa. 61:1; Jer. 34:8, 15, 17), the first of which (Lev. 25:10) is critical here: "You shall hallow the fiftieth year. You shall proclaim freedom [*d'ror*] throughout the land for all its inhabitants. It shall be a jubilee for you." The fiftieth, or jubilee, year comes at the end of seven cycles of seven years each. Each cycle was called a "sabbatical" cycle, and every seventh year was a "sabbatical" year when agricultural activity in the Land of Israel ceased and debts were canceled. The seventh (or sabbatical) year was in essence a yearlong "Shabbat" for the land, and in the fiftieth (or jubilee) year, one step higher still, land also reverted to its original owners (Lev. 25:10, 13) and slaves were freed (Jer. 34:9). The jubilee year is thus a time of great societal release in which (1) the land rested and (2) both ancestral holdings and people sold away during the previous fifty years were returned to their families. In a word, the

L. HOFFMAN (HISTORY)

(HISTORY)

D'ror Yikra ("Let Him Proclaim Freedom") One of the older *z'mirot, D'ror Yikra* is traditionally attributed to Dunash ibn Labrat (mid-tenth century), a poet and grammarian from Baghdad, who lived also for some time in Cordoba, which was part of the Spanish golden age under Islam. This Jewish renaissance was led by Chisdai ibn Shaprut (915–970), a Jewish businessman who became a significant diplomat in the Muslim hierarchy and the chief patron of Jewish renewal. Chisdai supported, among others, Menachem ben Saruk, who served as what we might consider a chief of staff. As language generally and poetry in particular were arts that were highly valued in Islamic circles; among Menachem's duties was the preparation of a dictionary, which Dunash attacked on halakhic and theological grounds, until Menachem lost his position in Chisdai's court.

D'ror Yikra appears first in the eleventh-century work *Machzor Vitry.* In several of the verses, the first letters of each line (taken together) spell out "Dunash," and because Dunash ibn Labrat was a poet with a colorful reputation, it was natural to attribute the work to him.

Alternatively, the poem is by yet another Dunash—Dunash ibn Tamim (c. 890–960), perhaps, another linguist and philosopher of the same period.

In either case, the writer probably lived in the tenth century and bequeathed a

J. HOFFMAN (TRANSLATION)

Hebrew word *yovel* just happens to sound like the Latin *iobelius,* meaning "celebrate," from which the very common, but wrong, translation "jubilee" derives.

[1] *"Apple of his eye"* Literally, "pupil of his eye."

[2] *"Vine"* The Hebrew word for vine here, *sorek,* is more poetic than the common *gefen.*

[2] *"Vineyard"* Unlike its English translation, the Hebrew word for vineyard, *kerem,* does not contain the word "vine." The Hebrew is thus more poetic than the redundant "vine in my vineyard."

[2] *"See my people's cry for help"* The Hebrew is considerably more poetic, using two rare words and alliteration. The word for "see" is *sh'e,* while the word for "cry" is *shav'a.*

[3] *"Bozrah [botsrah]"* Bozrah is a biblical town, perhaps the capital of Edom. But the name "Bozrah" seems to come from the root *b.ts.r,* which means "to harvest grapes," creating a verbal pun we cannot capture in English.

[3] *"Babylonia [bavel]"* Or "Babel." *Bavel* in Hebrew is called "Babel" in English when referring to the mythic biblical city (as in the story of the Tower of Babel), but

"Babylonia" or "Babylon" when referring to historical places. (The area called Babylonia is now in the country called Iraq.)

[3] *"Raging fury"* Literally, "nose" and "fury." "Nose" is commonly used to refer to anger.

[4] *"Elm"* Hebrew, *tidhar,* from Isaiah 41:19 and 60:13. It is not clear what kind of tree this was.

[4] *"One who warns and the one who is warned"* Although the root for "warn" is identical to the root for "shine," the particular verb forms here make it clear that the words have to do with "warning."

[5] *"My jealous God"* Literally, just "jealous God," but as we have done elsewhere, we add "my" to express the vocative. "O jealous God" seems archaic to us.

[5] *"Anguish"* We find the Hebrew word for "anguish" *(m'ginah)* only once in the Bible, Lamentations 3:65, where it appears with the word "heart," as in "anguish of the heart." *M'ginah* there is likely a word play on the similar-sounding *manginah,* "melody," which the author uses two verses earlier. Our line here is an oblique reference to Lamentations.

III. *Y'DID NEFESH* ("SOUL'S COMPANION")

[1] Soul's companion, source of mercy, draw your servant to your will.

Your servant like a deer shall run, to bow down low before your throne.

Your companionship will be sweeter than a honeycomb.

[2] Enthroned, adorned, light to the world, my lovesick soul pines for You.

O healer, heal this aching soul by shining forth your soothing light

With strength restored and health returned to be your servant day and night.

[3] Ancient One, compassionate, show kindness to your loving child.

So long I've yearned and still I yearn the glory of your might to see.

I plead my God, my heart's desire. Show mercy! Don't abandon me!

[4] Reveal Yourself, my precious One, envelop me with your sheltering peace.

Shine forth your glory on the world. We'll revel and rejoice in You.

Be quick my love. The time has come! And favor me with grace renewed.

III. *Y'DID NEFESH* ("SOUL'S COMPANION")

[1] Soul's companion, source of mercy, draw your servant to your will.
Your servant like a deer shall run, to bow down low before your throne.
Your companionship will be sweeter than a honeycomb.

[2] Enthroned, adorned, light to the world, my lovesick soul pines for You.
O healer, heal this aching soul by shining forth your soothing light
With strength restored and health returned to be your servant day and night.

[3] Ancient One, compassionate, show kindness to your loving child.
So long I've yearned and still I yearn the glory of your might to see.
I plead my God, my heart's desire. Show mercy! Don't abandon me!

[4] Reveal Yourself, my precious One, envelop me with your sheltering peace.
Shine forth your glory on the world. We'll revel and rejoice in You.
Be quick my love. The time has come! And favor me with grace renewed.

BRETTLER (BIBLE)

[1] *"Soul's companion, source of mercy"* As a poem concerned with mystical union, it is distant from the Bible, which tends to emphasize the chasm between God and humans. Stylistically speaking also, the Bible differs, in that only rarely (e.g., 2 Sam. 22:2–3) does it pile on divine epithets as here—"soul's companion," "source of mercy," "enthroned," "adorned," "light to the world," and so on.

Still, a few biblical texts contain incipient notions of mystical union, which are further developed in early post-biblical literature—Psalm 42:2–3, for example: "Like a deer crying for water, my soul cries for You, Adonai; my soul thirsts for God, the living God; O when will I come to appear before God!" Also, the poem draws much of its diction from the Bible. God is the "companion" in Isaiah 5:1, and "source of mercy" comes from Psalm 103:13: "As a father has compassion for his children, so Adonai has compassion for those who fear Him."

[1] *"Your servant"* The supplicant as God's servant *(eved)* is common in the Bible, as in ancient Near Eastern analogues. For example, the supplicant in Psalm 86:16 entreats Adonai, "Turn to me and have mercy on me; grant your strength to your servant...." In the Flood account preserved in the Mesopotamian *Gilgamesh Epic,* the flood hero Utnapishtim says, "Ea (the god of wisdom)...said to me, his servant" (tablet 11, lines 36–37).

[1] *"Like a deer* [ayal] *shall run"* An *ayal* is known for its speed (Song of

הַחַמָּה מֵרֹאשׁ הָאִילָנוֹת נִסְתַּלְּקָה— [1]
בֹּאוּ וְנֵצֵא לִקְרַאת שַׁבָּת הַמַּלְכָּה.
הִנֵּה הִיא יוֹרֶדֶת הַקְּדוֹשָׁה, הַבְּרוּכָה,
וְעִמָּהּ מַלְאָכִים צְבָא שָׁלוֹם וּמְנוּחָה.
בֹּאִי, בֹּאִי, הַמַּלְכָּה! [2]
בֹּאִי, בֹּאִי, הַמַּלְכָּה!—
שָׁלוֹם עֲלֵיכֶם, מַלְאֲכֵי הַשָּׁלוֹם! [3]
קִבַּלְנוּ פְּנֵי שַׁבָּת בִּרְנָנָה וּתְפִלָּה, [4]
הַבַּיְתָה נָשׁוּבָה, בְּלֵב מָלֵא גִילָה,
שָׁם עָרוּךְ הַשֻּׁלְחָן, הַנֵּרוֹת יָאִירוּ,
כָּל־פִּנּוֹת הַבַּיִת יִזְרָחוּ, יַזְהִירוּ.
שַׁבָּת שָׁלוֹם וּמְבֹרָךְ! [5]
שַׁבָּת שָׁלוֹם וּמְבֹרָךְ!
בֹּאֲכֶם לְשָׁלוֹם, מַלְאֲכֵי הַשָּׁלוֹם! [6]
שִׁבְעִי, זַכָּה, עִמָּנוּ וּבְזִיוֵךְ נָא אוֹרִי [7]
לַיְלָה וָיוֹם, אַחַר תַּעֲבֹרִי.
וַאֲנַחְנוּ נְכַבְּדֵךְ בְּבִגְדֵי חֲמוּדוֹת,
בִּזְמִירוֹת וּתְפִלּוֹת וּבְשָׁלֹשׁ סְעֻדוֹת.
וּבִמְנוּחָה שְׁלֵמָה, [8]
וּבִמְנוּחָה נָעֵמָה—
בָּרְכוּנוּ לְשָׁלוֹם, מַלְאֲכֵי הַשָּׁלוֹם! [9]
הַחַמָּה מֵרֹאשׁ הָאִילָנוֹת נִסְתַּלְּקָה— [10]
בֹּאוּ וּנְלַוֶּה אֶת־שַׁבָּת הַמַּלְכָּה.
צֵאתֵךְ לְשָׁלוֹם, הַקְּדוֹשָׁה, הַזַּכָּה—
דְּעִי, שֵׁשֶׁת יָמִים אֶל שׁוּבֵךְ נְחַכֶּה...
כֵּן לַשַּׁבָּת הַבָּאָה! [11]
כֵּן לַשַּׁבָּת הַבָּאָה:
צֵאתְכֶם לְשָׁלוֹם, מַלְאֲכֵי הַשָּׁלוֹם! [12]

² *"Day and night"* From the reference to redemption in Isaiah 35:10; 51:11: "The ransomed of Adonai shall return, and come with shouting to Zion, crowned with joy everlasting. They shall attain joy and gladness."

³ *"I've yearned"* A paraphrase of a biblical allusion to the mystical search: "I yearn for the courts of Adonai; my body and soul shout for joy to the living God" (Ps. 84:3).

³ *"Glory of your might"* Based on Psalm 89:18, "You are their strength in which they glory." The poet is making an oblique reference to messianic hope, assuming that the reader knows the last half of the biblical verse: "Our horn [the Davidic king] is exalted through your favor."

³ *"Don't abandon me"* Calls for God to "wake up" and act are frequent in Psalms—for example, "Rouse Yourself; why do You sleep, Adonai? Awaken, do not reject us forever!" (Psalm 44:24). This idea is softened here by removing explicit mention of God awakening. "Don't abandon me" is biblical (Ps. 55:2; Lam. 3:56).

⁴ *"Reveal yourself"* "Reveal" may denote either God's physical appearance or the technical sense, as in (p. 151)

Y'did Nefesh ("Soul's Companion") Like the Song of Songs, *Y'did Nefesh* can be understood as a spiritual love song rooted in human metaphor. However, unlike its biblical precursor, the speaker here exclusively addresses God, sometimes as lover, portrayed variously in the guise of the Jewish people, the individual Jew, and the soul; and other times as courtly envoy, speaking on behalf of his master waiting in the wings.

The language, though less graphically sensuous than (p. 152)

Songs 8:14); the *ayal* here alludes to the mystical connotation of Psalm 42:2, "Like a deer [*ayal*] crying for water, my soul cries for You, O God."

¹ *"Before your throne"* "Your throne" may refer to God, because "throne" appears frequently as a biblical epithet for God or the Temple (called "throne of glory" [Pss. 29:2; 96:9]). The poet combines both, by wishing to worship God at the (restored) Temple.

¹ *"Sweeter than a honeycomb"* A reapplication of Psalm 19:11, where God's commandments are "more Drawing upon kabbalistic ideas and imagery, he depicts the soul as the immanent *Sh'khinah,* longing for union with her consort, the transcendent Lord of the universe. Lovesick and weak, she hungers for dainties, *nofet tsuf*—literally, "honeycomb" (v. 1)—from her divine lover's hand.

How are contemporary Jewish women to relate to this seventeenth-century poem? Are we to identify with the soul? If we do, what happens to this identity when we become speakers in this poem? If we identify with the (p. 152) we're really only requesting that God will cure the lovesickness of this *present* moment. This will, however, in turn, create yet a new and more heightened awareness of our distance from God. And, in this way, the absence of intimacy with God will be even more keenly felt. It will serve as an impetus to

draw close again.

———◆———

הַחַמָּה מֵראֹש הָאִילָנוֹת נִסְתַּלְּקָה־¹
בֹּאוּ וְנֵצֵא לִקְרַאת שַׁבָּת הַמַּלְכָּה.
הִנֵּה הִיא יוֹרֶדֶת הַקְּדוֹשָׁה, הַבְּרוּכָה,
וְעִמָּהּ מַלְאָכִים צְבָא שָׁלוֹם וּמְנוּחָה.
בֹּאִי, בֹּאִי, הַמַּלְכָּה!²
בֹּאִי, בֹּאִי, הַמַּלְכָּה!־
שָׁלוֹם עֲלֵיכֶם, מַלְאֲכֵי הַשָּׁלוֹם!³

L. HOFFMAN (HISTORY)

THE ORIGINAL MANUSCRIPT OF Y'DID NEFESH EXISTS IN THE LIBRARY OF THE JEWISH THEOLOGICAL SEMINARY OF AMERICA IN NEW YORK. BUT IT HAS COME DOWN TO US IN MANY VARIED, AND OFTEN GARBLED, VERSIONS, TO WHICH COMMON MELODIES HAVE BEEN SET, MAKING IT HARD TO SUBSTITUTE THE ORIGINAL, EVEN WHEN WE KNOW IT IS ACCURATE AND THE ONE WE ARE USING IS NOT. THE COMMONEST SUCH VERSION IS CARRIED, AMONG OTHER PLACES, IN THE ARTSCROLL SIDDUR. THE REFORM MOVEMENT'S GATES OF PRAYER USES THAT VERSION, CHANGING ONLY A SINGLE LINE WHICH, AS IT STANDS, CANNOT BE GRAMMATICALLY CORRECT. OUR TRANSLATION FOLLOWS THE SCIENTIFIC TEXT, HOWEVER. JOEL M. (p. 154) HOFFMAN'S COMMENTARY desirable than gold" and "sweeter than honey, than a honeycomb."

2 *"Adorned [na'eh]"* In the Bible, God is never called *na'eh* (which could also mean "handsome"), though He is often modeled after kings who are considered handsome (e.g., 1 Sam. 16:18, of David).

2 *"My lovesick soul"* In the Song of Songs (2:5; 5:8), lovesickness reflects a deep desire to be with an unavailable lover.

2 *"Heal"* From Numbers 12:13, where Moses asks God to heal Miriam from *tsara'at,* a scaly skin disease, often incorrectly translated as "leprosy"; here, analogized as a request to heal the lovesick soul.

2 *"Your soothing [no'am] light"* *No'am* may also just mean "beauty." In any case, this is based on Psalm 27:4, "One thing I ask of Adonai...to live in the house of Adonai all the days of my life, to gaze upon the *no'am* of Adonai...." This is combined with a biblical idea that has Mesopotamian antecedents: that kings and deities have a glowing visage to reflect their power. This visage [*zivakh*] appears in the opening and closing lines of the stanza. It is God's radiance that will cure the soul's lovesickness (see comment above, "My lovesick soul").

קִבַּלְנוּ פְּנֵי שַׁבָּת בִּרְנָנָה וּתְפִלָּה,⁴
הַבַּיְתָה נָשׁוּבָה, בְּלֵב מָלֵא גִילָה.
שָׁם עָרוּךְ הַשֻּׁלְחָן, הַנֵּרוֹת יָאִירוּ,
כָּל־פִּנּוֹת הַבַּיִת יִזְרָחוּ, יַזְהִירוּ.
שַׁבָּת שָׁלוֹם וּמְבֹרָךְ!⁵
שַׁבָּת שָׁלוֹם וּמְבֹרָךְ!
בֹּאֲכֶם לְשָׁלוֹם, מַלְאֲכֵי הַשָּׁלוֹם!⁶
שְׁבִי, זַכָּה, עִמָּנוּ וּבְזִיוֵךְ נָא אוֹרִי⁷
לַיְלָה וָיוֹם, אַחַר תַּעֲבֹרִי.
וַאֲנַחְנוּ נְכַבְּדֵךְ בְּבִגְדֵי חֲמוּדוֹת,
בִּזְמִירוֹת וּתְפִלּוֹת וּבְשָׁלֹשׁ סְעֻדוֹת.
וּבִמְנוּחָה שְׁלֵמָה,⁸
וּבִמְנוּחָה נָעֵמָה–
בָּרְכוּנוּ לְשָׁלוֹם, מַלְאֲכֵי הַשָּׁלוֹם!⁹
הַחַמָּה מֵרֹאשׁ הָאִילָנוֹת נִסְתַּלְּקָה–¹⁰
בֹּאוּ וּנְלַוֶּה אֶת־שַׁבָּת הַמַּלְכָּה.
צֵאתֵךְ לְשָׁלוֹם, הַקְּדוֹשָׁה, הַזַּכָּה–
דְּעִי, שֵׁשֶׁת יָמִים אֶל שׁוּבֵךְ נְחַכֶּה...
כֵּן לַשַּׁבָּת הַבָּאָה!¹¹
כֵּן לַשַּׁבָּת הַבָּאָה:
צֵאתְכֶם לְשָׁלוֹם, מַלְאֲכֵי הַשָּׁלוֹם!¹²

DORFF (THEOLOGY)

"to reveal to a prophet." The poem's mystical context suggests the former.

[4] *"Shine forth"* Again (see comment above, "Reveal yourself"), the line may be literal or just a metaphoric reference to a better time. The latter is suggested by the use of "your glory" *(k'vodakh),* the Hebrew word that ends the first half of the line, and "We'll revel" *(nagilah),* which comes next and begins the second half. What we have is a play on words referring to the prophecy of restoration. Isaiah 40:5 reads: "The glory *(k'vod)* of Adonai shall appear *(niglah),* and all flesh, as one, shall behold...." *Nagilah* and *niglah* sound similar.

[4] *"We'll revel"* Song of Songs 1:4. In much of Jewish tradition, this ancient love song was understood as an allegory of the love between God and Israel.

[4] *"The time has come"* From Psalm 102:14, "You will surely arise and take pity on Zion, for it is time to be gracious to her; the time has come." The notion is that the destruction of Jerusalem will last for a certain predetermined period. Jeremiah (25:11–12; 29:10) sets it as "seventy years"; in Daniel 9 we see attempts at understanding what this seventy years really meant, because Jerusalem was not fully and permanently restored seventy years after Jeremiah.

[4] *"Renewed* [kimei olam]*"* More literally, "as in days of old." In prophetic rhetoric, "days of old" represents the idealized days of yore (e.g., Amos 9:11; Micah 7:14; Mal. 3:4).

———◆———

DORFF (THEOLOGY)

[1] *"Soul's companion"* The poem's expression of yearning for messianic times is deeply personal. God is my "soul's companion" (v. 1); "my lovesick soul pines for You" (v. 2). This is not a request to some distant deity; it is a prayer to a lover, as in Song of Songs. Verse 3 shifts the image to Israel as a beloved child, but the theme of God as lover returns in verse 4, where God is "my precious one" and "my love." God is to show compassion as a parent for a child and as a lover toward a beloved.

[2] *"Heal this aching soul"* Ultimately, the poem asks for the healing of soul that comes through seeing God's radiant splendor—meaning the messianic era when God will rule again.

[4] *"With sheltering peace"* A hope for peace, another aspect of the messianic dream.

[4] *"The time has come"* Friday evening is especially appropriate to voice messianic hope, "the time has come," the one that the Rabbis describe as "a foretaste of the world-to-come" (Gen. Rab. 17:5 [17:7 in some editions]), or "the holiness of the world-to-come" *(Mekhilta* to Exod. 31:13; *Batei Midrashot* 2: 46:9; 47:62; 48:61, according to

151

which it is a sixtieth of what we will experience in the world-to-come).

———◆———

FRANKEL (A WOMAN'S VOICE)

FRANKEL (A WOMAN'S VOICE)

that found in the Song of Songs, is no less intimate. God is here addressed as *y'did,* "companion" (v. 1); *chaviv,* "my precious one" (v. 4); and *ahuv,* "love" (v. 4). The speaker refers to himself as *ben ohavakh,* "your love-child" (v. 3)—"your loving child," in our translation— and yearns for the divine embrace. A cascade of verbs, adverbs, and phrases throughout the four stanzas convey urgency and longing: *yarutz...k'mo ayal,* literally, "run like a gazelle" (v. 1); *nikhsof nikhsaf,* "so long I've yearned and still I yearn" (v. 3); and *maher,* "be quick" (v. 4). The soul is depicted as physically ill with longing for her creator. In fact, the poem cites Moses' prayer for his afflicted sister Miriam—*El na r'fa na lah,* "Please, God, heal her" (v. 2; "O healer, heal" in our translation)—but here, in its new setting, it refers to lovesickness! Clearly, Elazar Azikri, the mystic poet who composed this hymn, meant to stir his audience through his words into an ecstatic state of expectancy.

Although it is only a grammatical coincidence that "soul," *nefesh,* is a feminine noun in Hebrew, Azikri takes advantage of this coincidence to dramatize his poetic conceit.

GRAY (TALMUD)

speaker who speaks on the soul's behalf, are we then divided against ourselves, speaking, as it were, through both sides of our mouths? And what about the beliefs concerning human nature implicit in this song? Is its vision offensive because it bends gender to fit a rigidly heterosexual, even misogynist, world-view, relegating women to mere receptacles of divine grace?

Significantly, *Y'did Nefesh* appears to have escaped the linguistic gender wars of our time. Perhaps this is because the melodies to which it has been set are so hauntingly beautiful as to transcend bad theology. Or perhaps it is because Azikri's poetic language is so tender and lyrical that we cannot believe that any offense is meant. If we look back to rabbinic times, we discover that the Rabbis were similarly torn when considering whether to include Song of Songs in the biblical canon. At that time, Rabbi Akiba argued that this clearly erotic work was *kodesh kodashim,* "the holiest of the holy," and deserved an honored place within our sacred Scripture. *Y'did Nefesh* seems a fitting sequel to that ancient valentine.

———◆———

GRAY (TALMUD)

[1] *"Soul's companion"* This *zemer* addresses God in deeply romantic, even erotic, terms—such as "my lovesick soul pines for You" (v. 2). Such an orientation to the divine characterizes the Kabbalah (particularly its major work, the *Zohar*), but it is also present in talmudic and halakhic piety. In the *Mekhilta D'rabbi Yishmael* (third century C.E.), Rabbi Akiba represents Israel as a lover, using Song of Songs to describe her beloved, God, to the nations of the world: "I am my beloved's and my beloved is mine" (2:16). In the Middle Ages, this erotic love of God shows up strikingly in *Sefer Hasidim* 14 (twelfth century, Germany), where the author interprets Deuteronomy 6:5 to say our love of God should be so intense that it dwarfs even the intense sexual pleasure experienced by a couple having intercourse after a prolonged separation.

Nevertheless the Talmud also channels the erotic energy of the Song of Songs into day-by-day piety. Just seeing the Song of Songs in a dream was said to herald a life of piety (Ber. 57b), and it was the Song of Songs (8:13) that served to prove the lesson that two Torah scholars who respect each other's views would merit having God listen to them (Shab. 63a).

◆

KUSHNER & POLEN (CHASIDISM)

Y'did Nefesh ("Soul's Companion") A contemporary rendition of *Y'did Nefesh* (from Lawrence Kushner, *The Way Into Jewish Mysticism*, [Woodstock, Vt.: Jewish Lights, 2001] pp. 46–48), which attempts to capture some of the Eros of this extraordinary mystical love poem:

> O Love of my soul, Father of Womb;
>   draw me to Your want,
> I can run like a deer;
>   reverent toward Your presence,
> Your love so soft;
>   even sweeter than liquid honey.
>
> Radiant brightness of Being;
>   my soul, faint with Your yearning,
> O God of seeking, heal her;
>   show her the ecstasy of Your light.
> Then at last recovery and vigor;
>   now Your servant and forever.
>
> O God, Your longing intimacy;
>   easy please for a child You love,
> I am only this endless waiting
>   and wanting;
>   just to peek Your Presence,
> Please God, my heart's desire;
>   hurry now with no more hiding.

Show me here Your love;
   cover me with the shade of Your time.
Your Presence lighting the sky;
   a wedding feast of Your joy,
Hurry now my darling, the time is here;
   loving like long, long ago.

[1] *"Honeycomb [tsuf]"* Rabbi Moshe Hayim Ephraim of Sudlikov, in his *Degel Machaneh Ephraim (Likkutim),* notes that the word *tsuf,* "honeycomb," in the last line of the first stanza is similar to one of the words for prophecy, *tsofeh.* Yet so great is our yearning for intimacy with God, he notes, that we choose it not only over honey but also even over being able to foretell the future.

[2] *"My lovesick soul pines for You...heal this aching soul"* Rabbi Yoshker Dov of Belz asked his father, Rabbi Joshua of Belz, "Why, if we're lovesick for God, do we want to be healed?" Shouldn't lovesickness for God be the ultimate goal? His father explained that

J. HOFFMAN (TRANSLATION)

DISCUSSES IT AND POINTS OUT WAYS IN WHICH IT DIFFERS FROM THE COMMONLY USED VERSION (SEE P. 137). ALL OTHER COMMENTARIES HERE FOLLOW THE COMMONLY USED TEXT, BECAUSE IT IS THE VERSION WE NORMALLY ENCOUNTER.

Y'did Nefesh ("Soul's Companion") A mystical poem fraught with esoteric allusions, and composed by Elazar Azikri (or Azkari), a sixteenth-century kabbalist from Safed (see pp. 27–28).

[3] *"My God, my heart's desire"* The common song "Eleh Chamdah Libi" is a garbled version of this. As the song stands, it cannot be correct. *Eleh* (meaning "these") is plural and has no referent (these "what"?) because it is followed by *chamdah libi* ("my heart's desire"), which is singular. Moreover, *chamdah libi* in itself is incorrect, because the proper form would be *chemdat,* the possessive, or genitive, case of *chemdah* (not *chamdah*). The proper version might be *eli chemdat libi,* meaning "my God, my heart's desire." But even that is not correct, as it happens. The manuscript original (which we use here) shows us *eli machmad libi,* meaning the same thing: "my God, my heart's desire."

———◆———

2

J. HOFFMAN (TRANSLATION)

[1] *Y'did Nefesh [1]* This currently exists in essentially two forms: the original poem and the version commonly used liturgically. The liturgical version—which is actually a set of versions, themselves with minor internal variations—differs from the original in the following key ways.

In terms of content, the imagery in the last line of the second verse of the original, which refers to "your (female) servant," has been eliminated. In place of the line that reads "[my soul] will forever be your servant," the liturgical versions give us, "[my soul] will always have eternal happiness." Unfortunately, this change destroys the parallelism between the first and second verses, both of which originally referred to serving God, and which offered rare egalitarianism, as discussed below.

The second major content change appears in the last verse, where the liturgical versions substitute "Be quick. Love [us] … and favor us with grace" for the original, "Be quick my love … and favor me with grace." The poem is thus transformed from a personal address to "my love" into a communal prayer asking for God's love.

Thirdly, the original "child of your love," which we translate here as "your loving child," has been changed in the liturgical versions to "child of your beloved."

Furthermore, most of the liturgical versions offer ungrammatical variations on the original ending of the third verse; the *GOP* version offers grammatical but still erroneous text.

[1] שָׁמְרוּ בְנֵי יִשְׂרָאֵל אֶת־הַשַּׁבָּת, לַעֲשׂוֹת אֶת־הַשַּׁבָּת לְדֹרֹתָם בְּרִית עוֹלָם. [2] בֵּינִי וּבֵין בְּנֵי יִשְׂרָאֵל אוֹת הִיא לְעֹלָם, כִּי שֵׁשֶׁת יָמִים עָשָׂה יְיָ אֶת־הַשָּׁמַיִם וְאֶת־הָאָרֶץ, וּבַיּוֹם הַשְּׁבִיעִי שָׁבַת וַיִּנָּפַשׁ.

[3] זָכוֹר אֶת־יוֹם הַשַּׁבָּת לְקַדְּשׁוֹ. [4] שֵׁשֶׁת יָמִים תַּעֲבֹד וְעָשִׂיתָ כָּל־מְלַאכְתֶּךָ. [5] וְיוֹם הַשְּׁבִיעִי שַׁבָּת לַיְיָ אֱלֹהֶיךָ, לֹא תַעֲשֶׂה כָל־מְלָאכָה, אַתָּה־וּבִנְךָ וּבִתֶּךָ עַבְדְּךָ וַאֲמָתְךָ וּבְהֶמְתֶּךָ, וְגֵרְךָ אֲשֶׁר בִּשְׁעָרֶיךָ. [6] כִּי שֵׁשֶׁת־יָמִים עָשָׂה יְיָ אֶת־הַשָּׁמַיִם וְאֶת־הָאָרֶץ אֶת־הַיָּם וְאֶת־כָּל־אֲשֶׁר־בָּם, וַיָּנַח בַּיּוֹם הַשְּׁבִיעִי [7] עַל כֵּן בֵּרַךְ יְיָ אֶת־יוֹם הַשַּׁבָּת וַיְקַדְּשֵׁהוּ.

[8] סַבְרֵי מָרָנָן וְרַבּוֹתָי.

[9] בָּרוּךְ אַתָּה יְיָ אֱלֹהֵינוּ מֶלֶךְ הָעוֹלָם, בּוֹרֵא פְּרִי הַגָּפֶן.

accurately as we might have, because we wanted to capture the more formal poetic aspects.

In terms of content, the poem is an erotic love poem between the author and God. The author is described with masculine imagery as *eved* ("servant") in the first verse, and then in feminine imagery as *shifchah* ("maidservant") in the second. The third and forth verses express the author's longing for God's love, ending with a plea for God to be quick and favor the author with love.

[1] *"Soul's"* The word for "soul" here, *nefesh,* is like the English "soul" in that it connotes a spiritual center within; but unlike English, it also connotes "person" (as in the English *(p. 158)*

Numbers calls on God to "heal her," where "her" is "Miriam." Here we find a wonderful bit of poetry: the "her" is "the lovesick soul," as described next.

[2] *"This aching soul"* The Hebrew is simply "her," referring to "the soul" mentioned in the first line. The "she" contrasts with "he" in the first verse (see above, "Sweeter"). We cannot use "she" or "he" here, and so we repeat the noun.

[2] *"Shining forth"* Literally, "by showing," but the word for "showing" is poetic, so we choose equally poetic English here to capture it.

[2] *"Light"* The same poetic word for light that we saw immediately above.

(p. 159)

IV. SHABBAT HAMALKAH ("THE SHABBAT QUEEN")

[1] The sun has disappeared from behind the treetops.
Come, let us go to meet the Shabbat queen,
For she is descending, holy, and blessed,
Accompanied by angels of peace and rest.
[2] Come forth, come forth, O queen.
Come forth, come forth, O queen.
[3] Peace to you, angels of peace!

[4] We'll greet Shabbat with joy and prayer,
Then return home with
hearts full of joy.   *(p. 160)*

Still, the point of all the versions is the same: "God is my heart's desire." (As it happens, the ungrammatical version has made its way into the popular song "Eileh Chamda Libi.")

Finally, the versions differ on minor grammatical points that affect the pronunciation (but not meaning) of many words.

Y'did Nefesh ("Soul's Companion") *[2]* Two general comments about *Y'did Nefesh* are in order, first about our translation, and then about the general content.

Know that we will wait six days for you to return.
[11] Yes, to the next Shabbat.
Yes, to the next Shabbat.
[12] Go in peace, angels of peace.

(p. 161)

beginning of Shabbat, going out to greet the Shabbat, Shabbat angels, Shabbat as a queen, anticipating the following Shabbat during the six weekdays—are not biblical in origin. What is striking is the way that a modern poet, unlike his medieval predecessors, can avoid biblical style and motifs.

———◆———

DORFF (THEOLOGY)

[1] *"Come, let us go meet"* A direct quotation from the Talmud (Shab. 119a), according to which Rabbi Chaninah would wrap himself in his prayer shawl as the sun was *(p. 163)*

bride, Shabbat's reception has arrived." (See forthcoming commentary in Volume 8, *Shabbat in the Synagogue.*)

Neither image logically excludes the other, for queens can be brides, and brides queens. The choice of each author is theologically based. Alkabetz emphasizes the bridal image because of the kabbalistic doctrine that on Shabbat, the masculine and feminine sides of God are united sexually in a divine marriage. Bialik, on the other hand, was a modern, Enlightenment figure. His deep interests in rationality and culture did not prevent him from using traditional poetic imagery, but a mystical perception of a God who is both male and female and who engages in sexual intercourse would *(p. 163)*

וְשָׁמְרוּ בְנֵי יִשְׂרָאֵל אֶת־הַשַּׁבָּת, לַעֲשׂוֹת אֶת־הַשַּׁבָּת לְדֹרֹתָם בְּרִית עוֹלָם. ²בֵּינִי וּבֵין בְּנֵי יִשְׂרָאֵל אוֹת הִיא לְעֹלָם, כִּי שֵׁשֶׁת יָמִים עָשָׂה יְיָ אֶת־הַשָּׁמַיִם וְאֶת־ הָאָרֶץ, וּבַיּוֹם הַשְּׁבִיעִי שָׁבַת וַיִּנָּפַשׁ.

³זָכוֹר אֶת־יוֹם הַשַּׁבָּת לְקַדְּשׁוֹ. ⁴שֵׁשֶׁת יָמִים תַּעֲבֹד וְעָשִׂיתָ כָּל־מְלַאכְתֶּךָ. ⁵וְיוֹם הַשְּׁבִיעִי שַׁבָּת לַיְיָ

Night and day, before you leave,
We will honor you with fine clothes,
with songs and prayers, and with
   three meals.
[8] And with complete rest.
And with pleasant rest.
[9] Bless us with peace, angels of
   peace.
[10] The sun has disappeared from
   behind the treetops.
Come, let us accompany the Shabbat
   queen.
(p. 161)

Like other lyric passages in this volume, "Soul's Companion" is a mixture of poetic language, meter, and rhyme. In this case, however, we have put more importance on preserving the meter and rhyme. For purposes of printing it on the page, the printed versions often give the impression that there are six lines to each stanza, but the original poem consists of only four lengthy verses of three lines each, forming an AAB rhyme scheme; each line consists of eight heavy syllables. Our translation, likewise, gives four three-line verses, with eight heavy syllables per line. Rather than an AAB rhyme scheme, which we found impossible to retain in the English, our translation offers an ABB scheme, which provides the flavor of the original Hebrew. To the extent possible, we have preserved the original imagery of the poem, but we have not translated the content as

אֱלֹהֶיךָ, לֹא תַעֲשֶׂה כָל־מְלָאכָה, אַתָּה־ וּבִנְךָ וּבִתֶּךָ עַבְדְּךָ וַאֲמָתְךָ וּבְהֶמְתֶּךָ, וְגֵרְךָ אֲשֶׁר בִּשְׁעָרֶיךָ. [6] כִּי שֵׁשֶׁת־יָמִים עָשָׂה יְיָ אֶת־הַשָּׁמַיִם וְאֶת־הָאָרֶץ אֶת־ הַיָּם וְאֶת־כָּל־אֲשֶׁר־בָּם, וַיָּנַח בַּיּוֹם הַשְּׁבִיעִי [7] עַל כֵּן בֵּרַךְ יְיָ אֶת־יוֹם הַשַּׁבָּת וַיְקַדְּשֵׁהוּ.

[8] סָבְרֵי מָרָנָן וְרַבּוֹתַי.

[9] בָּרוּךְ אַתָּה יְיָ אֱלֹהֵינוּ מֶלֶךְ הָעוֹלָם, בּוֹרֵא פְּרִי הַגָּפֶן.

***

BRETTLER (BIBLE)

"not a soul was left in the room"). It does not refer to the part of a person that lives on after death.

[1] *"Companion* [y'did]" Or "friend." The word returns in a related form (y'didut) in the third line.

[1] *"Source"* Literally, "father."

[1] *"Throne"* Literally, "glory," used metonymically to refer to God's power and might. See also below, "enthroned."

[1] *"Companionship"* Hebrew, y'didut, repeating the imagery from the first line.

[1] *"Sweeter"* Literally, "sweeter to him" *(lo)*, where "him" refers to "your servant." The "him" here contrasts with the "her" *(lah)* in the second verse, which is used to refer to the author's "soul." But this trick of using "his" and then "her," which works in Hebrew

because every word has gender, does not work in English.

[1] *"Honeycomb"* Literally, the Hebrew reads, "sweeter than the honeycomb's honey." But in Hebrew the word for "honeycomb" does not contain the word "honey," so we translate, simply, "sweeter than a honeycomb."

Additionally, it is worth noting that for "honey," the author chooses the rare *nofet,* not the more common *d'vash.*

Finally, the Hebrew finishes, "sweeter than honey or any other taste." We omit "than any other taste" to retain the rhyme scheme.

[2] *"Enthroned"* Hebrew, *hadur,* from the same root as *hadarakh* above, there translated as "your throne."

[2] *"Light"* Hebrew, *ziv,* which is a more poetic word than the more common *or.*

[2] *"Lovesick soul pines for You"* More literally, "my soul is lovesick for your love." It is important to translate the "sick" part of "lovesick," because the next verse asks for healing of this very lovesickness.

[2] *"O Healer, heal"* The repetition of "heal" mimics the repetitiveness of the original line, quoting Moses' plea on behalf of Miriam in Numbers 12:13. The original line in

DORFF (THEOLOGY)

[2] *"Servant day and night"* More literally, "maidservant forever," thus completing the feminine imagery in this verse, which contrasts with the masculine imagery in the first verse.

[3] *"Ancient One, compassionate"* To help retain the meter of the original poem, our English has the epithet "compassionate [One]" for God here, instead of the original Hebrew, which uses the verbal form, "let your compassion be abundant."

[3] *"Your loving child* [ben ohavakh]" One possible interpretation of the Hebrew. Also possible is "child of your love."

[3] *"Yearned and still I yearn* [nikhsof nikhsaf]" The repetition of "yearn" here matches the doubling of the word in Hebrew. In Hebrew, it is part of a construction, similar to "dream a dream," that we do not have in English.

[3] *"Show mercy"* The Hebrew is reminiscent of the second line of verse 2, a trick we miss in our translation.

[4] *"Reveal Yourself"* Or, more literally, "be revealed."

[4] *"Envelop me with"* Or "spread over me."

[4] *"Your sheltering peace* [sukat sh'lomakh]" The Hebrew here completes a direct

allusion to the *Hashkiveinu,* a prayer in the evening after the *Sh'ma,* which asks of God, "spread over us the shelter of your peace." In addition, the author belonged to a society of mystics that went by the same name, *sukat shalom.*

[4] *"Shine forth your glory on"* Literally, "light up with your glory."

[4] *"Revel and rejoice"* Hebrew, *nagilah v'nis'm'chah,* taken from Isaiah 25:9, and repeated in reverse order also as *nis'm'chah v'nagilah* in *L'khah Dodi,* a standard prayer for the synagogue service on Friday nights. (See forthcoming Volume 8, *Shabbat in the Synagogue.*)

[4] *"The time has come! And favor me with grace renewed."* The first part comes from Psalm 102:14. The context there is, "it is time [*et*] to favor Zion. The time [*mo'ed*] has come." The conjunction *vav* ("and") with which the second half begins is surprising. It is probably for euphony. But it may also be that the author wanted himself to be included along with Zion in receiving God's favor.

[4] *"Renewed"* Literally, "as in days of old."

◆ ◆ ◆

FRANKEL (A WOMAN'S VOICE)

There, the table is set, and candles will shine.
All the corners of the house will brightly glow.
[5] A blessed and peaceful Shabbat.
A blessed and peaceful Shabbat.
[6] Come in peace, angels of peace.

[7] Sit down with us, O pure one, shine your light upon us.

Night and day, before you leave,

We will honor you with fine clothes,

with songs and prayers, and with three meals.

[8] And with complete rest.

And with pleasant rest.

[9] Bless us with peace, angels of peace.

[10] The sun has disappeared from behind the treetops.

Come, let us accompany the Shabbat queen.

Go in peace, holy one, pure one.

GRAY (TALMUD)

IV. SHABBAT HAMALKAH ("THE SHABBAT QUEEN")

[1] The sun has disappeared from behind the treetops.

Come, let us go to meet the Shabbat queen,

For she is descending, holy, and blessed,

Accompanied by angels of peace and rest.

[2] Come forth, come forth, O queen.

Come forth, come forth, O queen.

[3] Peace to you, angels of peace!

[4] We'll greet Shabbat with joy and prayer,

Then return home with hearts full of joy.

There, the table is set, and candles will shine.

All the corners of the house will brightly glow.

[5] A blessed and peaceful Shabbat.

A blessed and peaceful Shabbat.

[6] Come in peace, angels of peace.

[7] Sit down with us, O pure one, shine your light upon us.

LANDES (HALAKHAH)

Go in peace, holy one, pure one.

Know that we will wait six days for you to return.

[11] Yes, to the next Shabbat.

Yes, to the next Shabbat.

[12] Go in peace, angels of peace.

BRETTLER (BIBLE)

[1] *"The sun"* In both vocabulary and theme, this modern composition resonates deeply with Shabbat as it developed in post-biblical eras. Its core images, however—the sunset

L. HOFFMAN (HISTORY)

setting Friday evening and say, "Come, let us go meet the Shabbat queen." Interestingly, Bialik selects this imagery, not the image that immediately follows it in the Talmud, in which Rabbi Yannai would don special clothes in honor of the Sabbath and say, "Come [Shabbat] bride, come [Shabbat] bride." Rabbi Shlomo Halevi Alkabetz, a sixteenth-century kabbalist, made the exact opposite choice for his Friday night poem, *L'khah Dodi:* the opening line and refrain of that poem says, "Go forth my love to meet the

J. HOFFMAN (TRANSLATION)

certainly have seemed to him as compromising God's holiness. He preferred the sexually sanitized and awesome image of the Shabbat queen, rather than the Shabbat bride with its inherent theological questions about monotheism, God's status, God's needs, and so forth.

[1] *"Accompanied by angels"* See "Peace to you, angels of service," pp. 66–70, regarding the talmudic belief that angels accompany us home from synagogue on Shabbat.

[4] *"Table is set, and candles will shine"* Bialik chooses two of the three things the Talmud (Shab. 119b) requires for a person to be blessed by the angels who accompany him home from synagogue on Friday night: Shabbat lights must be lit and the table set. (The third is that the bed is made.)

[7] *"Shine your light"* Shabbat spreads light and radiance to the rest of the week.

[7] *"We will honor you with fine clothes, with songs and prayers, and with three meals"* From the two versions of the Decalogue (Exod. 20:8–11; Deut. 5:12–15), we learn our obligation to *remember* and also to *observe* the Sabbath day; from Isaiah 58:13, the Rabbis deduced two additional commandments: to honor Shabbat and to rejoice thereon. Maimonides dedicates a full chapter of his Code ("Sabbath," chap. 30) to talmudic precedents (many of which are from Shab. 117b–118b) for these commandments. We honor Shabbat by consciously making sure during the preceding week that we will have proper food and clothes for the occasion. Jewish law requires new clothes for the three Pilgrimage Festivals, but that was too much to require for each Shabbat, especially for Jewish communities that were often poor. So Jewish law requires instead that our clothes be clean for Shabbat, a significant duty in a world before washing machines, when most people bathed and wore clean clothes only rarely.

3

(Queen Elizabeth was known as a fastidious queen because she bathed twice a year!) Songs and prayers are other ways to honor the Sabbath and rejoice on it; yet another is through eating three meals (Friday supper, Saturday lunch, and Saturday supper) a real treat in times and places when most people had little to eat. And then there is the Shabbat nap, a time-honored institution not to be trampled on or taken lightly! In this verse, Bialik captures these traditional modes of honoring Shabbat and making it a time of rejoicing.

^{10} *"The sun has disappeared"* As if we have come full circle, Bialik begins the final verse, describing the end of Shabbat, with the same words he used in verse 1, regarding its onset. As we greeted her, so now we accompany her as she leaves, the way we would a queen.

———◆———

FRANKEL (A WOMAN'S VOICE)

Shabbat Hamalkah ("The Shabbat Queen") Compared to the elevated theological language of most of the traditional Shabbat *z'mirot,* this poem by Chaim Nahman Bialik seems quaint and naïve. The subject of the four stanzas, corresponding to the four stanzas of *Shalom Aleikhem,* is the home celebration of Shabbat in all its concrete details—special meals and clean clothes, scrubbed floors and a festive atmosphere. Hardly a whiff of spirituality intrudes into the simple words of this song except, of course, the Shabbat queen and her ministering angels. Yet even these celestial beings seem remarkably down to earth. Like familiar house guests, they are expected on time each Sabbath. We greet them like old friends: *Shalom aleikhem,*

¹הִנֵּה אֵל יְשׁוּעָתִי, אֶבְטַח וְלֹא אֶפְחָד ,כִּי עָזִּי וְזִמְרָת יָהּ יְיָ, וַיְהִי לִי לִישׁוּעָה.

²וּשְׁאַבְתֶּם מַיִם בְּשָׂשׂוֹן מִמַּעַיְנֵי הַיְשׁוּעָה.

³לַיְיָ הַיְשׁוּעָה; עַל עַמְּךָ בִרְכָתֶךָ סֶּלָה.

⁴יְיָ צְבָאוֹת עִמָּנוּ, מִשְׂגָּב לָנוּ אֱלֹהֵי יַעֲקֹב, סֶלָה.

⁵יְיָ צְבָאוֹת, אַשְׁרֵי אָדָם בֹּטֵחַ בָּךְ.

⁶יְיָ, הוֹשִׁיעָה; הַמֶּלֶךְ יַעֲנֵנוּ בְיוֹם קָרְאֵנוּ.

⁷לַיְּהוּדִים הָיְתָה אוֹרָה וְשִׂמְחָה, וְשָׂשׂוֹן וִיקָר. כֵּן תִּהְיֶה לָּנוּ.

⁸כּוֹס יְשׁוּעוֹת אֶשָּׂא, וּבְשֵׁם יְיָ אֶקְרָא.

⁹סָבְרֵי מָרָנָן וְרַבּוֹתַי.

¹⁰בָּרוּךְ אַתָּה, יְיָ אֱלֹהֵינוּ, מֶלֶךְ הָעוֹלָם, בּוֹרֵא פְּרִי הַגָּפֶן.

¹¹בָּרוּךְ אַתָּה, יְיָ אֱלֹהֵינוּ, מֶלֶךְ הָעוֹלָם, בּוֹרֵא מִינֵי בְשָׂמִים.

¹²בָּרוּךְ אַתָּה, יְיָ אֱלֹהֵינוּ, מֶלֶךְ הָעוֹלָם, בּוֹרֵא מְאוֹרֵי הָאֵשׁ.

164

"Welcome back!" *Tseitkhem l'shalom,* "See you next week, same time, same place!"

God's name never appears in this song. Instead, it is human beings who are the heroes of Bialik's poem. Shabbat owes its weekly reappearance to the *pintele yidin* (pronounced PIN-t'-l' YEE-d'n), the "simple Jews" who each week sweep the corners of the house until they shine, commit themselves to transforming their ordinary houses into banquet halls fit for a queen. Despite our exhaustion from the workweek, we greet our special guests *b'lev malei gilah,* "with hearts full of joy" (v. 4); despite the frenzy of our stressful lives, we let it all go so we can truly relax with our company. What a wonderful counterweight to the headier notions of the kabbalists!

◆

GRAY (TALMUD)

[1] "*Come, let us go to meet the Shabbat queen*" Rabbi Chanina would wear nice clothes and stand outside at sunset on Friday, saying: "Come, let us go to meet the Shabbat queen" (Shab. 119a).

[1] "*Accompanied by angels of peace and rest*" An allusion to the talmudic tradition (Shab. 119b) that two angels accompany a person home from the synagogue every Friday night, a tradition carried in a four-line Shabbat song, *Shalom Aleikhem* (see "Angels of service," p. 66). Bialik continues this allusion in verse 3 ("peace to you, angels of peace"). Like *Shalom Aleikhem,* Bialik's poem too contains four stanzas, each stanza of which closes with a line

[13] בָּרוּךְ אַתָּה, יְיָ אֱלֹהֵינוּ, מֶלֶךְ הָעוֹלָם, הַמַּבְדִּיל בֵּין קֹדֶשׁ לְחוֹל, בֵּין אוֹר לְחֹשֶׁךְ, בֵּין יִשְׂרָאֵל לָעַמִּים, בֵּין יוֹם הַשְּׁבִיעִי לְשֵׁשֶׁת יְמֵי הַמַּעֲשֶׂה. בָּרוּךְ אַתָּה, יְיָ, הַמַּבְדִּיל בֵּין קֹדֶשׁ לְחוֹל.

should at least lower the hems then (Shab. 113a). Rashi explains that only the wealthy wore clothing of that length, because they did not have to worry about soiling their clothes during manual labor. But on Shabbat, even an ordinary Jew could wear clothes the way a wealthy person does, in honor of the day. The same recognition that not everyone could afford a set of special Shabbat clothes probably underlies the interesting tradition that Ezra instituted the requirement of doing laundry on Thursday, so that people would be sure to have clean clothes in honor of Shabbat (B.K. 82a; Maimonides, "Shabbat" 30:3). Meir of Rothenburg (thirteenth–fourteenth centuries; *Hagahot* *(p. 169)* *Maimuniyot* to

Saturday night, even if he only eats an olive's-bulk [worth of food]" (Shab. 119b; Maimonides, "Shabbat" 30:5; *Tur,* O. Ch. 300).

11 *"Yes, to the next Shabbat"* A subtle allusion to the words of the angels—in this case, of course, the good

(p. 169)

J. HOFFMAN (TRANSLATION)

1 *"Sun"* The Hebrew word for "sun" here is not the common *shemesh,* but the more poetic *chamah,* lending an immediate sense of poetry to the passage that our translation cannot mimic.

(p. 170)

KIDDUSHA RABBAH ("THE GREAT KIDDUSH")

1 The children of Israel shall keep Shabbat, observing Shabbat throughout their generations as an eternal covenant.

2 It is an eternal sign between Me and the children of Israel, for in six days Adonai made heaven and earth, and on the seventh day He rested.

3 Remember the day of Shabbat to make it holy. *(p. 172)*

of the older liturgical poem.

2 *"Come forth, come forth, O queen"* Rabbi Yannai would dress in his Shabbat finery on Friday night and say, "Come forth, O bride! Come forth, O bride!" (Shab. 119a).

4 *"There, the table is set"* Bialik alludes here to the "set table" *(shulchan arukh)* that must be waiting when a person returns home from the synagogue on Friday night (Shab. 119b). Maimonides (1135–1204) follows Shabbat 119b in ruling that we are to set the table on

9 Blessed are You, Adonai our God, ruler of the world, creator of the fruit of the vine.

(p. 172)

presents its proclamation about Shabbat in third person plural "The children of Israel shall keep Shabbat." But its complement, the passage beginning with "Remember" (*Zakhor;* Exod. 20:8–11), addresses the reader in second person singular: "Remember the Shabbat. For six days do your work, but do no work on the seventh day." Because Hebrew is such a highly gendered language, the imperative "you" is necessarily masculine. But are only men being addressed here? Are not women also expected to *(p. 175)*

(p. 175)

⁵ *"Animals"* Others, "cattle." The Hebrew here probably refers to animals that are likely to do work such as cattle, but not pets.

⁵ *"Midst"* Literally, "gates." JPS uses "settlements"; the NRSV says "towns."

⁶ *"Relaxed"* We have another word—different than the two used above—for "rest" here. To convey this third lexical choice, we opt for "relax" in our English translation. Most other translations use "rest."

⁷ *"Made it holy"* Most others, "sanctify." We want to preserve the connection expressed in the Hebrew between this line and the one above, *(p. 178)*

(p. 178)

¹הִנֵּה אֵל יְשׁוּעָתִי, אֶבְטַח וְלֹא אֶפְחָד, כִּי עָזִּי וְזִמְרָת
יָהּ יְיָ, וַיְהִי לִי לִישׁוּעָה.
²וּשְׁאַבְתֶּם מַיִם בְּשָׂשׂוֹן מִמַּעַיְנֵי הַיְשׁוּעָה.
³לַיְיָ הַיְשׁוּעָה; עַל עַמְּךָ בִרְכָתֶךָ סֶּלָה.
⁴יְיָ צְבָאוֹת עִמָּנוּ, מִשְׂגָּב לָנוּ אֱלֹהֵי יַעֲקֹב, סֶלָה.

A. *Havdalah* ("Separation")

short blessing over wine. But the Rabbis often bestow a positive title on what might otherwise be considered a deficit (Rabbi Meir, for example, who was blind, was called *sagi nahor,* "full of light"). Alternatively, the term may derive from the fact that the blessing over wine is common to all forms of *Kiddush* (see Rashi and Rashbam on Pes. 106a, rendering the meaning of *Kiddusha Rabbah,* "the universal *Kiddush*").

In any event, nowadays it is customarily introduced by *(p. 176)*

(p. 176)

(p. 179)

Friday and Saturday nights to honor
Shabbat as it enters and departs, even if
we eat only an olive's-bulk worth of
food ("Shabbat" 30:5).

[4] *"Candles will shine, all the corners
of the house will brightly glow"* A
reference to Shabbat candles (M. Shab.
2:6–7; Shab. 25b). The lights shine
brightly in all four corners of the home
to provide the requisite spirit of peace
and harmony (Tosafot to Shab. 25b).

[6] *"Come in peace, angels of peace"*
The stanza speaks of the peaceful
Shabbat scene awaiting those who enter
the home on Friday night; the line from
the song explicitly welcomes the angelic
visitors to this Shabbat scene.

[7] *"We will honor you with fine
clothes"* Both Rabbi Chanina and Rabbi
Yannai put on nice clothing to honor
Shabbat's arrival (Shab. 119a).
Elsewhere (Shab. 113a), the Talmud
interprets Isaiah 58:13 ("You shall
honor it by not following your own
ways") to mean, "Your clothing on
Shabbat should not be the same as your
clothing during the week." Although
the Talmud's ideal is that people should
wear clothing specifically designated for
Shabbat, it recognizes that not everyone
can afford to do so. Rav Huna,
therefore, rules that people who have to
wear weekday clothes on Shabbat

[5] יְיָ צְבָאוֹת, אַשְׁרֵי אָדָם בֹּטֵחַ בָּךְ.

[6] יְיָ, הוֹשִׁיעָה; הַמֶּלֶךְ יַעֲנֵנוּ בְיוֹם קָרְאֵנוּ.

[7] לַיְּהוּדִים הָיְתָה אוֹרָה וְשִׂמְחָה, וְשָׂשֹׂן
וִיקָר. כֵּן תִּהְיֶה לָנוּ.

[8] כּוֹס יְשׁוּעוֹת אֶשָּׂא, וּבְשֵׁם יְיָ אֶקְרָא.

[9] סָבְרֵי מָרָנָן וְרַבּוֹתַי.

[10] בָּרוּךְ אַתָּה, יְיָ אֱלֹהֵינוּ, מֶלֶךְ הָעוֹלָם,
בּוֹרֵא פְּרִי הַגָּפֶן.

[11] בָּרוּךְ אַתָּה, יְיָ אֱלֹהֵינוּ, מֶלֶךְ הָעוֹלָם,
בּוֹרֵא מִינֵי בְשָׂמִים.

[12] בָּרוּךְ אַתָּה, יְיָ אֱלֹהֵינוּ, מֶלֶךְ הָעוֹלָם,
בּוֹרֵא מְאוֹרֵי הָאֵשׁ.

[13] בָּרוּךְ אַתָּה, יְיָ אֱלֹהֵינוּ, מֶלֶךְ הָעוֹלָם,
הַמַּבְדִּיל בֵּין קֹדֶשׁ לְחוֹל, בֵּין אוֹר
לְחֹשֶׁךְ, בֵּין יִשְׂרָאֵל לָעַמִּים, בֵּין יוֹם
הַשְּׁבִיעִי לְשֵׁשֶׁת יְמֵי הַמַּעֲשֶׂה.
בָּרוּךְ אַתָּה, יְיָ, הַמַּבְדִּיל בֵּין קֹדֶשׁ
לְחוֹל.

BRETTLER (BIBLE)

Maimonides' "Shabbat" 30:3) quotes a source he claims is from the Yerushalmi in which Rabbi Yochanan expresses despair that people of his time and place must wear Shabbat clothes that are the same as their weekday attire.

[7] *"With three meals"* A reference to the three meals of Shabbat (Shab. 117b; Maimonides, "Shabbat" 30:9; *Shulchan Arukh,* O. Ch. 291). See "Food and meals," p. 118; and introductory essay by Michael Chernick, "*S'udah Sh'lishit:* A Rite of Modest Majesty," pp. 30–36.

[9] *"Bless us with peace, angels of peace"* Bialik closes the third stanza of his poem with a slight variation on the third line of the traditional *Shalom Aleikhem* hymn. He changes the wish for blessing to the plural, "Bless *us* with peace," to reflect the fact that the poem speaks for the Jewish people as a whole.

[10] *"The sun has disappeared"* Having used this line earlier to mark the beginning of Shabbat, Bialik now repeats it to indicate the setting of the sun as Shabbat ends.

[10] *"Come, let us accompany the Shabbat queen"* Earlier (v. 1), Bialik borrowed the line from Shabbat 119a: "Come, let us go to meet the Shabbat Queen." Now he says, "Come, let us accompany the Shabbat Queen," a reference to accompanying her exit until next week. The Hebrew verb *l.v.h* ("accompany") alludes to the traditional custom of *m'laveh malkah* (pronounced m'-lah-VEH MAHL-kah or, commonly, the Yiddishized m'-LAH-v' MAHL-k'), the "accompaniment of the queen," a festive Saturday night gathering to mark the end of Shabbat. The *m'laveh malkah* has a talmudic basis in Rabbi Chanina's teaching that "a person should set his table on

DORFF (THEOLOGY)

angel—who accompany a person home from the synagogue on Friday night. (See "Angels of service," p. 68).

[12] *"Go in peace, angels of peace"* The fourth and final stanza concludes with the fourth and final line of the traditional song. The song is sung as an entire piece on Friday night; but Bialik distributes it throughout his description of an entire Shabbat day, making the angels' departure coincide with Shabbat's own departure. By spreading the song throughout his poem, Bialik interprets the song to keep the angels with us over the entire Shabbat—and while he is at it, he does away with the medieval objection that it is rude to ask angels to leave (*Machatzit Hashekel* and *Sha'arei T'shuvah* to *Shulchan Arukh,* O. Ch. 262). (See "Go in peace," p. 71.)

L. Hoffman (History)

Shabbat Hamalkah ("The Sabbath Queen") Although not intended originally as a Shabbat table song, this poem by Chaim Nachman Bialik is sung as such in many homes today. (See pp. 28–29.)

———◆———

Ellenson (Modern Liturgies)

[1] *"To meet"* Literally, "toward" *(likrat),* a direct reference to *L'khah Dodi,* a Friday evening synagogue prayer (see forthcoming Volume 8) that depicts Shabbat as a bride and queen.

[1] *"Blessed...rest"* By coincidence, "blessed" (one syllable, once spelled "bless'd" in poetry) and "rest" rhyme in English, as do their counterparts in Hebrew. In this poem, we have abandoned the goal of making the English rhyme, preferring instead to capture more closely the meaning of the words. As it happens, in this instance, we can do both.

[1] *"Accompanied by"* Literally, "with her."

[3] *"Peace to you, angels of peace"* A reference to *Shalom Aleikhem* (see "Peace to you," p. 67). The final line of each verse here refers to the three motifs of each verse there.

[4] *"Greet Shabbat"* A reference to *L'khah Dodi;* but beyond that, the idea goes back to the Talmud, from which *L'khah Dodi,* too, is derived.

[4] *"Table is set"* A reference to the midrash according to which the visiting good angels see the table set beautifully for Shabbat and say, "So may it be next week," to which the visiting bad angels are forced to say, "Amen."

[4] *"Brightly glow"* Literally, "shine and shine," using two synonymous words for "shine," both of which differ from the word for "shine" used in the last line.

[7] *"Before you leave"* Literally, "then you may move on."

———◆◆◆———

Kiddusha Rabbah *("The Great* Kiddush *")*

[1] The children of Israel shall keep Shabbat, observing Shabbat throughout their generations as an eternal covenant.

[2] It is an eternal sign between Me and the children of Israel, for in six days Adonai made heaven and earth, and on the seventh day He rested.

[3] Remember the day of Shabbat to make it holy.

[4] Six days you shall labor and do all your work.

[5] The seventh day is Shabbat, for Adonai your God. You shall not do any work, you or your son or your daughter, your male or female slave, or your animals, or the stranger in your midst.

[6] For in six days Adonai made heaven and earth, and the sea, and everything in them, and He relaxed on the seventh day. [7] Therefore Adonai blessed the seventh day and made it holy.

[8] With our masters' and teachers' approval:

[9] Blessed are You, Adonai our God, ruler of the world, creator of the fruit of the vine.

FRANKEL (A WOMAN'S VOICE)

⁴ Six days you shall labor and do all your work.

⁵ The seventh day is Shabbat, for Adonai your God. You shall not do any work, you or your son or your daughter, your male or female slave, or your animals, or the stranger in your midst.

⁶ For in six days Adonai made heaven and earth, and the sea, and everything in them, and He relaxed on the seventh day.

⁷ Therefore Adonai blessed the seventh day and made it holy.
⁸ With our masters' and teachers' approval:

GRAY (TALMUD)

BRETTLER (BIBLE)

¹ *"The children of Israel shall keep Shabbat"* Both the *Kiddush* for Friday night (see Kiddush p. 93) and for Saturday morning are comprised of passages composed by priestly authors after the return from the Babylonion exile, where Shabbat became especially significant. The first quotation (Exod. 31:16–17) begins in the middle of the instructions for constructing the Tabernacle (Exod. 31:12–17). This placement of the ban on Shabbat labor in the middle of the Tabernacle account served as the basis for the rabbinic decision to define forbidden Shabbat work as activities involved in the construction of the Tabernacle. It is uncertain why the entire unit (from vv. 12–17, instead of just 16–17) was not incorporated into the *Kiddush;* perhaps it was felt to be too repetitive, or its emphasis on capital punishment (vv. 14–15) was seen as inappropriate.

² *"Sign"* The priestly authors were especially active in the Babylonian exile, and it is likely that the Shabbat became particularly important during this period (586–538 B.C.E.), as sacred time (the Shabbat) filled the role previously played by sacred space (the Temple). Here, then, is the crucial priestly notion that not just circumcision (Genesis 17), but Shabbat too is an eternal "covenant" *(b'rit). Ot* (see Ezek. 20:12, 20), or "marker," is a technical term denoting a thing that signifies something else. Here, Shabbat is the priestly covenant marker that signifies Israel's fealty to God. Observing Shabbat (as God did) signifies acknowledgment of God as creator.

³ *"Remember the day of Shabbat"* The Shabbat commandment from the Decalogue of Exodus, which fits the priestly emphasis on Shabbat as a commemoration of creation (Exod. 20:8–11). By contrast, the Decalogue in Deuteronomy links Shabbat to the Exodus (Deut. 5:15). Whereas the Friday night *Kiddush* blends these traditions, the Saturday afternoon version focuses on the first Shabbat, when God rested after creation.

⁵ *"Shabbat, for Adonai"* The Hebrew is ambiguous: either "Adonai's Shabbat"—

Shabbat legislated by, so belonging to, Adonai; or "a Shabbat [that we keep to commemorate] Adonai."

[5] *"You shall not do any work, you or your son or your daughter, your male or female slave"* The commandment against Shabbat labor extends to the whole household, male and female—as opposed to the final commandment against coveting (Exod. 20:14), which is addressed only to men. Complete rest is mandated for everything and everyone under Israelite control, but not for non-Israelites outside of Israelite control, because Shabbat is a sign of the covenant between God and Israel only.

[6] *"For in six days"* A paraphrase of the priestly creation story. Surprisingly, only in that story, and in its retelling here, is there explicit biblical reference to creation in six days. Most people think that six days of creation is the predominant biblical story of creation—in reality, it is just a minority tradition.

—◆—

DORFF (THEOLOGY)

[2] *"An eternal sign"* Shabbat is a "sign" (as, by extension, are the High Holy Days and the three Pilgrimage Festivals), but so too are *t'fillin* (Deut. 6:8). *T'fillin* are therefore not worn on Shabbat and holidays, for the Talmud rules that one sign is enough (Eruv. 96a; *Shulchan Arukh,* O. Ch. 31:1). *T'fillin* provide graphic, physical reminders of our covenant with God. But so also do the laws of Shabbat, which obviate the need for any other reminder.

[2] *"Between Me and the children of Israel"* But, the Rabbis deduce, "Not between Me and the other nations of the world" (*Mekhilta,* Ki Tissa, on Exod. 31:17), so non-Jews are not subject to the laws of Shabbat. Of ongoing debate is the question of whether Jews may benefit from work that a non-Jew does on Shabbat. The Mishnah (Shab. 16:8) rules, "If a gentile kindles a lamp, an Israelite may use its light; but if the gentile does it for the sake of the Israelite, it is forbidden." One talmudic opinion restricts permission for the Jew to use the light to cases where (a) the gentile does not know the Jew, so would not be tempted to do the Jew a favor, or (b) the gentile kindles the light when the Jew is not present. A fourth-century Rabbi, Rava, extends permission to use it even if those conditions are absent, for "a lamp for one is a lamp for a hundred" (Shab. 122a). Balancing these principles under a variety of circumstances became a major topic for medieval and modern Jewish law. In antiquity, Jews (like everyone else) owned slaves, and the Exodus version of the Decalogue (20:10) prohibits Jews and their "male or female slave" from Sabbath work. Slaves, however, have no option but to obey their master, so the Torah's prohibition may be only for slaves, to protect them from having to work seven days a week. Historically, after slavery was long gone, the issue became gentiles who freely choose to do something for a Jew on Shabbat, either as a favor or for compensation.

173

In general, gentiles may choose to use Saturday to complete a project they are doing for a Jew when they are being paid for the product but not by the hour, and according to many authorities, they may agree to a contract to provide a variety of services for Jews on Shabbat. Other Jewish jurists, however, discourage or even forbid the use of a "Shabbos goy," because (a) Jews might be tempted to do the tasks themselves if the designated non-Jews do not show up or cannot do them, or (b) because they find it disdainful for Jews to evade Shabbat restrictions through the use of non-Jews.

1–2 "Throughout their generations…He rested" Two short verses (Exod. 31:16–17) combine a particularistic reason for observing Shabbat with a universalistic one: we should set Shabbat aside both because Jews have done so for generations and also because God rested from the process of creating the whole universe. This combination of reasons is reflected in the two versions of the Decalogue: Deuteronomy 5:12–15 refers to God's particularistic redemption of the Israelites from slavery; Exodus 20:8–11 cites God's resting on the seventh day of creation. These differing rationales complement rather than contradict each other, providing equally significant ways to find meaning in the Sabbath.

3 "Remember the Sabbath day to make it holy" From Exodus 20. Because the Deuteronomic parallel (chap. 5) begins instead with "Observe the Sabbath day to keep it holy," the Talmud concludes, "Remember and observe were said [by God] as one word, what the [human] mouth cannot say and the [human] ear cannot hear" (R.H. 27a). Their point was not only to reconcile two variant versions of the same thing by attributing a miracle to God, but also to link Shabbat observance to an appropriate Shabbat spirit and to link the Shabbat spirit to specific acts of observance that establish the day as special. Thus, acts that may be justified in terms of how Jewish law defines "observe" may nonetheless be inappropriate to the Shabbat spirit, as, for example, shouting specifically to annoy someone. Conversely, activities that we love as recreation may still be banned by the laws of "observe."

3 "Remember the Sabbath day" The Rabbis applied this also to how we plan Shabbat during the prior week: "Elazar, son of Chananiah…says: 'Remember the Sabbath day to make it holy': remember it from the first day of the week, so that if you happen upon a nice portion of food [then], fix it for Shabbat. Rabbi Isaac says: Do not count [the days of the week] the way others do; count them instead for the sake of Shabbat (i.e., the first day until next Shabbat, the second day until next Shabbat, etc.)" (*Mekhilta,* Bachodesh, chap. 7, on Exod. 20:8).

———◆———

FRANKEL (A WOMAN'S VOICE)

1 "The children of Israel shall keep [v'shamru] *Shabbat"* The passage known as *V'shamru*

KUSHNER & POLEN (CHASIDISM)

remember the Sabbath day, to hallow it and refrain from their labors?

Lest there be any doubt that all Israelites are being commanded to observe the Sabbath day, the third verse of our passage specifies who is being included in the injunction to "do no work": "you or your son or daughter, your male or female slave, or your animals, or the stranger who is within your midst." By not listing "your wives" after "you," the verse clearly includes both men and women in the second person imperative. The passage then goes on to specify the gender of all the others bound by this commandment—"your son or daughter, your male or female slave." (Significantly, in the Tenth Commandment presented four verses later, male Israelites are commanded in the second person singular—not to covet "your neighbor's wife").

This passage affirms that women are meant to enjoy Sabbath rest as well as its demands. Thank God, in our own day, under the influence of feminism, reality is finally catching up with this ancient ideal.

◆

GRAY (TALMUD)

Kiddusha Rabbah ("The Great *Kiddush*") The principal *Kiddush* is the Friday night version (Pes. 106a; Maimonides, "Shabbat" 29:4). But from the Torah's admonition to "remember the Shabbat to keep it holy" (Exod. 20:8), the Talmud derives a requirement to "remember [Shabbat] over wine" on the day of Shabbat as well (Pes. 106a). According to Rabbi Judah, this *Kiddush* consists simply of the blessing over wine (Pes. 106a).

The Talmud unwittingly testifies to the fact that between the third century C.E. (the time of Rabbi Judah) and the fourth to fifth centuries C.E., the Shabbat morning *Kiddush* had not made much headway. The story is told of Rav Ashi (fourth–fifth centuries C.E., a principal Rabbi of his generation), who visited the town of Mechoza and was invited to recite *Kiddusha Rabbah*. Rav Ashi was unsure of what to do. He reasoned that because every *Kiddush* opens with the blessing over wine, he would begin with that and then see whether people answered "Amen" but paused expectantly for more to be recited. He recited the blessing slowly and then saw an elderly man drink his wine. Rav Ashi thus realized that no more was expected: *Kiddusha Rabbah* consisted merely of the blessing over wine. He applied to himself Ecclesiastes 2:14: "The wise man has eyes in his head" (Pes. 106a).

If the "Great *Kiddush*" consists only of the blessing over wine, why did people call it by that name? Rashi and his grandson Rashbam (Rabbi Samuel b. Meir, twelfth century) opine that the wine blessing by itself can properly be called the "great" *Kiddush* because every *Kiddush* begins with it. The *Maggid Mishneh* (Vidal Yom Tov of Tolosa, fourteenth century) more persuasively suggests that the name "Great *Kiddush*" is a euphemism meant to increase the prestige of a form of *Kiddush* that is short enough to be easily overlooked. Adding other verses to *Kiddusha Rabbah* is a matter of *minhag* ("custom") that likely stems from the desire to enhance its status.

———◆———

LANDES (HALAKHAH)

Kiddusha Rabbah ("The Great *Kiddush*") The *Kiddusha Rabbah* is also called *Kiddush Hayom* ("*Kiddush* of the Day"), because it is said at Saturday noon rather than Friday night. Its title, "The Great *Kiddush*," is ironic, because it consists essentially of only the

LANDES (HALAKHAH)

several biblical verses that outline laws and concepts of Shabbat. After the verses comes the formalized Aramaic "request" to recite the blessing, "With our masters' and teachers' approval" (see "With our masters' and teachers' approval," p. 107) and then the blessing. The Lithuanian tradition is to omit the introduction and say just the "request" (to get people's attention) followed by the blessing. Indeed, the blessing alone suffices.

Kiddusha Rabbah is rabbinic, derived from close attention to Exodus 20:8, "Remember the Sabbath day to sanctify it," thereby extending the commandment to "remember" Shabbat to the day, not just the evening when the larger *Kiddush* is recited. Requisite *kavod* ("honor") is thereby accorded the day, which, halakhically, is more important than the night. If, for instance, one lacks sufficient food or wine for the entire Shabbat, more should be reserved for the day than for the night (Pes. 105a–b). Still, the more extensive *Kiddush* is said at night when the Shabbat actually begins, on the principle that "a *mitzvah* is especially precious at its appointed time." The *Kiddush* of the evening introduces a meal filled with social, sensual, and spiritual *oneg* ("joy"). The daytime *Kiddusha Rabbah* outfits the noontime meal with spiritual *kavod* ("honor"). On Friday night, the meal augments the *Kiddush;* on Saturday, the *Kiddush* augments the meal. The Friday night principle is *ein kiddush ela bim'kom s'udah,* "There can be no *Kiddush* without a [Shabbat] meal." On Saturday, as my teacher the Rav (Rabbi Joseph B. Soloveitchik, 1903–1993, halakhic master and philosopher; Lithuania, Berlin, Boston, New York) explained to us in class, the principle is reversed: *ein s'udah ela bim'kom kiddush,* "There can be no [Shabbat] meal without a *Kiddush*."

Modernity created a new wrinkle. Traditionally, Shabbat morning services ended early enough for people to go home, make *Kiddush,* have lunch (what we would call brunch), and take a Shabbat rest. Now, people live farther away, so services begin later; they feature additional *chazzanut* ("cantorial singing," pronounced chah-zah-NOOT) and choral music, as well as a sermon, so that the lunchtime meal is greatly delayed. The custom therefore arose to recite *Kiddush* at synagogue with cake and dainties, as a semi-meal ("semi" because there is no bread, and halakhically, a full "meal" is defined by the inclusion of bread within it). This collation became popularly known also as the *Kiddush.* As long as this *Kiddush* does not replace the actual Shabbat meal at home, it is a worthy custom, because it brings *oneg* ("joy") to the Shabbat day in the milieu of community. But *Kiddusha Rabbah* should be repeated at home to contextualize the meal there with appropriate *kavod* ("honor").

The noontime meal is called *s'udah sh'niyah* (pronounced s'oo-DAH sh'nee-YAH), "the second meal," the first one being the evening meal of the night before. Breakfast cannot be considered a Shabbat meal because one is technically not allowed to eat in the morning before prayers. A "little something" is allowed by some authorities only to settle the mind. Therefore, the second meal—as explained earlier, definitionally, as sit-down—follows Shabbat morning prayer.

[9] *"Fruit of the vine"* As *Kiddusha Rabbah* indicates, the second meal starts with wine. But because the point of *Kiddusha Rabbah* is the joy of Shabbat, and because it is enacted rabbinically but not biblically, the Rabbis permitted *chamar dim'dinah,* any popular alcoholic drink other than wine, for the occasion. Many communities nowadays "make *Kiddush*" over a fine schnapps or other spirits.

——◆——

L. HOFFMAN (HISTORY)

[9] *"Fruit of the vine"* Rabbinical or cantorial students who find themselves in situations where they are expected to know more than what they have learned should take heart! The Talmud tells of Rav Ashi, who found himself celebrating Shabbat in a strange town and was asked, on Shabbat noon after services, to lead the "Great *Kiddush.*" Rav Ashi (usually dated 335–427) is the most-cited authority in the entire Babylonian Talmud and is said even to have initiated its canonization. Yet even he is described as being baffled by the request. He did what most students would do, made an educated guess and hoped he was right. He therefore says the normal blessing over wine, then pauses, and sees one of the elders drink his wine in apparent approval. Ever since, the simple blessing over wine, if said for Shabbat afternoon, is known as the "Great *Kiddush.*"

The biblical citations prior (vv. 1–7) were added later, in part, no doubt, as a means of outfitting the ordinary blessing sufficiently to make it look "great."

——◆——

J. HOFFMAN (TRANSLATION)

[1] *"Children of Israel"* We translate this literally. More colloquial would be "Israelites."

[1] *"Observing"* Literally, "doing." The Hebrew verb *'.s.h,* literally "to do" or "to make," seems out of context here. Usually one "keeps" the Shabbat; one does not "do" it. (Deut. 5:15 is the only other biblical exhortation to "do Shabbat.") Perhaps the verb "to do" is chosen here to emphasize the parallel nature of the covenant. God "did" (see below, "Made") six days of work and we "do" Shabbat.

[2] *"For"* Others: "that...."

2 *"Made"* This is the same verb in Hebrew from the root *'.s.h* that we translated above as "observing," and which means, more generally, "to do."

2 *"Rested"* The Hebrew contains two verbs for "to rest" here. The first is from the root for "Shabbat." The second, probably reflecting nuances we have not fully appreciated, comes from the root *n.f.sh,* commonly translated as "soul" but more accurately understood as referring to the physical aspect of human life. (See Volume 1, *The Sh'ma and Its Blessings,* pp. 100, 102.)

3 *"Make it holy"* Others, "keep it holy." We translate this verb elsewhere as "sanctify." Here, people make Shabbat holy, while in verse 7, God will make Shabbat holy.

4 *"Labor"* We would like to use "work" here, but we will need that word at the end of the verse; we do not want to use the same word in English for two different words in Hebrew.

L. HOFFMAN (HISTORY)

in which people are commanded to make Shabbat holy.

◆ ◆ ◆

Bidding Shabbat Farewell

J. HOFFMAN (TRANSLATION)

[1] God is my salvation. I trust. I am not afraid. God is my strength and might, and will be my salvation.

[2] You shall draw forth water in gladness from the wells of salvation.

[3] Salvation is God's. May You bless your people forever.

[4] The Lord of Hosts is with us, Jacob's God is our stronghold.

[5] Lord of Hosts, happy is the one who trusts in You.

[6] Adonai, save us. May our king answer us when we cry out.

[7] The Jews enjoyed light and happiness and joy and honor. May we have these, too!

[8] I lift up the cup of salvations, and call on the name of God.

[9] With our masters' and teachers' approval:

[10] Blessed are You, Adonai our God, ruler of the world, creator of the fruit of the vine.

[11] Blessed are You, Adonai our God, ruler of the world, creator of varied spices.

[12] Blessed are You, Adonai our God, ruler of the world, creator of the lights of fire.

[13] Blessed are You, Adonai our God, ruler of the world, who distinguishes between holy and ordinary, between light and dark, between Israel and the nations, between the seventh day and the six days of work. Blessed are You, Adonai, who distinguishes between holy and ordinary.

A. HAVDALAH ("SEPARATION")

[1] God is my salvation. I trust. I am not afraid. God is my strength and might, and will be my salvation.

[2] You shall draw forth water in gladness from the wells of salvation.

[3] Salvation is God's. May You bless your people forever.

[4] The Lord of Hosts is with us, Jacob's God is our stronghold.

[5] Lord of Hosts, happy is the one who trusts in You.

[6] Adonai, save us. May our king answer us when we cry out.

[7] The Jews enjoyed light and happiness and joy and honor. May we have these, too!

[8] I lift up the cup of salvations, and call on the name of God.

[9] With our masters' and teachers' approval:

[10] Blessed are You, Adonai our God, ruler of the world, creator of the fruit of the vine.

[11] Blessed are You, Adonai our God, ruler of the world, creator of varied spices.

[12] Blessed are You, Adonai our God, ruler of the world, creator of the lights of fire.

[13] Blessed are You, Adonai our God, ruler of the world, who distinguishes between holy and ordinary, between light and dark, between Israel and the nations, between the seventh day and the six days of work. Blessed are You,

[1] הַמַּבְדִּיל בֵּין קֹדֶשׁ לְחֹל חַטֹּאתֵינוּ הוּא יִמְחֹל;
זַרְעֵנוּ וְכַסְפֵּנוּ יַרְבֶּה כַּחוֹל וְכַכּוֹכָבִים בַּלָּיְלָה.

[2] שָׁבוּעַ טוֹב.

181

[1] *"God is my salvation"* Unlike both versions of *Kiddush* (see *Vay'hi erev* and *V'shamru*, pp. 91, 155), there is no "obvious" biblical passage to introduce *Havdalah;* instead, we find a selection of eight biblical verses: Isaiah 12:2; 12:3; Psalms 3:9; 46:12; 84:13; 20:10; Esther 8:16 (with the addition of the words "May we have these too! [*Ken tihyeh lanu*]); and Psalm 116:13. None is directly connected to Shabbat, but they all relate to deliverance. Four use the noun "salvation" *(y'shu'ah),* and one the verb "save" *(hoshi'a).* Of the remaining verses, two depict God as "Lord of hosts," an epithet suggesting the image of God as military general, leading angelic hosts to battle. The only prose verse, Esther 8:16, refers to the rejoicing of the Jewish community after the defeat of Haman. This theme of deliverance seems unrelated to *Havdalah,* which follows it, but as we saw in some of the *z'mirot,* in the Middle Ages, Shabbat came to anticipate military deliverance.

[10–12] *"Fruit of the vine...spices... fire"* As Shabbat began with wine and lights, so it ends that way; in addition we get spices, a luxury item in antiquity.

[13] *"Who distinguishes"* Four pairs through which God has created distinctions. Each pair is longer than the preceding one, following a general rule called the law of increasing members, by which lists move from short to long items. This list concludes climactically with Shabbat itself, but the preceding elements of the list are connected, because Shabbat is holy, ends at darkness, and is a sign of God's special relationship with Israel. Each of the first three pairs has a biblical basis: in Genesis 1:4, God distinguishes between light and darkness; in Leviticus 10:10, priests are told to distinguish between holy and ordinary; and in Leviticus 20:24, God distinguishes Israel from other nations. The only

Adonai, who distinguishes between holy and ordinary.

phrase without explicit biblical precedent is the fourth and climactic one distinguishing Shabbat from the six days of creation, but it is assumed here, and subsumed into the biblical pattern used for the other three.

[13] *"Between holy"* A paraphrase of Leviticus 10:10 (cf. Ezek. 44:23), where priests, not God, play this role. The conclusion of this blessing parallels the conclusion of the evening *Kiddush,* where, in contrast to biblical precedents, it is God who is given the role of sanctifying Shabbat.

—◆—

¹הַמַּבְדִּיל בֵּין קֹדֶשׁ לְחֹל חַטֹּאתֵינוּ הוּא יִמְחֹל; זַרְעֵנוּ וְכַסְפֵּנוּ יַרְבֶּה כַחוֹל וְכַכּוֹכָבִים בַּלָּיְלָה.

²שָׁבוּעַ טוֹב.

DORFF (THEOLOGY)

[1] *"My salvation"* These verses, drawn from a variety of places in the Bible, all speak of God's salvation. For Christians, Jesus saves us from sin and its punishment: hellfire and damnation. Jews deny salvation from sin, for if we could never sin, we would be without free will, which makes sense only if we can choose to do right or wrong. Were we to be saved from committing sins, we would become automata, hard-wired to do the good. Jeremiah (31:30–33) actually threatens such a state, when God will "write it [my Torah] on their hearts," so that they cannot do otherwise but obey it, but because we still have free will, God clearly did not carry out that threat. Instead, God has chosen to create human beings with the ability to choose right or wrong, and in love, God has given Jews a book of instruction (the literal meaning of "Torah") to help us exercise our ability to choose. Judaism conceives of God as all the greater for not creating us in such a way that we are determined to do good, for it is much harder to teach and convince human beings to do the good when they have the ability to do otherwise. Salvation, then, is not from sin; instead, Jews hope for salvation from poverty, illness, ignorance, and the like. As we exchange Shabbat with its foretaste of a world-to-come for our broken world that still suffers from these limitations, we voice our hope for a future when Shabbat will be an everyday occurrence.

[13] *"Between…"* In the process of creation, God separates out the various

אֵ֠לִיָּהוּ הַנָּבִיא אֵלִיָּהוּ הַתִּשְׁבִּי [1]
אֵלִיָּהוּ הַגִּלְעָדִי. בִּמְהֵרָה יָבוֹא
אֵלֵינוּ עִם מָשִׁיחַ בֶּן דָּוִד.

Havdalah ("Separation") Both Abraham Geiger and Isaac Mayer Wise, "the founding fathers of Reform Judaism," included *Havdalah* in their prayer books. The *Union Prayer Book* of 1895, however, omitted it, thereby setting the pattern for almost one hundred years. The liturgical revolution that began with *Gates of Prayer* in 1975 reversed that pattern, and by now, *Havdalah* has been restored almost everywhere, from the American *GOP* to the Israeli *Ha-avodah Shebalev.* The Conservative *Siddur Sim Shalom* (1998) is noteworthy for its appended section entitled *"B'rachot Uminhagei Bayit:* Observances in the Home," a unit that provides home liturgies with transliterations for families who do not enjoy Hebrew competence. It includes there a lengthy Friday night home liturgy, as well as a Chanukah ritual of candle lighting. Yet it omits *Havdalah* *(p. 188)*

that despite the movement's formal requirement of *Havdalah* as a *mitzvah,* American Conservative Judaism imagines that only the reasonably Hebraically competent are likely to include *Havdalah* at home and that is why no transliterated version of *Havdalah* is included in the home unit *(B'rachot Uminhagei Bayit).* Alternatively, it may be that *Sim Shalom* is a compilation of at least two original manuscripts, each reflecting a different philosophy regarding transliteration. The first one, *(p. 188)*

begin again."

[10] *"Creator of the fruit of the vine"* Marcia Falk here offers a substitute blessing over the wine for the traditional formula. Her blessing states, "Let us bless the source of life that ripens fruit on the vine as we hallow the week, calling to mind our history." In Falk's words, this blessing attempts, "at the transitional moment of the Sabbath's departure," to speak of "what leaves and what enters." *(p. 188)*

beings from the primordial, global chaos. According to some interpretations, God also created the original chaos out of nothing. We cannot do the latter, but we can manage the former, making distinctions, as God did, "between light and dark, between Israel and the nations, between the seventh day and the six days of work…between holy and ordinary."

———◆———

ELLENSON (MODERN LITURGIES)

GRAY (TALMUD)

Havdalah ("Separation") Maimonides sees *Havdalah* as a biblically required aspect of the sanctification of Shabbat called for by Exodus 20:8 ("Remember the Sabbath day to sanctify it"). *Kiddush* and *Havdalah* are thus two aspects of one sanctification of Shabbat, he says: "[A Jew] must remember [Shabbat] at its entrance and exit; at its entrance with *Kiddush* and at its exit with *Havdalah*" ("Shabbat" 29:1). Maimonides' estimate of *Havdalah* as having biblical status like the *(p. 190)* evening from *Havdalah al Hakos* ("over a cup [of wine]"), which is to say, the *Havdalah* we have here, the *Havdalah* for the home (Ber. 33a; Pes. 105b). The Talmud even wonders whether both recitations of *Havdalah* are needed (Ber. 33a). An initial claim is made that the Men of the Great Assembly instituted the home *Havdalah* only for a time when people were wealthy enough to afford the extra wine, whereas during hard times, the *Havdalah* in the evening *Amidah* suffices. Another tradition claims that the Men of the *(p. 190)*

[1] *"God is my strength and might, and will be my salvation"* In Isaiah 12:2, and here as well, the Hebrew verse juxtaposes two names of God: Yah and Adonai. But Adonai is missing from Exodus 15:2 and Psalm 118:14, where parallel verses occur but with only the name Yah. Rashi (to Isaiah 12:2) interprets the juxtaposition of both divine names as a hint that God's name remains incomplete until the perfection of God's earthly rule.

[2] *"You shall draw forth water in gladness from the wells of salvation"* Targum Jonathan to Isaiah 12:3 translates this verse as "You shall receive a new teaching in joy from the elect of the righteous." The "water" of the verse is thus rendered as "teaching," and the "wells of salvation" are the "elect of the righteous." Rashi and Radak (David Kimchi, twelfth–thirteenth centuries, Provence) suggest that the new "teaching" from the "elect of the righteous" implies the end of exile, when Israel is no longer beset by persecution and will be able to develop insights into Torah that will seem entirely new. This interpretation by Rashi and Radak is well suited to the end of Shabbat, itself a hint of the world-to-come (Ber. 57b).

¹אֵלִיָּהוּ הַנָּבִיא אֵלִיָּהוּ הַתִּשְׁבִּי אֵלִיָּהוּ הַגִּלְעָדִי. בִּמְהֵרָה יָבוֹא אֵלֵינוּ עִם מָשִׁיחַ בֶּן דָּוִד.

[7] *"The Jews enjoyed light and happiness"* Esther 8:16, recited, perhaps, because *Havdalah* evokes its reference to "light." But there may be more to it, as we see from a talmudic story (PT Ber. 1:1, 2c) of *(p. 190)*

BRETTLER (BIBLE)

there, placing it instead at the end of the Saturday night synagogue service, where the same text serves as *Havdalah* at home and/or in synagogue. Part of the ritual is transliterated (a single line of the introduction [*Lay'hudim...*, from Esther 8:16], *Eliyahu Hanavi*, and the chorus for *Shavu'a Tov*), but the rest of it, including the blessings, is not. By contrast, such staples as the Friday night candle blessings and *Shehecheyanu* are fully translated in the "Observances in the Home" unit that follows.

Several explanations for the inconsistency come to mind. It may be, for instance,

ELLENSON (MODERN LITURGIES)

reflective of the book as a whole, had selective transliterations throughout the synagogue service, including *Havdalah,* which was part of the liturgy for synagogue prayer, but also prescribed for the home. Later, however, it was thought that certain home ceremonies (liturgies to inaugurate Shabbat and Chanukah) demanded their own unit and should have complete transliterations, including the basic blessings. But the first, and original, manuscript, which assumed enough Hebrew competence to say at least the basic blessings of *Havdalah,* was omitted from the new unit and remained unchanged where it already was.

In her ceremony for *Havdalah,* Marcia Falk "puts aside the hierarchical overview of the traditional ritual and considers the relationship between Sabbath and weekday in a new light." The aim of the *Havdalah* ritual found in *The Book of Blessings* is to celebrate the "rest" and "joy" that characterize the Sabbath, while simultaneously rejoicing in "the hope of fruitfulness, of accomplishment and achievement" that mark the days of the week. Falk therefore opens her *Havdalah* with an "Opening Psalm" that reads, "The arc of evening slowly turning, the sun's blue shadows washed away, the gate still open as three stars wait to pierce the sky, in the corridor where night bares its maze you begin to

FRANKEL (A WOMAN'S VOICE)

[11] *"Creator of varied spices"* Marcia Falk's *Book of Blessings* provides a blessing over the spices that celebrates "the uniqueness of every living being." The blessing reads, "Let us celebrate the breath of all living things and praise all essences."

[12] *"Creator of the lights of fire"* Here, Falk's *Book of Blessings* states, "Let us seek the unseen sparks that kindle the greater lights." This new blessing seeks to illuminate "the less visible aspects of identities."

[13] *"Between Israel and the nations"* Although Isaac Mayer Wise retained this phrase in his *Minhag America,* Abraham Geiger departed from his American colleague at this

point and omitted this phrase from both the 1854 and the 1870 editions of his prayer book, objecting to its wording as "too particularistic." The British *Lev Chadash* follows Geiger on this score, as does the 1975 edition of *Gates of Prayer* and the 1995 Reconstructionist *Kol Haneshamah*. On the other hand, *Gates of Repentance,* the High Holy Day liturgy of American Reform Judaism, and the Israeli *Ha-avodah Shebalev* do insert this phrase in their *Havdalah* texts, as does the 1994 American Reform home prayer book, *On the Doorposts of Your House.*

Obviously, the sensibilities of liberal prayer book authors are divided on the theological and ethical implications contained in distinguishing Israel from "the [other] nations." In America, at least, the earliest contemporary thinking (1975, *GOP*) was divided enough to retain the *Union Prayer Book* suspicion of such particularism here and (in its synagogue services) to include the traditional *Alenu* as a valid option, despite that prayer's claim that God "did not make us like…the [other] families of the earth" (see Volume 6, *Tachanun and Concluding Prayers,* pp. 134–135). By *GOR,* only three years later (1978), the particularistic line was restored here in the *Havdalah* also.

—◆—

FRANKEL (A WOMAN'S VOICE)

[7] *"The Jews enjoyed light and happiness"* It has often been noted by rabbinic authorities that the Book of Esther is the only biblical book in which God's name never once appears. Yet the hand of God is clearly present in the story, nowhere more so than in the Persian Jews' miraculous escape from Haman's intended genocide. The opening verse of the *Havdalah* ceremony makes this point explicit. The liturgist cites a verse from Esther—"The Jews enjoyed light and happiness and joy and honor" (8:16)— embedding it among seven other biblical verses that all involve the theme of messianic redemption. And if we place the verse from Esther back into its original context, we discover that it, too, concerns redemption. Due to Esther's intercession, the Jews in the Persian Empire are permitted to defend themselves against the soldiers sent to destroy them; it is our verse cited here that proclaims the happy results of their efforts. By appropriating this verse and inserting it here within this liturgical pastiche from Psalms and Isaiah, it too has been redeemed from its original profane setting. And with it, Esther takes her place, albeit belatedly and through a back door, as a psalmist and prophet in Israel.

—◆—

GRAY (TALMUD)

Kiddush is not shared by everyone (*Maggid Mishneh* to "Shabbat" 29:1), nor is that view clearly supported by the Babylonian Talmud, which sees the institution as a rabbinic or proto-rabbinic innovation by the Men of the Great Assembly (Ber. 33a).

The Talmud differentiates the *Havdalah* insertion into the *Amidah* of Saturday

KUSHNER & POLEN (CHASIDISM)

Great Assembly always intended that both be said—a position that wins the day (Ber. 33a). This talmudic discussion testifies to a fluidity of practice, at least regarding *Havdalah,* in the talmudic period.

[1-2] *"God is my salvation.... You shall draw forth waters from the wells of salvation"* These two verses almost exactly correspond to Isaiah 12:2–3, although the phrase *ki ozi v'zimrat Yah Adonai vay'hi li li'shua* ("God is my strength and might, and will be my salvation") has parallels in Exodus 15:2 (the "Song of the Sea") and in Psalm 118:14 (a psalm in the Egyptian *Hallel*). The *Tur* (O. Ch. 299) attributes the recitation of Isaiah 12:2 to *Seder Rav Amram* (our first prayer book, ca. 860 C.E.), which, however, is said to have advocated it after the *Havdalah* ceremony, not before. Moses Isserles (R'ma, 1530–1575) mentions its recitation before *Havdalah,* as we have (R'ma to *Shulchan Arukh,* O. Ch. 296:1).

L. HOFFMAN (HISTORY)

Rabbi Chiya the Great and Rabbi Shimon Chalafta, who are out walking shortly before sunrise. As dawn breaks and the sun slowly rises, Rabbi Chiya observes that Israel's ultimate redemption too will unfold gradually, similar to Mordecai's gradual elevation to power in the Book of Esther. He cites none other than Esther 8:16, the verse we have here, as the verse corresponding to Israel's complete redemption. This is a perfect verse for the end of the Shabbat. As our "taste of the world-to-come" (Ber. 57b) ends, we gladly anticipate the real messianic redemption said to arrive if Israel keeps Shabbat properly (see "Renew our Temple," p. 123). We add, "May we have these, too!" expressing our wish that the joy felt by the Jews of Esther's day will be ours as well.

[10] *"Fruit of the vine"* Moses Isserles (*Shulchan Arukh,* O. Ch. 296:1) tells us to let some wine overflow onto the ground, because any home that is not lucky enough to be able to spill wine like water will not see a blessing. Moreover, pouring wine, using it to extinguish the *Havdalah* candle, and then passing some over the eyes promotes good luck for the coming week.

[11] *"Varied spices"* Maimonides ("Shabbat" 29:29) explains that the spices cheer the

About the Contributors

MARC BRETTLER

Marc Brettler, Ph.D., is Dora Goldberg Professor of Biblical Studies and chair of the Department of Near Eastern and Judaic Studies at Brandeis University. His major areas of research are biblical historical texts, religious metaphors, and gender issues in the Bible. Brettler is author of *God Is King: Understanding an Israelite Metaphor* (Sheffield Academic Press) and *The Creation of History in Ancient Israel* (Routledge) as well as a variety of articles and books on the Bible. He is also associate editor of the new edition of the *Oxford Annotated Bible,* and coeditor of *The Jewish Study Bible* (Oxford University Press).

MICHAEL CHERNICK

Dr. Michael Chernick is an Orthodox rabbi ordained by R. Isaac Elchanan Theological Seminary. He received his doctorate in Talmud and rabbinic literature from the Bernard Revel Graduate School of Yeshiva University. Dr. Chernick is the Deutsch Family Professor of Jewish Jurisprudence and Social Justice at the Hebrew Union College–Jewish Institute of Religion, New York School, where he teaches rabbinic literature. He is the author of several works on rabbinic hermeneutics and of articles on the history of Jewish law, the interplay of Jewish law and ethics, and the literary and cultural study of the talmudic story.

ELLIOT N. DORFF

Elliot N. Dorff, Ph.D., is rector and Sol and Anne Dorff Distinguished Professor of Philosophy at the University of Judaism in Los Angeles. His book *Knowing God: Jewish Journeys to the Unknowable* (Jason Aronson) includes an extensive analysis of the nature of prayer. Ordained a rabbi by the Jewish Theological Seminary of America, Dorff is a member of the Conservative Movement's Committee on Jewish Law and Standards, its Commission on the Philosophy of the Conservative Movement, and its Commission to write a new Torah commentary for the Conservative Movement. Winner of the National Jewish Book Award for *To Do the Right and the Good: A Jewish Approach to Modern Social Ethics,* he has written ten books and more than 150 articles on Jewish thought, law, and ethics, and he has served on several federal government commissions on issues in bioethics.

DAVID ELLENSON

David Ellenson, Ph.D., is president of Hebrew Union College–Jewish Institute of Religion. He holds the Gus Waterman Herrman Presidential Chair and is the I. H. and Anna Grancell Professor of Jewish Religious Thought. Ordained a rabbi by Hebrew Union College–Jewish Institute of Religion, he has served as a visiting professor at Hebrew University in Jerusalem, at the Jewish Theological Seminary in New York, and at the University of California at Los Angeles. Ellenson has also taught at the Pardes Institute of Jewish Studies and at the Shalom Hartman Institute, both in Jerusalem. Ellenson has published and lectured extensively on diverse topics in modern Jewish thought, history, and ethics.

ELLEN FRANKEL

Dr. Ellen Frankel is currently the CEO and editor in chief of The Jewish Publication Society. A scholar of Jewish folklore, Frankel has published eight books, including *The Classic Tales; The Encyclopedia of Jewish Symbols,* co-authored with artist Betsy Teutsch; *The Five Books of Miriam: A Woman's Commentary on the Torah; The Jewish Spirit;* and *The Illustrated Hebrew Bible.* Frankel travels widely as a storyteller and lecturer, speaking at synagogues, summer study institutes, Hillels, Jewish women's groups, Jewish community centers, museums, schools, retirement communities, and nursing homes, and to radio audiences.

ALYSSA GRAY

Alyssa Gray, Ph.D., J.D., is assistant professor of codes and responsa literature at Hebrew Union College–Jewish Institute of Religion in New York. She has also taught at The Jewish Theological Seminary in New York. Her principal research interests are the redactions and interrelationship of the Babylonian and Palestinian Talmuds, Jewish law and legal theory, and the history of Jewish law, especially the topics of *tzedakah,* Jewish–non-Jewish interactions, and martyrdom. She is currently working on a book about the literary dependency of Bavli tractate *Avodah Zarah* on Yerushalmi tractate *Avodah Zarah.*

JOEL M. HOFFMAN

Joel M. Hoffman, Ph.D., teaches advanced Hebrew, translation, and the history of Hebrew at Hebrew Union College–Jewish Institute of Religion in New York; he has also taught at Brandeis University, and lectured in the United States, Europe, and Israel. He has served as Hebrew consultant to Harper/San Francisco and Jewish Lights Publishing. Hoffman's research in theoretical linguistics brings him to a new approach to ancient Hebrew, viewing it not merely as a dead language, but as a spoken language of antiquity. In addition to his graduate-level teaching, Hoffman teaches youngsters at various Hebrew schools. He considers teaching his greatest joy.

LAWRENCE A. HOFFMAN

Lawrence A. Hoffman, Ph.D., has served for more than two decades as the Barbara and Stephen Friedman Professor of Liturgy Worship and Ritual at Hebrew Union College–Jewish Institute of Religion in New York, where he was ordained a rabbi. Widely recognized for his liturgical scholarship, Hoffman has combined research in Jewish ritual, worship, and spirituality with a passion for the spiritual renewal of contemporary Judaism. He has written and edited numerous books, including *The Art of Public Prayer, 2nd Edition: Not for Clergy Only* (SkyLight Paths)—now used nationally by Jews and Christians as a handbook for liturgical planners in church and synagogue, as well as a revision of *What Is a Jew?,* the best-selling classic that remains the most widely read introduction to Judaism ever written in any language. He is also the author of *Israel—A Spiritual Travel Guide: A Companion for the Modern Jewish Pilgrim* and *The Way Into Jewish Prayer* (both Jewish Lights Publishing). Hoffman is currently a developer of Synagogue 2000, a transdenominational project designed to envision and implement the ideal synagogue of the spirit for the twenty-first century.

LAWRENCE KUSHNER

Lawrence Kushner is the Emanu-El scholar at Congregation Emanu-El in San Francisco and is an adjunct faculty member at Hebrew Union College–Jewish Institute of Religion. He served as spiritual leader of Congregation Beth El in Sudbury, Massachusetts, for twenty-eight years and is widely regarded as one of the most creative religious writers in America. Ordained a rabbi by Hebrew Union College–Jewish Institute of Religion, Kushner led his congregants in publishing their own prayer book, *V'taher Libenu (Purify Our Hearts),* the first gender-neutral liturgy ever written. Through his lectures and many books, including *The Way Into Jewish Mystical Tradition; Invisible Lines of Connection: Sacred Stories of the Ordinary; The Book of Letters: A Mystical Hebrew Alphabet; Honey from the Rock: An Introduction to Jewish Mysticism; God Was in This Place and I, i Did Not Know: Finding Self, Spirituality, and Ultimate Meaning; Eyes Remade for Wonder: A Lawrence Kushner Reader,* and *Jewish Spirituality: A Brief Introduction for Christians,* all published by Jewish Lights, he has helped shape the Jewish community's present focus on personal and institutional spiritual renewal.

DANIEL LANDES

Daniel Landes is director and Rosh HaYeshivah of the Pardes Institute of Jewish Studies in Jerusalem and was an adjunct professor of Jewish law at Loyola University Law School in Los Angeles. Ordained a rabbi by Rabbi Isaac Elchanan Theological Seminary, Landes was a founding faculty member of the Simon Wiesenthal Center and the Yeshiva of Los Angeles. He has lectured and written various popular and scholarly articles on the subjects of Jewish thought, social ethics, and spirituality.

NEHEMIA POLEN

Nehemia Polen is professor of Jewish thought and director of the Hasidic Text Institute at Boston's Hebrew College. He is the author of *The Holy Fire: The Teachings of Rabbi Kalonymus Shapira, the Rebbe of the Warsaw Ghetto* (Jason Aronson), as well as many academic and popular articles on Chasidism and Jewish spirituality. He received his Ph.D. from Boston University, where he studied with and served as teaching fellow for Nobel laureate Elie Wiesel. In 1994 he was Daniel Jeremy Silver Fellow at Harvard University, and he has also been a Visiting Scholar at the Hebrew University in Jerusalem. He was ordained a rabbi at the Ner Israel Rabbinical College in Baltimore, Maryland, and served as a congregational rabbi for twenty-three years. In 1998–1999 he was a National Endowment for the Humanities Fellow, working on the writings of Malkah Shapiro (1894–1971), the daughter of a noted Chasidic master, whose Hebrew memoirs focus on the spiritual lives of women in the context of pre-war Chasidism in Poland. This work is documented in his book *The Rebbe's Daughter*.

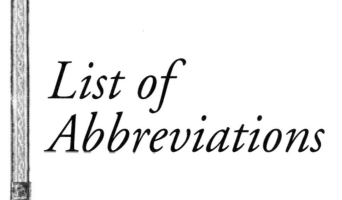

List of Abbreviations

Artscroll	*Siddur Kol Ya'akov*, 1984.
Birnbaum	*Daily Prayer Book: Hasiddur Hashalem*, 1949.
FOP	*Forms of Prayer*, 1997.
Fox	Everett Fox, *The Five Books of Moses* (New York: Schocken Books, 1995).
GOP	*Gates of Prayer*, 1975.
HS	*Ha'avodah Shebalev*, 1982.
KH	*Kol Haneshamah*, 1996.
JPS	*Jewish Publication Society Bible* (Philadelphia: Jewish Publication Society, 1985).
NRSV	*New Revised Standard Bible*, 1989.
SLC	*Siddur Lev Chadash*, 1995.
SOH	*Service of the Heart*, 1967.
SSS	*Siddur Sim Shalom*, 1985; revised, 1998.
SVT	*Siddur Va'ani T'fillati*, 1998.
UPB	*Union Prayer Book*, 1894–1895.

Glossary

The following glossary defines Hebrew words used regularly throughout this volume and provides the way the words are pronounced. Sometimes two pronunciations are common, in which case the first is the way the word is sounded in proper Hebrew, and the second is the way it is sometimes heard in common speech, under the influence of Yiddish, the folk language of Jews in northern and eastern Europe (it is a combination, mostly, of Hebrew and German). Our goal is to provide the way that many Jews actually use these words, not just the technically correct version.

- The pronunciations are divided into syllables by dashes.

- The accented syllable is written in capital letters.

- "Kh" represents a guttural sound, similar to the German (as in "sprach").

- The most common vowel is "a" as in "father," which appears here as "ah."

- The short "e" (as in "get") is written as either "e" (when it is in the middle of a syllable) or "eh" (when it ends a syllable).

- Similarly, the short "i" (as in "tin") is written as either "i" (when it is in the middle of a syllable) or "ih" (when it ends a syllable).

- A long "o" (as in "Moses") is written as "oe" (as in the word "toe") or "oh" (as in the word "Oh!").

Acharonim (pronounced ah-khah-roe-NEEM or, commonly, akh-ROE-nim): The name given to Jewish legal authorities from roughly the sixteenth century on. The word means, literally, "later ones," as opposed to the "earlier ones," authorities prior to that time who are held in higher regard and are called *Rishonim* (pronounced ree-shoh-NEEM or, commonly, ree-SHOH-nim). Singular: *Acharon* (pronounced ah-khah-RONE) and *Rishon* (pronounced ree-SHONE).

Adon Olam (pronounced ah-DOHN oh-LAHM): An early morning prayer of unknown authorship, but dating from medieval times, and possibly originally intended as a nighttime prayer, because it praises God for watching over our souls when we sleep.

Nowadays, it is used also as a concluding song for which composers have provided a staggering variety of tunes.

Adonai elohei yisra'el (pronounced ah-doh-NAH'y eh-loh-HAY yis-rah-AYL): Literally, "Adonai God of Israel." A common appellation for God, used in this series to designate the opening words, and hence, the name of a prayer, that is added to *Tachanun* on Mondays and Thursdays.

Akedah (pronounced ah-kay-DAH): Literally, "binding"; the technical term for the Genesis 22 account of the binding of Isaac on the altar; read liturgically as part of the *Birkhot Hashachar*. By extension, a genre of poem, especially for the High Holy Days, pleading for forgiveness on account of the merit of Isaac's near self-sacrifice.

Al chet (pronounced ahl KHEHT): Literally, "For the sin…" See ***Vidui Rabbah***.

Alenu (pronounced ah-LAY-noo): The first word and, therefore, the title of a major prayer compiled in the second or third century as part of the New Year (Rosh Hashanah) service, but from about the fourteenth century on, used also as part of the concluding section of every daily service. *Alenu* means "it is incumbent upon us…" and introduces the prayer's theme: our duty to praise God.

Amah (pronounced ah-MAH): A rabbinic measure, amounting, roughly, to a forearm: the distance from the elbow to the tip of the little finger.

Amidah (pronounced either ah-mee-DAH or, commonly, ah-MEE-dah): One of three commonly used titles for the second of two central units in the worship service, the first being the *Sh'ma* and Its Blessings. It is composed of a series of blessings, many of which are petitionary, except on Sabbaths and holidays, when the petitions are removed out of deference to the holiness of the day. Also called ***T'fillah*** and ***Sh'moneh Esreh***. *Amidah* means "standing," and refers to the fact that the prayer is said standing up.

Amora (pronounced ah-MOE-rah): A title for talmudic authorities and, therefore, those living from roughly the third to the sixth centuries. Plural: *Amoraim* (pronounced ah-moe-rah-EEM or, commonly, ah-moe-RAH-yim). Often used in contrast to a *Tanna* (pronounced TAH-nah), the title of authorities in the time of the Mishnah, that is, prior to the third century. Plural: *Tannaim* (pronounced tah-nah-EEM or, commonly, tah-NAH-yim).

Arvit (pronounced ahr-VEET or, commonly, AHR-veet): From the Hebrew word *erev* (pronounced EH-rev) meaning "evening." One of two titles used for the evening worship service (also called ***Ma'ariv***).

Ashamnu (pronounced ah-SHAHM-noo): Literally, "We have sinned." See **Vidui Zuta**.

Ashkavah (pronounced ahsh-kah-VAH or, commonly, ahsh-KAH-vah): Sometimes spelled *Hashkavah* (pronounced hahsh-kah-VAH or, commonly, hahsh-KAH-vah). A traditional Sefardi prayer for the dead, recited by mourners following the reading of Torah during the regular service. Said also at the graveside and during the evening service of Yom Kippur.

Ashkenazi (pronounced ahsh-k'-nah-ZEE or, commonly, ahsh-k'-NAH-zee): From the Hebrew word *Ashkenaz*, meaning the geographic area of northern and eastern Europe; Ashkenazi is the adjective, describing the liturgical rituals and customs practiced there, as opposed to Sefardi, meaning the liturgical rituals and customs that are derived from *Sefarad*, Spain (see **Sefardi**).

Ashre (pronounced ahsh-RAY or, commonly, AHSH-ray): The first word and, therefore, the title of a prayer said three times each day, composed primarily of Psalm 145. *Ashre* means "happy" and introduces the phrase "Happy are they who dwell in Your [God's] house."

Atarah (pronounced ah-tah-RAH): A stole worn by some Reform service leaders (in place of an actual *tallit* with *tsitsit*) prior to the liturgical renewal of the late twentieth century that featured a recovery of tradition and the reuse of the traditional *tallit*. (See **tallit**.)

Av harachamim (pronounced AHV hah-rah-khah-MEEM or, commonly, ahv hah-RAH-khah-meem): Literally, "Father of mercy," a prayer composed in the wake of the Crusades to commemorate the death of German Jewish martyrs; now part of the weekly Shabbat service (after reading Torah) and one of the main prayers comprising the Memorial Service *(Yizkor)*.

Avodah (pronounced ah-voe-DAH): Literally, "sacrificial service," a reference to the sacrificial cult practiced in the ancient Temple until its destruction by the Romans in the year 70 C.E.; also the title of the third to last blessing in the *Amidah*, a petition for the restoration of the Temple in messianic times. Many liberal liturgies either omit the blessing or reframe it as a petition for divine acceptance of worship in general.

Avot (pronounced ah-VOTE): Literally, "fathers" or "ancestors," and the title of the first blessing in the *Amidah*. The traditional wording of the blessing recollects the covenantal relationship between God and the patriarchs: Abraham, Isaac, and Jacob. Most liberal liturgies also include explicit reference to the matriarchs: Sarah, Rebekah, Rachel, and Leah.

[The] Bach (pronounced BAHKH): An acronym for Rabbi Joel Sirkes (1561–1640, Poland), formed by juxtaposing the two Hebrew initials of his major legal work, *Bayit Chadash* (BaCH).

Bakashot (pronounced bah-kah-SHOTE; singular, *bakashah*, pronounced bah-kah-SHAH): Petitions; technically, the middle thirteen blessings of the daily **Amidah**.

Baleh busteh (pronounced bah-l' BUS-tah [the U of "BUS" rhymes with the OU of "could]): A virtually untranslatable Yiddish phrase meaning "good homemaker."

Bar'khu (pronounced bah-r'-KHOO or, commonly, BOH-r'khoo): The first word and, therefore, the title of the formal Call to Prayer with which the section called the *Sh'ma* and Its Blessings begins. *Bar'khu* means "praise," and it introduces the invitation to the assembled congregation to praise God.

Barukh k'vod (pronounced bah-RUKH k'-VOD): The first two words of a response in the third blessing of the *Amidah* taken from Ezekiel 3:12, meaning "the glory of Adonai is blessed from His place."

Barukh she'amar (pronounced bah-ROOKH sheh-ah-MAHR): Literally, "Blessed is the One by whose speech [the world came to be]," the first words and, therefore, the title of the blessing that opens the *P'sukei D'zimrah,* the "warm-up" section to the morning service composed mainly of biblical material (chiefly psalms) that were intended to be sung as praise of God.

Benediction (also called a "blessing"): One of two terms used for the Rabbis' favorite prose formula for composing prayers. The worship service is composed of many different literary genres, but most of it is benedictions. Long benedictions end with a summary line that begins *Barukh atah Adonai…* "Blessed are You, Adonai…" Short blessings have the summary line alone.

Ben Sirah (pronounced behn SIH-rah): Author of a book of wisdom similar in style to Proverbs, probably dating to 180 or 200 B.C.E., and containing, among other things, a moving description of the High Priest in the Jerusalem Temple. Although not included in the Bible, it is known because it became part of Catholic Scripture. The book carries the author's name, but it is called, by Catholics, Ecclesiasticus. A recently discovered Hebrew edition of Ben Sirah contains a prayer that some identify (probably incorrectly) as an early version of the *Amidah* (see **Amidah**).

Bet Yosef (pronounced bayt yoh-SAYF): Commentary to the *Tur* by Joseph Caro, sixteenth century, Land of Israel, and a precursor to his more popular code, the *Shulchan Arukh.*

Binah (pronounced bee-NAH or, commonly, BEE-nah): Literally, "knowledge" or "understanding," and the title of the fourth blessing in the daily *Amidah*. It is a petition for human knowledge, particularly insight into the human condition, leading to repentance. In kabbalistic circles, it is one of the uppermost *s'firot,* representing a stage of divine thought prior to creation.

Birkat (pronounced beer-KAHT): Literally, "Blessing of..." The titles of many blessings are known as "Blessing of...," for example, "Blessing of Torah" and "Blessing of Jerusalem." Some titles are commonly shortened so that only the qualifying last words are used (such as "Jerusalem" instead of "Blessing of Jerusalem"), and they are listed in the glossary by the last words, e.g., *Y'rushalayim* instead of *Birkat Y'rushalayim* ("Jerusalem" instead of "Blessing of Jerusalem"). Those blessings that are more generally cited with the full title appear under *Birkat.*

Birkat Hashir (pronounced beer-KAHT hah-SHEER): Literally, "Blessing of song," and the title, therefore, of the final blessing to the *P'sukei D'zimrah,* the "warm-up" section to the morning service composed mainly of biblical material (chiefly psalms) that were intended to be sung as praise of God. Technically, a *Birkat Hashir* concludes any *Hallel* (see **Hallel**), in this case, the Daily *Hallel,* which is the central component of the *P'sukei D'zimrah.*

Birkat Hatorah (pronounced beer-KAHT hah-toe-RAH): Literally, "Blessing of Torah," the title for the second blessing in the liturgical section called the *Sh'ma* and Its Blessings; its theme is the revelation of the Torah to Israel on Mount Sinai.

Birkat Kohanim (pronounced beer-KAHT koe-hah-NEEM): Literally, "Blessing of the Priests," but usually referred to as "the priestly benediction," a reference to Numbers 6:24–26. Also the title of the final blessing of the *Amidah.* See also **Kohanim**.

Birkat yayin (pronounced beer-KAHT YAH-yin or, commonly, BEER-kaht YAH-yin): Literally, "blessing over wine," hence, the benediction recited before drinking wine or grape juice and used especially as part of the *Kiddush* (a prayer announcing sacred time).

Birkhot Hashachar (pronounced beer-KHOT hah-SHAH-khar): Literally, "Morning Blessings," the title of the first large section in the morning prayer regimen of Judaism; originally said privately upon arising in the morning, but now customarily recited immediately upon arriving at the synagogue. It is composed primarily of benedictions thanking God for the everyday gifts of health and wholeness, as well as study sections taken from the Bible and rabbinic literature.

Birkhot mitzvah (pronounced beer-KHOT meetz-VAH): Blessings said upon performing a commandment; normally of the form, "Blessed are You, Adonai our God, ruler of the universe, who sanctified us with commandments and commanded us to...."

Birkhot nehenin (pronounced beer-KHOT neh-heh-NEEN): Blessings said upon enjoyment of God's world (e.g., eating food, seeing rainbows, hearing a thunderstorm, seeing a flower); normally of the form, "Blessed are You, Adonai our God, ruler of the universe, who…."

Bo'i khallah, Bo'i khallah (pronounced boh-EE khah-LAH, boh-EE khah-LAH): Literally, "Come O bride, come O bride," the invitation to Shabbat that concludes *L'khah Dodi* in the Friday night evening *(Ma'ariv)* service (see *L'khah Dodi*).

B'rakhah (pronounced b'-rah-KHAH): The Hebrew word for "benediction" or "blessing." See **Benediction**. Plural ("benedictions") is *b'rakhot* (pronounced b'-rah-KHOTE).

Chanukah (pronounced khah-noo-KAH, or commonly, KHAH-noo-kah): An eight-day festival beginning on the twenty-fifth day of the Hebrew month of Kislev, corresponding, usually, to some time in December. Chanukah celebrates the miraculous deliverance of the Jews as described in the books known as *Maccabees* (pronounced MA-kah-beez). Although not canonized in the Bible, Maccabees is carried in Catholic Scripture and describes the heroic acts of a priestly family, known also as the Hasmoneans (pronounced has-moe-NEE-'ns), in 167 B.C.E.

Chanuki'ah (pronounced khah-noo-kee-YAH or, commonly, khah-noo-KEE-yah): An eight-branch candelabra for Chanukah candles.

Chasidei Ashkenaz (pronounced khah-see-DAY Ahsh-k'-NAHZ or, commonly, khah-SEE-day AHSH-k'-nahz): Literally, "The pious of Germany," a loosely knit philosophical school of thought from twelfth- to thirteenth-century Germany, which pioneered a mystical understanding of the liturgy and emphasized an ascetic way of life and a negative view of humanity. See **Kavod**.

Chasidism (pronounced KHAH-sih-dizm): The doctrine generally traced to an eighteenth-century Polish Jewish mystic and spiritual leader known as the Ba'al Shem Tov (called also the BeSHT, an acronym composed of the initials of his name B, SH, and T). Followers are called *Chasidim* (pronounced khah-see-DEEM or khah-SIH-dim; singular, *Chasid,* pronounced khah-SEED or, commonly, KHA-sid) from the Hebrew word *chesed* (pronounced KHEH-sed), meaning "loving-kindness" or "piety."

Chatimah (pronounced khah-tee-MAH): The final summary line of a benediction (see **Benediction**).

Chatzi Kaddish (pronounced khah-TSEE kah-DEESH or, commonly, KHAH-tsee KAH-d'sh): Literally, "Half *Kaddish,*" a short version of the *Kaddish*, a sort of "oral punctuation," in this case, an "oral semicolon," used to indicate a separation between one major rubric of the service and another.

Cheshvan (pronounced KHESH-vahn): A Hebrew month corresponding to late October or November.

Chokhmah (pronounced khokh-MAH or, commonly, KHOKH-mah): Literally, "wisdom," but in kabbalistic circles, one of the uppermost *s'firot*, representing a stage of divine thought prior to creation.

Chuppah (pronounced khoo-PAH or, commonly, KHUH-pah): A wedding canopy.

Confession: See **Vidui Rabbah, Vidui Zuta**.

Daily Hallel (pronounced hah-LAYL or, commonly, HAH-layl): English for *Hallel Sheb'khol Yom*. See **Hallel**.

David (pronounced dah-VEED): Literally, "David," a reference to the biblical King David, and the title of the fifteenth blessing of the daily *Amidah*, a petition for the appearance of the messianic ruler said by tradition to be a descendent of King David. Some liberal liturgies omit the blessing or reframe it to refer to a messianic age of perfection, but without the arrival of a human messianic ruler.

Doxology: Technical term for a congregational response to an invitation to praise God; generally a single line of prayer affirming praise of God forever and ever. Examples in the *Sh'ma* and Its Blessings are the responses to the Call to Prayer and to the *Sh'ma* itself. From the Greek word *doxa*, meaning "glory."

D'vekut (pronounced d'vay-KOOT): Literally, "clinging" to God, a mystical term meaning the soul's temporary separation from the body and its loving unification with God.

Ein Keloheinu (pronounced ayn kay-loh-HAY-noo): Literally, "There is none like our God," a concluding prayer of the *Musaf* service.

El Adon (pronounced ayl ah-DOHN): An early medieval (or, perhaps, ancient) poem celebrating God as a king enthroned on high; it is arranged as an acrostic, that is, each line begins with a different letter of the alphabet. Nowadays, *El Adon* is a popular Sabbath morning hymn.

Elohai n'tsor (pronounced eh-loh-HA'y n'-TSOR): Literally, "My God, keep [my tongue from evil]"; the first words and, therefore, the title of a silent prayer following every **Amidah**, attributed by the Talmud (Ber. 17a) to a fourth-century Babylonian sage known for his piety.

Eretz Yisrael (pronounced EH-retz yis-rah-AYL): Hebrew for "the Land of Israel."

Gaon (pronounced gah-OHN; plural: *Geonim,* pronounced g'-oh-NEEM): Title for the leading Rabbis in Babylon (present-day Iraq) from about 750 to 1038. From a biblical word meaning "glory," which is equivalent in the title to saying "Your Excellence."

Gematria (pronounced g'-MAHT-ree-ah): The system of assigning a numerical value to each Hebrew letter according to its sequence in the alphabet, then matching the total represented by a word or phrase to another word or phrase with the same value, thereby applying the meaning implicit in one word or phrase to the other.

Genizah (pronounced g'-NEE-zah): A cache of documents, in particular the one discovered at the turn of the twentieth century in an old synagogue in Cairo; the source of our knowledge about how Jews prayed in the Land of Israel and vicinity prior to the twelfth century. From a word meaning "to store or hide away," "to archive."

Gra (pronounced GRAH): Elijah of Vilna, known also as the Vilna Gaon, outstanding halakhic authority of Lithuania (1720–1797).

Graveside Kaddish: See **Kaddish L'it'chad'ta**.

G'ullah (pronounced g'-oo-LAH): Literally, "redemption" or "deliverance," and the title of the seventh blessing of the daily *Amidah,* as well as the third blessing in the *Sh'ma* and Its Blessings; its theme affirms God's redemptive act of delivering the Israelites from Egypt and promises ultimate deliverance from suffering and want at the end of time.

G'vurot (pronounced g'voo-ROTE): Literally, "strength" or "power," and the title of the second blessing in the *Amidah.* It affirms the power of God to bring annual rain and new growth in nature and, by extension, to resurrect the dead. Some liberal liturgies omit the belief in resurrection or replace it with wording that suggests other concepts of eternal life.

Hachnasat orchim (pronounced hahkh-nah-SAHT ohr-KHEEM): Literally, "bringing guests in," hence, the *mitzvah* of welcoming guests for such things as Shabbat dinner.

Hadas (pronounced hah-DAHS): Myrtle sprigs used on Sukkot as one of the four required species ("You shall take the produce of good trees, branches of palm trees, boughs of leafy trees, and willows of the brook" [Lev. 23:40]); preferred in antiquity for the spices that became part of the *Havdalah* ritual.

Hadlakat nerot (pronounced hahd-lah-KAHT nay-ROHT): Literally, "candle lighting," the liturgical act of kindling lights to inaugurate Shabbat and the Festivals.

Haftarah (pronounced hahf-tah-RAH or, commonly, hahf-TOE-rah): The section of Scripture taken from the prophets and read publicly as part of Shabbat and holiday worship services. From a word meaning "to conclude," because it is the "concluding reading," that is, it follows a reading from the Torah (the Five Books of Moses).

Haggadah (pronounced hah-gah-DAH or, commonly, hah-GAH-dah): The liturgical service for the Passover eve Seder meal. From a Hebrew word meaning "to tell," because the Haggadah is a telling of the Passover narrative.

Hakafah (pronounced hah-kah-FAH): Literally, "going around [the room]," a procession in which the Torah is taken from the ark and carried to the *bimah* during the introductory prayers. As the procession winds its way to the *bimah,* people approach the Torah, even kiss it.

Halakhah (pronounced hah-lah-KHAH or, commonly, hah-LAH-khah): The Hebrew word for "Jewish law." Also used as an anglicized adjective, halakhic (pronounced hah-LAH-khic), meaning "legal." From the Hebrew word meaning "to walk" or "to go," denoting the way in which a person should walk through life.

Hallel (pronounced hah-LAYL or, commonly, HAH-layl): A Hebrew word meaning "praise" and, by extension, the name given to sets of psalms that are recited liturgically in praise of God: Psalms 145–150, the Daily *Hallel,* is recited each morning; Psalm 136, the Great *Hallel,* is recited on Shabbat and holidays and is part of the Passover Seder. Psalms 113–118, the best-known *Hallel,* known more fully as the Egyptian *Hallel,* is recited on holidays and gets its name from Psalm 114:1, which celebrates the moment "when Israel left Egypt."

Hallel Sheb'khol Yom (pronounced hah-LAYL [or, commonly, HAH-layl] sheh-b'-khol YOHM): The Hebrew term for "The Daily *Hallel.*" See **Hallel**.

Halleluyah (pronounced hah-l'-loo-YAH, but sometimes anglicized as hah-l'-LOO-yah): A common word in Psalms, meaning "praise God," and the final word of a congregational response within the third blessing of the *Amidah* (from Ps. 146:10).

Hat'fillah (pronounced hah-t'-fee-LAH): Literally, "the *T'fillah,*" another name for the *Amidah.* See **T'fillah**.

Hatov v'hameitiv (pronounced hah-TOHV v'-hah-mei-TEEV): Literally, "the one who is good and does good," that is, the conclusion of a blessing recited on several occasions such as hearing good news; the name, therefore, for the blessings in question, including the final blessing in the *Birkat Hamazon* (Grace after Meals).

Havdalah (pronounced hahv-dah-LAH or, commonly, hahv-DAH-lah): Literally "separation," hence, the name of the prayer that separates Shabbat from the following week, said as an insertion into the Saturday evening *Amidah* and at home later in the evening. The latter instance, which is accompanied by wine, is called *Havdalah al Hakos* (pronounced hahv-dah-LAH ahl hah-KOHS), "*Havdalah* over a cup [of wine]."

Hoda'ah (pronounced hoe-dah-AH): Literally, a combination of the Hebrew words for "gratitude" and "acknowledgment," so translated here as "grateful acknowledgment." The title of the second to last blessing in the *Amidah,* an expression of our grateful acknowledgment to God for the daily wonders that constitute human existence.

Hoeche K'dushah (pronounced HAY-kh' k'DOO-shah): A Yiddish term combining German and Hebrew and meaning, literally, "the High *K'dushah*." Refers to a way to shorten the time it takes to say the *Amidah* by avoiding the necessity of having the prayer leader repeat it all after it is said silently by the congregation.

Inclusio (pronounced in-CLOO-zee-oh): A rhetorical style common to biblical prayer, whereby the end of a composition reiterates the theme or words with which the composition began.

Kabbalah (pronounced kah-bah-LAH or, commonly, kah-BAH-lah): A general term for Jewish mysticism, but used properly for a specific mystical doctrine that began in western Europe in the eleventh or twelfth centuries; recorded in the *Zohar* (see **Zohar**) in the thirteenth century, and then further elaborated, especially in the Land of Israel (in Safed), in the sixteenth century. From a Hebrew word meaning "to receive" or "to welcome," and secondarily, "tradition," implying the receiving of tradition from one's past.

Kabbalat Shabbat (pronounced kah-bah-LAHT shah-BAHT): Literally, "Welcoming Shabbat." The preamble to the evening synagogue service *(Ma'ariv)* for Friday night, climaxing in the well-known mystical prayer *L'khah Dodi* (see **L'khah Dodi**).

Kaddish (pronounced kah-DEESH or, more commonly, KAH-d'sh): One of several prayers from a Hebrew word meaning "holy," and therefore the name given to a prayer affirming God's holiness. This prayer was composed in the first century but later found its way into the service in several forms, including one known as the Mourner's *Kaddish* and used as a mourning prayer.

Kaddish D'rabbanan (pronounced d'-rah-bah-NAHN): A form of the *Kaddish* (see **Kaddish**) containing a unique paragraph requesting well-being for all who study Torah. It appears liturgically as a conclusion to study passages.

Kaddish L'it'chad'ta (pronounced l'-it-KHAH-d'-tah): Also called *Kaddish L'chad'ta* (pronounced l'-KHAH-d'-tah). Literally, *Kaddish* "of renewal," the only form of *Kaddish* that includes a reference to the resurrection of the dead and the rebuilding of

Jerusalem at the end of days. Recited after concluding a tractate of the Talmud or after a funeral (nowadays, some Jews substitute the Mourner's *Kaddish* for it. See **Kaddish Yatom**).

Kaddish Shalem (pronounced shah-LAYM): Literally, "The Complete *Kaddish*," the same words as **Kaddish Yatom** (The Mourners' *Kaddish*), but with an added line asking that our prayers be accepted on high. A sort of "oral punctuation," in this case, an "oral period," marking the completion of the *Amidah*, which (other than the reading of Torah, on specific days only) is the final major rubric in the service. Known also as *Kaddish Titkabal,* from the first word of the added line *Titkabal* [*tsalot-hon*], pronounced tit-kah-BAHL [tsa-lot-HOHN], meaning, "[May our prayer] be accepted."

Kaddish Titkabal: See **Kaddish Shalem**.

Kaddish Yatom (pronounced yah-TOHM): That version of the *Kaddish* that is said by mourners specifically to memorialize the deceased.

Kavod (pronounced kah-VOHD): Literally, "glory," but used philosophically and liturgically by the German pietists (see **Chasidei Ashkenaz**) to refer to the manifest aspect of God, as opposed to the unknown and unknowable divine essence.

Kavod Shabbat (pronounced kah-VOHD shah-BAHT): Literally, "honor [due to] Shabbat."

Kavvanah (pronounced kah-vah-NAH): From a word meaning "to direct," and therefore used technically to denote the state of directing one's words and thoughts sincerely to God, as opposed to the rote recitation of prayer.

K'dushah (pronounced k'-doo-SHAH or, commonly, k'-DOO-shah): From the Hebrew word meaning "holy," and therefore one of several prayers from the first or second century occurring in several places and versions, all of which have in common the citing of Isaiah 6:3: *Kadosh, kadosh, kadosh...,* "Holy, holy, holy is the Lord of hosts. The whole earth is full of his glory."

K'dushat Hashem (pronounced k'-doo-SHAHT hah-SHEM): Literally, "sanctification of the name [of God]," and the full name for the prayer that is generally called *K'dushah* (see **K'dushah**). Best known as the third blessing in the *Amidah,* but found also prior to the morning *Sh'ma.* Used also in variant form *kiddush hashem* (pronounced kee-DOOSH hah-SHEM) as a term to describe dying for the sanctification of God's name, that is, martyrdom.

K'dushat hayom (pronounced k'-doo'-SHAHT ha-YOHM): Literally, "the holiness of the day," hence, the technical name of prayers that express the presence of a sacred day (Shabbat or holidays). There are three instances: the *Kiddush* that inaugurates the day either at the dinner table or at the opening evening *(Ma'ariv)* service; the fourth benediction of the Shabbat or holiday *Amidah;* and the final benediction after the *Haftarah* is recited.

Keva (pronounced KEH-vah): A Hebrew word meaning "fixity, stability," and, therefore, the aspect of a service that is fixed and immutable: the words on the page, perhaps, or the time at which the prayer must be said. In the early years, when prayers were delivered orally and improvised on the spot, *keva* meant the fixed order in which the liturgical themes had to be expressed.

Kibbuts G'luyot (pronounced kee-BOOTS g'-loo-YOTE): Literally, "gathering the exiles," and the title of the tenth blessing of the daily *Amidah,* a petition for Jews outside the Land of Israel to return home to their land as a sign that messianic times are imminent. Some liberal liturgies omit the blessing or interpret it more broadly to imply universal messianic liberation, but without the literal belief that Jews outside the Land of Israel are in "exile," or that they need to or want to "return home."

Kiddush (pronounced kee-DOOSH but, commonly, KIH-d'sh): Literally, "sanctification," hence, a form of *k'dushat hayom* (see **K'dushat hayom**); in this case, the prayer for the eve of Shabbat and holidays, intended to announce the arrival of sacred time, and accompanied by *birkat yayin,* the blessing over wine. See also **Birkat yayin**.

Kiddusha Rabbah (generally pronounced kih-DOO-shah RAH-bah): Literally, "the Great *Kiddush*." The name for the *Kiddush* (see **Kiddush**) recited at noon on Saturdays and holidays and, ironically, consisting essentially of only the blessing over wine.

Kohanim (pronounced koe-hah-NEEM): Literally, "priests," plural of *kohen* (pronounced koe-HAYN), a reference to the priests who offered sacrifices in the ancient Temple until its destruction by Rome in the year 70 C.E. Also the name of modern-day Jews who claim priestly descent and who are customarily given symbolic recognition in various ritual ways—as, for instance, being called first to stand beside the Torah reader and to recite a blessing over the reading. It is also the title of the last blessing in the *Amidah,* which contains the priestly benediction from Numbers 6:24–26. Another more popular name for that blessing is *Shalom* (pronounced shah-LOME), "peace," because the priestly benediction requests peace. See also **Birkat Kohanim**.

Korbanot (pronounced kohr-bah-NOHT; singular: *korban,* pronounced kohr-BAHN): Literally, "sacrifices," but used liturgically to denote passages from Torah and rabbinic literature that explain how sacrifices are to be offered. These are inserted especially in the *Birkhot Hashachar* and the *Musaf* service.

K'riat Hatorah (pronounced k'ree-AHT hah-toe-RAH): The public reading of the Torah.

K'riat Sh'ma (pronounced k'-ree-YAHT sh'-MAH): Literally, "reciting the *Sh'ma*," and therefore a technical term for the liturgical act of reading the prayer known as the *Sh'ma* (see **Sh'ma**).

L'chayim (generally pronounced l'-KHAH-yim): Literally, "To life," the common Jewish expression used as a sort of "toast" before drinking wine together, as in the *Kiddush*.

Lechem mishneh (pronounced LEH-khem MISH-neh): "Double bread," referring to the double portion of manna that fell on Fridays (to provide also for Saturdays, when Israel could not collect food because it was the Sabbath).

Licht bentschen (pronounced LIKHT behn-ch'n): Literally, "kindling lights," the Yiddish equivalent of *hadlakat nerot* (see **Hadlakat nerot**).

Liturgy: Public worship, from the Greek word *leitourgia,* meaning "public works." Liturgy in ancient Greece was considered a public work, the act of sacrificing or praising the gods, from which benefits would flow to the body politic.

L'khah Dodi (pronounced l'-KHAH doh-DEE): Literally, "Come, friend." A mystic sixteenth-century prayer that climaxes the Friday night service of **Kabbalat Shabbat** (welcoming Shabbat).

Long Confession (in Hebrew, *Vidui Rabbah,* pronounced vee-DOO'y rah-BAH or, commonly, VEE-doo-y RAH-bah): A lengthy litany arranged alphabetically and recited on Yom Kippur. The acrostic is formed by the initial letter of the first word after the opening phrase for each line, *Al chet shechatanu* (pronounced ahl KHEHT she-chah-TAH-noo), meaning "For the sin that we have committed." Referred to also as *Al chet*.

Ma'ariv (pronounced mah-ah-REEV or, commonly, MAH-ah-reev): From the Hebrew word *erev* (pronounced EH-rev), meaning "evening": one of two titles used for the evening worship service (also called **Arvit**).

Machzor Vitry (commonly pronounced MAKH-zohr VEET-ree): Earliest comprehensive compendium of liturgical custom in France (eleventh to twelfth century).

Mah Tovu (pronounced mah TOH-voo): Technically, the prayer to be said upon approaching or entering a synagogue; in practice, the first prayer of *Birkhot Hashachar*.

Maimonides, Moses (known also as Rambam, pronounced RAHM-bahm): Most important Jewish philosopher of all time; also a physician and very significant legal authority. Born in Spain, he moved to Egypt, where he lived most of his life (1135–1204).

Massekhet Sofrim (pronounced mah-SEH-khet sohf-REEM): Literally, "Tractate [dealing with issues relevant to] scribes," an eighth-century compilation (with some later interpolations) dealing with such matters as the writing of Torah scrolls, but also including much detail on the early medieval (and possibly ancient) prayer practice of Jews in the Land of Israel.

Menorah (pronounced m'-noh-RAH, or commonly, m'-NOH-rah): A candelabra, originally the one in the desert Tabernacle of Exodus, with seven branches. The term was once commonly used also for the eight-branch candelabra for Chanukah, but now the term **chanuki'ah** is preferred for that one.

Mid'ora'ita (pronounced mee-d'-oh-RYE-tah): Strictly speaking, commandments derived directly from Torah, which are of a higher order than those rooted only in rabbinic ordinance (called **Mid'rabbanan**), but all are binding.

Mid'rabbanan (pronounced mee-d'-rah-bah-NAHN): Commandments rooted only in rabbinic ordinance. See **Mid'ora'ita**.

Midrash (pronounced meed-RAHSH or, commonly, MID-rahsh): From a Hebrew word meaning "to ferret out the meaning of a text," and therefore a rabbinic interpretation of a biblical word or verse. By extension, a body of rabbinic literature that offers classical interpretations of the Bible.

Minchah (pronounced meen-KHAH or, more commonly, MIN-khah): Originally the name of a type of sacrifice, then the word for a sacrifice offered during the afternoon, and now the name for the afternoon synagogue service usually scheduled just before nightfall. *Minchah* means "afternoon."

Minhag (pronounced meen-HAHG or, commonly, MIN-hahg): The Hebrew word for custom and, therefore, used liturgically to describe the customary way that different groups of Jews pray. By extension, *minhag* means a "rite," as in *Minhag Ashkenaz*, meaning "the rite of prayer, or the customary way of prayer for Jews in *Ashkenaz*"—that is, northern and eastern Europe.

Minhag hamakom (pronounced min-HAHG hah-mah-KOHM or, commonly, MIN-hahg hah-mah-KOHM): "The usual custom of the community." In cases where liturgical or ritual practice varies, but where the alternative practices are equally permitted, the rule is to follow *minhag hamakom*.

Minim (pronounced mee-NEEM): Literally, "heretics" or "sectarians," and the title of the twelfth blessing of the daily *Amidah*, a petition that heresy be eradicated and heretics punished. Liberal liturgies frequently omit the blessing, considering it an inappropriate malediction, not a benediction at all, or reframe it as a petition against evil in general.

Minyan (pronounced meen-YAHN or, commonly, MIN-y'n): A quorum, the minimum number of people required for certain prayers. *Minyan* comes from the word meaning "to count."

Mi sheberakh (pronounced, commonly, MEE sheh-BAY-rakh): A standard blessing beginning, "May the One who blessed [our ancestors]…," which could be adapted for any number of instances. This set of prayers requesting God's blessing on those who receive an *aliyah* or on their family members is perhaps the best-known addition to the service.

Mishnah (pronounced meesh-NAH or, commonly, MISH-nah): The first written summary of Jewish law, compiled in the Land of Israel about the year 200 C.E., and, therefore, our first overall written evidence for the state of Jewish prayer in the early centuries.

Mishneh Torah (pronounced MISH-n' TOH-rah): Code of Jewish law by Moses Maimonides (composed in 1180), called also the *Yad* (pronounced YAHD), a Hebrew word made of the letters that, together, stand for the number fourteen—a reference to the fact that the Code is divided into fourteen books. Unlike other Codes, the *Mishneh Torah* sums up every aspect of Jewish law, even hypothetical precepts relevant only in messianic times, as well as philosophical introductions on the nature of God and prayer.

Mishpat (pronounced meesh-PAHT): Literally, "justice," and the title of the eleventh blessing of the daily *Amidah;* a petition for just rulership, a condition associated with the messianic age.

Mitzvah (pronounced meetz-VAH or, commonly, MITZ-vah; plural: *mitzvot,* pronounced meetz-VOTE): A Hebrew word used commonly to mean "good deed," but in the more technical sense, denoting any commandment from God and, therefore, by extension, what God wants us to do. Reciting the *Sh'ma* morning and evening, for instance, is a *mitzvah*.

Mitzvat aseh shehaz'man g'ramah (pronounced meets-VAHT ah-SAY sheh-hah-z'-MAHN g'rah-MAH): Literally, a "positive commandment dependent on time," a category of commandments from which women are normally exempt.

Mitzvah l'ma'alah min haz'man (pronounced meets-VAH l'-mah-ah-LAH meen hahz-MAHN): Literally, "a commandment that transcends time," a theological correction to *mitzvot* (commandments) that seem otherwise to be "commandments dependent on time" (see ***Mitzvat aseh shehaz'man g'ramah***), and which would then exempt women from required observance.

M'kadesh (pronounced m'kah-DESH), or, commonly, m'-KAH-desh): Literally, "to sanctify" or "declare sacred," hence the person who recites *Kiddush,* the home evening prayer that inaugurates Shabbat and holidays.

Modeh/ah ani (pronounced moh-DEH ah-NEE [for women, moh-DAH ah-NEE]): Literally, "I gratefully acknowledge [...that You have returned my soul to me]"—therefore, the standard prayer to be said upon awakening.

Modim D'rabbanan (pronounced moe-DEEM d'-rah-bah-NAHN, or commonly, MOE-dim d'-rah-bah-nahn): *Modim* is the first word of the second to last blessing of the *Amidah* and, therefore, a shorthand way of referring to that prayer. *Modim D'rabbanan* is the name given to the form of the prayer that is reserved for congregational recitation during the repetition of the *Amidah* by the prayer leader. Literally, it means "the *Modim* of our Rabbis," and refers to the fact that the prayer is composed of what were once several alternative responses, each of which was the custom of one of the Rabbis of the Talmud.

Motsi (pronounced MOH-tsee): Literally, "brings forth, extracts," from the blessing over bread, "Blessed are You...who brings forth bread from the earth," and used as a shorthand reference to that blessing (as in, "It is time to make the *Motsi*").

Musaf (pronounced moo-SAHF or, commonly, MOO-sahf): The Hebrew word meaning "extra" or "added," and, therefore, the title of the additional sacrifice that was offered in the Temple on Shabbat and holy days. It is now the name given to an added service of worship appended to the morning service on those days.

M'zuzah (pronounced m'-zoo-ZAH or, commonly, m'-ZOO-zah): The Hebrew word in the Bible meaning "doorpost" and, by extension, the term now used for a small casement that contains the first two sections of the *Sh'ma* (Deut. 6:4–9; 11:13–21) and is affixed to the doorposts of Jewish homes.

Naches (pronounced NAH-kh's): Pride (in another person), as in the *naches* a parent feels for a son or daughter.

N'filat apayim (pronounced n'-fee-LAHT ah-PAH-yim): Literally, "falling on one's face," and, therefore, a technical term for the ***Tachanun***, the section of the daily service that features supplications and is said with head resting on forearm, as if "prostrate" before God.

N'illah (pronounced n'-ee-LAH or, commonly, n'-EE-lah): The concluding service for Yom Kippur.

Nishmat kol cha'i (pronounced neesh-MAHT kohl KHA'i): A blessing mentioned in the Talmud as one of two benedictions in use as the *Birkat Hashir* (pronounced beer-KAHT hah-SHEER), the blessing that ends a psalm collection known as *Hallel*. (See **Hallel**.) Nowadays, we use it (1) as part of a longer **Birkat Hashir**, after the Daily *Hallel*, that constitutes the central section of the **P'sukei D'zimrah** for Sabbaths and festivals; and (2) to conclude a similar *Hallel* in the Passover Haggadah.

N'kadesh (pronounced n'kah-DAYSH): The *Amidah* is first recited silently by each worshiper and then repeated aloud by the prayer leader, at which time its third blessing appears in extended form. *N'kadesh* (literally, "Let us sanctify…") is the first Hebrew word of that extended blessing and is thus, by extension, a common way of refering to it.

Notarikon (pronounced noh-TAH-ri-kohn): A system of acrostics, by which each letter of a single word is treated as the initial letter of another word, until a secret meaning is revealed by the set of new words.

N'shamah y'teirah (pronounced n'-shah-MAH y'-tei-RAH): Literally, "extra soul," referring to the talmudic promise that all who keep Shabbat are granted an extra soul for the day.

Oneg Shabbat (pronounced OH-neg shah-BAHT): Literally, "joy of Shabbat."

Orach Chayim (pronounced OH-rakh KHA-yim): Abbreviated as O. Ch. Literally, "The Way of Life," one of four sections in the *Tur* and the *Shulchan Arukh,* two of Judaism's major law codes; the section containing the rules of prayer.

Over la'asiyatan (pronounced oh-VEHR lah-ah-see-yah-TAHN): Literally, "before doing them," the principle that a blessing over an act (such as lighting Shabbat candles) precedes the act.

Payy'tan (pronounced pah-y'-TAHN; plural: *payy'tanim,* pronounced pah-y'-tah-NEEM): A poet; the name given particularly to classical and medieval poets whose work is inserted into the standard prayers for special occasions.

Perek (pronounced PEH-rek; plural: *p'rakim,* pronounced p'-rah-KEEM): Literally, a "section" or "chapter" of a written work; used liturgically to mean the sections of the *Sh'ma*. Each of its three biblical sections is a different *perek*.

Piyyut (pronounced pee-YOOT; plural: *piyyutim,* pronounced pee-yoo-TEEM): Literally, "a poem," but used technically to mean liturgical poems composed in classical and medieval times and inserted into the standard prayers on special occasions.

P'sukei D'zimrah (pronounced p'-soo-KAY d'-zeem-RAH or, commonly, p'-SOO-kay d'-ZIM-rah): Literally, "verses of song," and therefore the title of a lengthy set of opening morning prayers that contain psalms and songs and serve as spiritual preparation prior to the official Call to Prayer.

Purim (pronounced poo-REEM or, commonly, PU-rim): A festival falling on the fourteenth day of the Hebrew month of Adar, generally corresponding to late February or early March. It celebrates the miraculous deliverance referred to in the biblical Book of Esther. Literally, *purim* means "lots," as in the phrase "drawing of lots," because the date on which the Jews were to have been killed was chosen by lot.

Rashba (pronounced rahsh-BAH): Halakhic authority Shlomo ben Aderet, (1235–1310, Barcelona).

Rashi (pronounced RAH-shee): Solomon ben Isaac (1040–1105), most significant Jewish biblical exegete and founder of French Jewry.

R'fuah (pronounced r'-foo-AH or, commonly, r'-FOO-ah): Literally, "healing," and the title of the eighth blessing of the daily *Amidah,* a petition for healing.

Rosh (pronounced ROHSH): The Rosh (1250–1328), otherwise known as Rabbeinu Asher, or Asher ben Yechiel, was a significant halakhic authority, first in Germany and later in Spain. His son, Jacob ben Asher, codified many of his father's views alongside his own in his influential law code, the *Tur.*

Rosh Chodesh (pronounced rohsh KHOH-desh): Literally, "the head of the month," and, therefore, the Hebrew name for the one- or two-day new moon period with which lunar months begin. It is marked as a holiday in Jewish tradition, a period of new beginnings.

Rubric (pronounced ROO-brick): A technical term for any discrete section of liturgy, whether a prayer or a set of prayers. The *Sh'ma* and Its Blessings is one of several large rubrics in the service; within that large rubric, the *Sh'ma* or any one of its accompanying blessings may be called a rubric as well.

Seder (pronounced SEH-der or, commonly, SAY-der): The Hebrew word meaning "order" and, therefore, (1) the name given to the ritualized meal eaten on Passover eve, and (2) an early alternative term for the order of prayers in a prayer book. The word Siddur (see **Siddur**) is now preferred for the latter.

Seder Rav Amram (pronounced SAY-dehr rahv AHM-rahm): First known comprehensive Jewish prayer book, emanating from Rav Amram Gaon (c. 860 C.E., a leading Jewish scholar and head of Sura, a famed academy in Babylonia (modern-day Iraq).

Sefardi (pronounced s'-fahr-DEE or, commonly, s'-FAHR-dee): From the Hebrew word *Sefarad* (pronounced s'-fah-RAHD), meaning the geographic area of modern-day

Spain and Portugal. Sefardi is the adjective, describing the liturgical rituals and customs that are derived from *Sefarad* prior to the expulsion of Jews from there at the end of the fifteenth century, as opposed to Ashkenazi (see **Ashkenazi**), meaning the liturgical rituals and customs common to northern and eastern Europe. Nowadays, Sefardi refers also to the customs of Jews from North Africa and Arab lands, whose ancestors came from Spain.

S'firot (pronounced s'-fee-ROTE; singular: *s'firah,* pronounced s'-fee-RAH): According to the Kabbalah (Jewish mysticism, see **Kabbalah**), the universe came into being by a process of divine emanation, whereby the divine light, as it were, expanded into empty space, eventually becoming physical matter. At various intervals, this light was frozen in time, as if captured by containers, each of which is called a *s'firah.* Literally, *s'firah* means "number," because early theory conceptualized the stages of creation as primordial numbers.

S'firotic (pronounced s'fee-RAH-tik): Relating to one or more *s'firot* or to the system of *s'firot.*

Shabbat (pronounced shah-BAHT): The Hebrew word for "Sabbath," from a word meaning "to rest."

Shabbos (pronounced SHAH-b's): Yiddish for *Shabbat,* "Sabbath."

Shacharit (pronounced shah-khah-REET or, commonly, SHAH-khah-reet): The name given to the morning worship service; from the Hebrew word *shachar* (SHAH-khar), meaning "morning."

Shalom (pronounced shah-LOME): Literally, "peace," and a popular title for the final benediction of the *Amidah,* more properly entitled *Kohanim* (pronounced koe-hah-NEEM), "priests," or, more fully, *Birkat Kohanim* (pronounced beer-KAHT koe-hah-NEEM), "blessing of the priests," "priestly benediction." See also **Birkat Kohanim, Kohanim**.

Shanim (pronounced shah-NEEM): Literally, "years," and the title of the ninth blessing of the daily *Amidah;* a petition for a year of agricultural abundance, such as that associated with messianic days.

Shefa (pronounced SHEH-fah): In kabbalistic worship, the plenitude of blessing that flows vertically through the *s'firot* to the world we inhabit.

Shirat Hayam (pronounced shee-RAHT hah-YAHM): Literally, "Song of the Sea," the song of praise and gratitude sung by Israel after the splitting of the Red Sea and, since the Middle Ages, a prominent constituent of the *P'sukei D'zimrah,* the "warm-up" section to the morning service composed mainly of biblical material (chiefly psalms) that were intended to be sung as praise of God.

Shi'ur (pronounced shee-OOR): A talmudic lesson, frequently accompanying (or even fully constituting) the *s'udah sh'lishit* (the "third meal" of Shabbat).

Shiva (pronounced, shee-VAH or, commonly, SHIH-vah): Literally, "seven," denoting the seven days of mourning. A *shiva* home is a home where the seven days of mourning are being observed.

Shivah d'n'chemta (pronounced shih-VAH d'-n'-KHEM-tah): "Literally, the seven weeks of comfort." The seven Sabbaths following Tisha B'av, which take us all the way to Rosh Hashanah, call for *Haftarot* that guarantee hope.

Sh'liach tsibbur (pronounced sh'-LEE-ahk tsee-BOOR): Literally, the "agent of the congregation," and, therefore, the name given to the person who leads the prayer service.

Sh'lom bayit (pronounced shah-LOHM BAH-yit): Literally, "peace of the home."

Sh'ma (pronounced sh'-MAH): The central prayer in the first of the two main units in the worship service, the second being the *Amidah* (see ***Amidah***). The *Sh'ma* comprises three citations from the Bible, and the larger unit in which it is embedded (called the *Sh'ma* and Its Blessings) is composed of a formal Call to Prayer (see ***Bar'khu***) and a series of blessings on the theological themes that, together with the *Sh'ma,* constitute a liturgical creed of faith. *Sh'ma,* meaning "hear," is the first word of the first line of the first biblical citation, "Hear O Israel: Adonai is our God; Adonai is One," which is the paradigmatic statement of Jewish faith, the Jews' absolute commitment to the presence of a single and unique God in time and space.

Sh'mini Atseret (pronounced sh'-MEE-nee ah-TSEH-ret): Literally, "the eighth day of solemn assembly," and the name given to the eighth and final day of the autumn festival of Sukkot.

Sh'moneh Esreh (pronounced sh'-MOE-neh ES-ray): A Hebrew word meaning "eighteen" and, therefore, a name given to the second of the two main units in the worship service that once had eighteen benedictions in it (it now has nineteen), known also as the *Amidah* (see ***Amidah***).

Shomer Shabbat (pronounced shoh-MAYR shah-BAHT—using the Yiddish pronunciation—SHO-mare SHAH-b's, or even SHOI-mare SHAH-b's). Literally, "keeping Shabbat," meaning the observance of Shabbat regulations.

Shomer Yisra'el (pronounced shoh-MAYR yis-rah-AYL or, commonly, SHOH-mayr yis-rah-AYL): Literally, "keeper of Israel," a designation of God and the opening words—hence, the title—of a medieval poem that is found in *Tachanun*.

Short Confession (in Hebrew, *Vidui Zuta,* pronounced vee-DOO'y ZOO-tah or, commonly, VEE-doo-y ZOO-tah): A short confession of sin, arranged alphabetically, so that each sin that is listed begins with a different letter of the Hebrew alphabet. Also referred to by the opening word, *Ashamnu* (pronounced ah-SHAHM-noo), meaning "We have sinned."

Shul (pronounced SHOOL): Yiddish for synagogue.

Shulchan Arukh (pronounced shool-KHAN ah-ROOKH or, commonly, SHOOL-khan AH-rookh): The name given to the best-known code of Jewish law, compiled by Joseph Caro in the Land of Israel and published in 1565. *Shulchan Arukh* means "The Set Table" and refers to the ease with which the various laws are set forth—like a table prepared with food ready for consumption.

Shulchan Arukh D'rav (pronounced shool-KHAHN ah-ROOKH d'-RAHV or, popularly, SHOOL-khahn AH-rukh d'-RAHV): Halakhic compendium by Rabbi Shneur Zalman of Liady, eighteenth-century founder of Chabad Chasidism.

Siddur (pronounced see-DOOR or, commonly, SIH-d'r): From the Hebrew word *seder* (see ***Seder***), meaning "order," and therefore, by extension, the name given to the "order of prayers," or prayer book.

S'lichah (pronounced s'lee-KHAH or, commonly, s'LEE-khah): Literally, "pardon" or "forgiveness," and the title of the sixth blessing of the daily *Amidah,* a petition for divine forgiveness of our sins.

S'mikhah (pronounced s'-mee-KHAH or, commonly, s'-MEE-khah): Literally, "the laying on [of hands], a biblical (Lev. 16:21) and early rabbinic reference to the priestly act of laying hands on a sacrifice, but also Moses' act of passing authority on to Joshua by laying his hands on him (Num. 27:23)—from which is derived the further meaning of laying hands on a candidate for ordination.

Tachanun (pronounced TAH-khah-noon): A Hebrew word meaning "supplications" and, by extension, the title of the large unit of prayer that follows the *Amidah,* which is largely supplicatory in character.

Tallit (pronounced tah-LEET; plural: *tallitot,* pronounced tah-lee-TOTE): The prayer shawl equipped with tassels (see ***Tsitsit***) on each corner and generally worn during the morning *(Shacharit)* and additional *(Musaf)* synagogue services.

Tallit katan (pronounced tah-LEET kah-TAHN): Literally, "a little *tallit*," used originally as an undergarment to allow the wearing of *tsitsit* privately, all day long, in cultures where Jews wanted to look the same as everyone else.

Talmud (pronounced tahl-MOOD or, more commonly, TAHL-m'd): The name given to each of two great compendia of Jewish law and lore compiled over several centuries and ever since, the literary core of the rabbinic heritage. The Talmud Yerushalmi (pronounced y'-roo-SHAHL-mee), the "Jerusalem Talmud," is earlier, a product of the Land of Israel generally dated about 400 C.E. The better-known Talmud Bavli (pronounced BAHV-lee), or "Babylonian Talmud," took shape in Babylonia (present-day Iraq) and is traditionally dated about 550 C.E. When people say "the" Talmud without specifying which one they mean, they are referring to the Babylonian version. Talmud means "teaching."

T'chin's (pronounced t'-KHEE-n's): Literally, Yiddish for "supplications," but used technically to denote liturgies for women, common mostly in eastern Europe from the seventeenth- to nineteenth-century liturgy.

Tetragrammaton: The technical term for the four-letter name of God that appears in the Bible. Treating it as sacred, Jews stopped pronouncing it centuries ago, so that the actual pronunciation has been lost; instead of reading it according to its letters, it is replaced in speech by the alternative name of God, Adonai.

T'fillah (pronounced t'-fee-LAH or, commonly, t'-FEE-lah): A Hebrew word meaning "prayer" but used technically to mean a specific prayer, namely, the second of the two main units in the worship service. It is known also as the *Amidah* or the *Sh'moneh Esreh* (see **Amidah**). Also the title of the sixteenth blessing of the *Amidah,* a petition for God to accept our prayer.

T'fillin (pronounced t'-FIH-lin or, sometimes, t'-fee-LEEN): Two cube-shaped black boxes containing biblical quotations (Exod. 13:1–10; 13:11–16; Deut. 6:4–9; 11:13–21) and affixed by means of attached leather straps to the forehead and left arm (right arm for left-handed people) during morning prayer.

T'hillah l'David (pronounced t'-hee-LAH l'-dah-VEED): Literally, "a psalm of David," and the first two words of Psalm 145; hence, the rabbinic name for Psalm 145, which eventually became known, more popularly, as *Ashre* (pronounced ahsh-RAY or, commonly, AHSH-ray). See **Ashre**.

T'lata d'puranuta (pronounced t'-LAH-tah d'-poo-rah-NOO-tah): "The three readings of retribution." As the Rabbis saw it, God must have allowed, and perhaps even caused, the Temple to fall as punishment for Israel's sins. The three weeks prior to Tisha B'av, therefore, anticipate the fall, culminating in Shabbat *Chazon* (pronounced khah-ZOHN), "The Sabbath of 'the Vision,'" which features Isaiah's premonitory vision of Jerusalem's fall and the expectation of ultimate recovery (Isa. 1:1–27).

T'murah (pronounced t'-moo-RAH): A substitution code by which one letter takes the place of another, revealing new meanings.

Tosefet k'dushah (pronounced toh-SEH-feht k'-doo-SHAH or commonly, toh-SEH-feht k'-DOO-shah): Literally, "adding holiness," a halakhic concept that extends the commandment to start Shabbat or holidays early and end them later.

Tsadikim (pronounced tsah-dee-KEEM): Literally, "the righteous," and the title of the thirteenth blessing of the daily *Amidah,* a petition that the righteous be rewarded.

T'shuvah (pronounced t'shoo-VAH or, commonly t'SHOO-vah): Literally, "repentance," and the title of the fifth blessing in the daily *Amidah,* a petition by worshipers that they successfully turn to God in heartfelt repentance.

Tsitsit (pronounced tsee-TSEET): A Hebrew word meaning "tassels" or "fringes" and used to refer to the tassels affixed to the four corners of the *tallit* (the prayer shawl, see ***Tallit***) as Numbers 15:38 instructs.

Tur (pronounced TOOR): The shorthand title applied to a fourteenth-century code of Jewish law, compiled by Jacob ben Asher in Spain, and the source for much of our knowledge about medieval liturgical practice. *Tur* means "row" or "column." The full name of the code is *Arba'ah Turim* (pronounced ahr-bah-AH too-REEM), "The Four Rows," with each row (or *Tur*) being a separate section of law on a given broad topic.

Un'taneh Tokef (pronounced oo-n'-TAH-neh TOH-kehf): A *piyyut* (liturgical poem) for the High Holy Days emphasizing the awesome nature of these days when we stand before God for judgment. Widely, but incorrectly, connected with a legend of Jewish martyrdom in Germany, the poem more likely derives from a Byzantine poet, circa sixth century. It is known for its conclusion: "Penitence, prayer, and charity avert a bad decree."

V'hu rachum (pronounced v'HOO rah-KHOOM): Literally, "He [God] is merciful," and, because of its sentiment, a common introductory line to prayers lauding God's gracious beneficence. The best example is a seven-paragraph penitential prayer that makes up the bulk of the version of *Tachanun* (pronounced TAH-khah-noon) that is said Mondays and Thursdays.

Vidui Rabbah (pronounced vee-DOO'y RAH-bah or, commonly, VEE-doo-y RAH-bah): Literally, "long confession." See **Long Confession.**

Vidui Zuta (pronounced vee-DOO-y ZOO-tah or, commonly, VEE-doo-y ZOO-tah): Literally, "short confession." See **Short Confession.**

Yahrzeit (pronounced YOHR-tseit): A Yiddish word meaning the practice of marking the anniversary of a loved one's death by saying *Kaddish*. People speak of "having *yahrzeit*" on a given day, at which time the name of the person being memorialized may be mentioned aloud at services prior to the Mourner's *Kaddish* (see **Kaddish**).

Yichud (pronounced yee-KHOOD): Literally, "unification"; in kabbalistic worship, prayers have esoteric significance, generally the unification of the letters that make up God's name, but standing also for the conjoining of God's masculine and feminine aspects and, deeper still, the coming together of the shattered universe in which we live.

Yigdal (pronounced yig-DAHL): A popular morning hymn that encapsulates the thirteen principles of faith composed by prominent medieval philosopher Moses Maimonides (1135–1204). These thirteen principles were arranged poetically as *Yigdal* in the fourteenth century by Daniel ben Judah Dayan (pronounced dah-YAHN) of Rome.

Yishtabach (pronounced yish-tah-BAKH): The first word and, therefore, the title of the blessing used as the *Birkat Hashir* for weekdays (see **Birkat Hashir**). On Sabbaths and festivals, it is expanded by the addition of *Nishmat kol cha'i* (pronounced neesh-MAHT kohl KHA'i), a blessing mentioned in the Talmud (see **Nishmat kol cha'i**).

Yizkor (pronounced yeez-KOHR or, commonly, YIZ-k'r): The Memorial Service, said on Yom Kippur and the three Festivals (Passover, Shavuot, and Sh'mini Atseret).

Yotser (pronounced yoe-TSAYR or, commonly, YOE-tsayr): The Hebrew word meaning "creator" and, by extension, the title of the first blessing in the *Sh'ma* and Its Blessings, which is on the theme of God's creation of the universe.

Y'rushalayim (pronounced y'roo-shah-LAH-yeem): Literally, "Jerusalem," and the title of the fourteenth blessing of the daily *Amidah;* a petition for the divine building up of Jerusalem, a condition associated with the imminence of the messianic age. Some liberal liturgies interpret it more broadly to include the restoration of modern-day Jerusalem, currently under way.

Z'mirot (pronounced z'mee-ROHT, or commonly, z'-MEE-roht), sometimes referred to in the Yiddish, *z'meer's* (pronounced z'MEE-r's): Literally, "songs," but used technically for table songs during meals of Shabbat. It is also the preferred Sefardi title for the "warm-up" section of the morning liturgy, called *P'sukei D'zimrah* by Ashkenazim. (See **P'sukei D'zimrah.**)

Zohar (pronounced ZOE-hahr): A shorthand title for *Sefer Hazohar* (pronounced SAY-fer hah-ZOE-hahr), literally, "The Book of Splendor," which is the primary

CPSIA information can be obtained
at www.ICGtesting.com
Printed in the USA
LVOW02s1703080217
523626LV00005B/310/P